Face Your Fears

A Proven Plan to Beat Anxiety, Panic, Phobias, and Obsessions

DAVID F. TOLIN, Ph.D.

WILEY

John Wiley & Sons, Inc.

Published by John Wiley & Sons, Inc., Hoboken, New Jersey
Published simultaneously in Canada

Design by Forty-Five Degree Design LLC

The information contained in this book is not intended to serve as a replacement for professional medical advice. Any use of the information in this book is at the reader's discretion. The author and the publisher specifically disclaim any and all liability arising directly or indirectly from the use or application of any information contained in this book. A health care professional should be consulted regarding your specific situation.

For general information about our other products and services, please contact our Customer Care Department within the United States at (800) 762-2974, outside the United States at (317) 572-3993 or fax (317) 572-4002.

Wiley also publishes its books in a variety of electronic formats and by print-on-demand. Some content that appears in standard print versions of this book may not be available in other formats. For more information about Wiley products, visit us at www.wiley.com.

ISBN 978-1-118-01673-2 (cloth); ISBN 978-1-118-14623-1 (ebk.);
ISBN 978-1-118-14624-8 (ebk.); ISBN 978-1-118-14625-5 (ebk.)

Printed in the United States of America

10 9 8 7 6 5 4 3 2 1

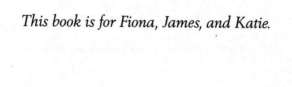

This book is for Fiona, James, and Katie.

Contents

Part III. Face Your Fears for Life

Acknowledgments

This book was created with the help and support of all of my colleagues at the Institute of Living's Anxiety Disorders Center. My sincere thanks to my graduate students Janine Domingues, Kristin Slyne, and Andrea Umbach, as well as my literary agent Jill Marsal, who provided important comments and insights on earlier drafts of this book. And of course, I want to thank all of the patients who have taught me about anxiety disorders, particularly the seven who were kind enough to lend their stories to this book.

PART I

The Face Your Fears Program to Beat Anxiety

Faces of Fear

He who fears something gives it power over him.
—*Moorish proverb*

I t's fitting that as I write the opening sentences to a book about fear, I am sitting on a commercial airplane, somewhere over the Midwestern United States, flying through severe turbulence. As the plane lurches and bounces through the dark skies, its engines whining (okay, maybe that's my interpretation of what they are doing), I am aware that my palms have become moist and clammy with perspiration. Putting a hand to my chest, I feel my heart beating faster. My breathing has become more rapid and shallow, my muscles tense. I find that I am paying much more attention than usual to the sounds of the airplane, waiting for any unexpected noises that might signal impending disaster. I am thinking about airplane crashes I have read about in the news and considering the possibility that my plane might be next. I even notice that I am white-knuckle gripping the armrests, as if to somehow hold the plane up in the sky.

Yup, even doctors who study and treat fear experience fear. In fact, we all do. In this case, my fear didn't get the better of me—I was able to deal with it and eventually feel better, rather than panicking—but the experience certainly got me thinking about fear. Most of the time, when we experience fear, it's not a big deal (and, in fact, it can be quite helpful in the right context). Yet when fear escalates out of control, the impact can be devastating. Over one-quarter of Americans either have or will have an anxiety disorder, such as *panic disorder, specific or social phobias, obsessive-compulsive disorder, generalized anxiety disorder*, or *posttraumatic stress disorder*—significantly more than the number of people who suffer from depression, substance abuse, or other mental health conditions. These anxiety disorders can have a very serious effect on someone's quality of life, as evidenced by countless stories of marital and financial problems, impaired social relationships, problems at work or attending school, and so on. People with anxiety disorders are suffering, often quite badly.

Fortunately, help is available. Having worked with hundreds of patients during the last two decades and having conducted federally supported research on the treatment of anxiety disorders, I can teach you skills to help you beat your fears. One crucial finding from my research and that of many, many colleagues is that *exposure therapy*—directly and gradually confronting feared objects, activities, and situations—is the key to overcoming most forms of fear.

Lots of books have been written about mastering anxiety. Some of them are good; others are not so good. Perhaps you've seen them and even tried one (or more). This book is different. Why? Everything in it is backed by hard science showing that these methods work. I won't send you off to do things that I can't prove are helpful. This book will give you what works and only what works. No fluff. No BS. This book will provide you with a clear, user-friendly program that makes exposure therapy accessible to everyone, from mildly fearful individuals to people who are debilitated by their fears and anxieties.

If you're like most people reading this book, you are bothered by fears that seem as if they are out of control (or starting to get out of control). Perhaps your fears are so intense that they severely affect your quality of life. In my clinic, I've met countless people who told me that their fears were diminishing their ability to work, to perform in school, to have social lives, or to maintain good relationships with family members. If you find that fear has affected your ability to live a happy and healthy life, the program in this book will get you back on track toward the life you want and deserve.

That might not be your story, however. Although the people in my clinic tend to represent the more severe end of the continuum, countless others suffer—often privately—from fears that don't necessarily affect their ability to function but are bothersome, nevertheless. These people might simply feel nervous and afraid a lot of the time or find themselves becoming irritable or run down. Even though they can function just fine, they simply don't like the way they feel and wish things could be better. If you're closer to this end of the continuum, read on—this book is for you, too, and can help you feel much better.

There are lots of ways to divide fears into categories. Mental health professionals use the diagnoses listed in the *Diagnostic and Statistical Manual of Mental Disorders*, 4th edition, Text Revision (*DSM-IV-TR*), published by the American Psychiatric Association. If you've talked to a health-care professional about your fear, you might have heard things like "Your condition is called a specific phobia," or "You have OCD." These are *DSM-IV-TR* diagnoses.

I have mixed feelings about diagnoses such as these. On one hand, I understand that in the era of modern health care, it's necessary to come up with labels for record keeping, billing, and so on. I also know that the use of diagnoses has led to a wealth of research on how to treat anxiety effectively—some of which I'll share with you in this book. On the other hand, I think that the *DSM-IV-TR* isn't always the best way to understand fear—especially if you're the person suffering from it.

Lots of fears, such as the ones I'll discuss further on, cut across the conventional diagnostic boundaries, with the result that these diagnoses often overlap substantially. The *DSM-IV-TR* diagnoses also don't give us much guidance in terms of what someone should do to get better. Knowing the name for a fear isn't nearly as helpful as understanding exactly what is feared and why.

In this book, I don't put tremendous emphasis on *DSM-IV-TR* diagnoses. I will discuss them, but I think there's a much simpler, more intuitive, and more helpful way to break them down—and this is how the book will be arranged. Most people's fears fall into one or more of these categories:

- Fears of specific situations or objects
- Fears of body sensations
- Social and performance fears
- Obsessive fears
- Excessive worries
- Post-traumatic fears

As I describe each of these types of fear in detail, I'd like to introduce you to some people I've met in my clinic who have also experienced fear and anxiety-related problems. Perhaps you'll see a bit of yourself in their stories. Your fear might not match theirs exactly. Yet as you read their stories, look for aspects of your fears that seem to overlap with theirs. This should give you a sense of which categories your fears belong to.

Fears of Specific Situations or Objects

Fears of specific situations or objects are among the most common fears. People may be afraid of flying, heights, animals, receiving an injection, seeing blood, or many other things. They can become anxious simply by anticipating an encounter with these objects or situations and often try very hard to avoid coming into contact with them.

Audrey's Story

Audrey, a sixty-four-year-old retired health-care worker, was a little sheepish about her severe fear of snakes. There was no need for her to be ashamed—lots of people have this exact fear. Her fear was really getting to her, though. Here's how she described it:

> When I was five years old, I saw a large snake and thought it was going to attack my little sister. I couldn't do anything about it, and our mom had to rescue us. Ever since then, I've been unable to deal with any kind of snake, even on TV or in a book. I'm a very rational person, but I just couldn't overcome this irrational fear. If I see a snake, or even think I see a snake, I freeze in fear and want to scream at the top of my lungs, but nothing comes out. Several years ago, I lived in a basement apartment that had some flooding. I opened my linen closet and saw five little baby snakes. They were no more than five or six inches long, but I started screaming and ran out of the apartment. Even though the building manager brought in an exterminator, for the next year I couldn't be comfortable in my own home. I was constantly checking everything to make sure there were no snakes.

Audrey is a good example of someone who is afraid of specific situations or objects: in this case, snakes. In fact, she didn't even need to see a snake in order to feel afraid; the mere anticipation that she *might* see a snake was enough to paralyze her. A big part of her problem was that she tended to magnify, in her thoughts, what would happen if she actually saw a snake. In her mind, the prospect of seeing a snake was not only uncomfortable—it meant panicking and not being able to feel comfortable ever again.

Michelle's Story

Despite the fact that Michelle, age thirty-five, worked as a registered nurse, she was terrified that she might see or hear someone vomit. She worried that if a person vomited anywhere near her, it would cause her to vomit. So she specifically chose nursing jobs that minimized the likelihood of this happening. She describes it this way:

> I can remember the exact moment I became afraid of throwing up. I was nine years old and enjoying an evening at the Ice Capades with my Brownie troop. A girl threw up near my feet. In my mind, it was so close, it was unbearable. I woke up in the middle of the night that very same night, telling my mom I was going to be sick. She was very consoling and sat with me while I lay awake nervous all night, thinking I was going to get the stomach bug. After that, I woke up almost every night, afraid I was going to throw up. I would become physically nauseous and shaky. I would not want to eat. I would pace back and forth when the nerves would really amp up. To me, puke was my enemy. The best way to beat it was to avoid it. And so that became me in a nutshell for many, many years. I became great at avoiding vomit. If friends were too drunk, I was not going to be the one holding their hair back. If a family member was sick, I would run out of the room pretending I was looking for something to help them with. For me, as long as I could seem nice but still avoid the situation, it was all under control. My fear of vomiting was at its worst when I became a mother. I became a germophobe, really. I was constantly placing Purell in the palms of my kids' hands, wiping tables clean, avoiding "germy" play places, and keeping my secret. I probably seemed normal, but the words *puke, throw up,* and *vomit* were starting to become buzz words in my head on a constant basis. I would wash dishes and think of vomit. I would play a game and think of throwing up.

Like Audrey, Michelle also had a fear of specific situations or objects. In this case, she was afraid of the sight, sound, or idea of people vomiting. She became a master of avoidance, learning to keep away from things that scared her. Yet once her children were born, she was no longer able to rely on her old ways of coping with the fear.

Fears of Body Sensations

Some people are afraid of sensations that come from inside their bodies—such as racing heart, dizziness, lightheadedness, or shortness of breath. People with a fear of body sensations often experience recurrent, unexpected *panic attacks*, which are "bursts" of fear and associated physical discomfort. In many cases, the person will start to avoid certain activities or places in order to prevent a panic attack or to make sure he or she can escape from situations easily in case of panic.

Susan's Story

Susan is a twenty-six-year-old single woman who began to develop paralyzing anxiety attacks, seemingly out of nowhere. Here's how she described one particularly terrifying attack:

> On my ride to work, I felt this weird numbness trickle down my temple. I tried to tell myself I was just fine, but when I got to work, I started to get the dizzies. I tried breathing deep, but I had a tendency to just hold my breath, and when I would let go, I'd breathe heavier. Within two minutes the feelings just intensified, and I could barely stand. I ran to my desk and sat with my head between my legs and started rocking back and forth because I was so petrified. My manager ran over and started yelling for someone who would know what to do because she had no idea how to handle someone with such crazy panic attacks. My friend was by my side with a fan, trying to cool down the hot flashes I was having. They had three people walk me to the break room and lay me on the couch. I was crying and so, so scared. My

manager was so freaked out, she called 911, and they ran in with a wheelchair and an oxygen mask. It was so overwhelming and so embarrassing because I thought I was going to die—over nothing. Over a small sensation I felt in my head that most people feel and hardly notice. I hate thinking about that day.

In talking with Susan, it became clear that her concerns centered on a fear of body sensations. She was afraid of sensations that came from inside her body, such as numbness, dizziness, and hot flashes. When she noticed sensations like these, she would think to herself, "Oh my God, I'm having a heart attack!" or "Oh no, I'm about to faint!" These thoughts, in turn, made her feel even more anxious, until her anxiety reached a peak—a panic attack. Panic attacks are certainly scary when they happen—so scary, in fact, that Susan had pretty much stopped driving her car, for fear that a panic attack would cause her to lose control of the vehicle and have an accident. In the next chapter, I'll talk about why panic attacks happen and where they come from.

Social and Performance Fears

Many people's fears center around the concern that they will do or say something stupid or embarrassing, or that others will be able to see how nervous they are and will therefore think less of them. Some people with this kind of fear are afraid of only a few social/performance situations, such as public speaking; others are afraid of virtually all social encounters. Many people with social and performance fears have particular difficulty starting and maintaining conversations, talking to members of the opposite sex, asserting themselves, or talking to authority figures.

Steven's Story

Steven is a fifty-year-old attorney with a wife and two children. Although he was doing okay at work, privately he was becoming increasingly withdrawn from others. He was going out less, gave up participating on the local library board, and stopped doing readings at his church services. It's not that he wasn't interested in socializing. What stopped him was his crippling fear of being embarrassed, humiliated, or rejected. Here's what he told me:

> At a dinner for my bar association, I was sitting at a table with a judge and several other attorneys I didn't know very well. My face started getting red, and I was sweating. My mouth was dry, and I felt like it was hard to talk. I felt like I was being judged. I stayed quiet and withdrawn throughout the dinner. Later, when I was anticipating going to another function, I dreaded the idea. I quit being a lector at my church because I found it so difficult to read in front of the congregation, thinking that they were scrutinizing me and judging me. I would break into a sweat. I gradually began to avoid social and professional functions, thinking that everything I said and did had to be perfect, or else I'd be humiliated.

Steven was mainly bothered by social and performance fears. It wasn't so much that he was afraid of people; rather, he was afraid of his own behavior in situations where other people could scrutinize him—such as while socializing or speaking in front of an audience. He was afraid that he would do or say something that would prove embarrassing or humiliating or that others would be able to see how nervous he was (for example, that they would see him tremble or blush). Over time, this fear became so all-consuming that simply interacting with others became painful. So, like a lot of people with anxiety disorders, he avoided these situations to try to keep his fear under control.

Obsessive Fears

People with obsessive fears can have a range of recurrent and intrusive thoughts, ideas, or images that come to mind over and over and cause the person to feel anxious or uncomfortable; we call these *obsessions*. The obsessions are usually accompanied by a need to perform *compulsions*, which are behaviors or mental acts that the person does in an effort to prevent disasters or to try to feel better.

Rachel's Story

Rachel is a fifty-one-year-old wife and mother. When she was forty-two years old, she watched TV news stories about people in the United States becoming contaminated by the anthrax virus. She worried that anthrax was in her mail, but that fear quickly spread. She became fearful that anthrax was on the ground, on the floor of her house, and on anything that had touched the floor of her house. From there, she began worrying about all kinds of potential contamination, not only anthrax. Here's how she described it:

> It got to the point where I wasn't so much afraid of anthrax as I was of "something"—it often didn't even have a name. I was just afraid there was "something" bad on things. Maybe it was something from the toilet, maybe from someone in public, maybe from undercooked food—it just generalized into fear of contamination. I wasn't as afraid that I would be made sick by these things—I was more afraid that my seven-year-old son would and that it would be my fault if I didn't prevent that. In addition to washing my hands and overshowering to remove any contamina- tion, I began cleaning compulsively with bleach. I also began to avoid things—not touching them, opening doors with the corner of my shirt, walking around things, leaving things on the floor when they really should have been picked up, getting a new and "clean" pair of pants to put on because the ones I'd taken off the night before had "accidentally" touched the carpeting. I felt on edge all the time. As if I was wired for sound. I was on constant vigil for any contamination. My mind never rested—if I wasn't

worried about one thing, I'd start worrying about another thing. I was completely drained and exhausted. I couldn't eat. I lost so much weight that people thought I was anorexic. I felt like a freak. Everyone just told me to stop it, snap out of it. They kept saying, "But look at your hands . . . can't you *just* stop washing?" And I couldn't, at least not without experiencing an overwhelming amount of anxiety.

It was clear to me that Rachel was suffering from obsessive fears. Obsessions are recurrent, intrusive thoughts, ideas, or images that come to mind over and over again, and cause the person to feel anxious or uncomfortable. Obsessive fears come in many forms. Some people might be afraid of things such as contamination and germs. Others are afraid that they will make a mistake and cause some kind of disaster or harm to another person. Some people are bothered by unwanted, intrusive thoughts that seem horrific or repugnant. Other people are afraid of throwing things away, for fear of making a mistake. Still others have severe discomfort when things are not symmetrical, exact, or "just right." Like most people with obsessive fears, Rachel was also wrapped up in compulsions, ritualized behaviors that she felt that she had to perform in order to prevent the worst from happening (in this case, catching or spreading a disease).

Excessive Worries

Many people with excessive and uncontrollable worries use up a lot of energy trying to get control of these worries. People with excessive worries often fall into the habit of trying to control their anxiety by jumping from worry to worry—so that when a scary image pops up, they start worrying about something else. They can also get hung up on trying to control their thoughts and on not upsetting themselves, which can become a full-time job.

Samantha's Story

Samantha, a forty-eight-year-old married woman with a twenty-year-old son, was troubled by worried thoughts that would pop into her mind even when she didn't want them to. Here's an example she gave me:

> I was consumed by fears about my son's safety and my own safety. I would think about my son dying in a fire, dying in a car crash, or being killed by an intruder. I had similar fears about myself, particularly about riding in a car. If a trip was planned, I would lie awake for weeks, picturing horrible crashes. I also had an overwhelming fear about the world ending. Whenever some doomsday story was run on the news or in the paper, I would shut down and go into terror mode. A few years ago, I went to a comedy show, and the comedian went into a rant about how the bees were disappearing. Then she said, "Einstein said, when the bees disappear, humans have three years left." I went into an immediate panic mode. I grew cold and numb and didn't even hear the rest of the show. My stomach clenched, and I felt sick. That night after going to sleep, I woke up about two hours later and had a full-blown panic attack: my whole body started shaking violently and uncontrollably, my bowels cramped, and I had to get up and spend the rest of the night in the bathroom.

Samantha had experienced a panic attack, too, as Susan had. Yet instead of being afraid of her own body sensations, Samantha's fear reaction was the result of excessive worries. Even though most of us worry about a few things from time to time, Samantha found that she was worrying about these issues for most of the day, day in and day out. She created worst-case scenarios in her head and felt intensely frightened by them. Often, she didn't limit her worrying to only one topic; instead, her mind raced from worry to worry. The result of all of this worrying was that she was literally making herself sick.

Post-Traumatic Fears

Some fears can develop after a horrific or life-threatening experience. People with post-traumatic fears often feel afraid of certain activities or situations that are not dangerous but that remind them of their traumatic experiences and make them feel unsafe. Some people might develop a fear of driving after a car accident, a fear of war movies after serving in the military, and so on. In addition, people with post-traumatic fears are often afraid of their own *memories* of the traumas. They react to mental images of their traumatic experience as if these could somehow harm them—as if they can't really believe that this is only a bad memory and not something happening in the present.

Andrea's Story

Andrea is a thirty-one-year-old dentist. A few years ago, when she was in dental school, she woke up in the middle of the night to find a man in her bedroom, sexually assaulting her. She screamed, and the man ran out. Yet Andrea was left with emotional scars that didn't go away. Images of the assault kept coming into her mind, even when she was trying to pay attention in class. She had frequent nightmares about the assault. She became extremely worried about her safety: even when she moved to a new, safer neighborhood, she felt as if she was constantly looking over her shoulder.

> I felt afraid when I was walking to the house at night from my car. I made sure the doors were locked and installed a lock on my bedroom door, but I didn't feel safe in that area. I moved out quickly and rented a room in a different area. One of the people at the new place belonged to the same ethnic group as the man who broke in, and I didn't feel safe there either. A few months later, while living in a different state and in a pretty safe area, I still had the same fears. I was afraid someone was going to break in. I installed locks on the bedroom door and felt afraid if I heard a noise

in the apartment at night or in the hallway. I had night-mares and got startled easily. I watched my surroundings very carefully when walking at night. I still went out with friends, but I was nervous and wary on the street. I felt afraid if someone was walking behind me, and I had to turn around to see who it was.

Andrea's sad story is one of post-traumatic fears. After being assaulted, she developed a fear not only of situations that reminded her of the assault or that made her feel vulnerable (such as going out of her house alone) but also of the memories themselves (for example, a mental picture of the man who assaulted her). That is, she reacted to mental images of her assailant as if they, too, were a threat to her. It was as if she could not put the traumatic event into perspective—as a bad part of her history—and instead, she felt as if she was reliving it over and over again in her present life.

If you recognize yourself in any of these stories, you're not alone. Audrey, Michelle, Susan, Steven, Rachel, Samantha, and Andrea all have anxiety disorders: problems of excessive fear, worry, and anxiety, as well as a strong tendency to avoid activities and situations they find scary. Later in this book, you'll learn more about the anxiety disorders, why they happen, and how to recognize them. As we proceed through the program, you'll hear more from each of these people as they go through the process with you.

What Are You Afraid Of?

To get a sense of whether this book can help you, let's start with a quiz, which groups fears into six categories. Look at each item and indicate the extent to which you would be afraid to do, confront, or experience it using the following scale:

Not at all
A little bit
Moderately
Extremely

As you review the items, imagine for now that you would have to do each thing without using any "tricks" to make yourself feel better or feel safer—for example, for item 9, "flying in an airplane," imagine that you do this without taking a tranquilizer or having an alcoholic drink to calm down. For item 17, "situations that are hard to escape from in case of panic sensations," imagine that this means not having a cell phone to call home in case of emergency. For item 28, "touching things that seem dirty or contaminated," imagine that you touch these things without washing your hands afterward.

How much are you afraid of the following:

Fears of Specific Situations or Objects
1. Going to the doctor or the dentist
2. Eating food you could choke on
3. Being near spiders
4. Being near cats, dogs, birds, or other animals
5. Being in stormy weather
6. Receiving injections or having blood drawn
7. Being near snakes
8. Hearing or seeing someone vomit or be sick
9. Flying in an airplane
10. Seeing blood or injuries
11. Being in a high place
12. Being in an enclosed space
13. Being in or near water

Fears of Body Sensations
14. Physical symptoms that feel as if they could be a heart attack or a stroke
15. Situations where it would be dangerous to lose control in the event of panic sensations, such as driving a car
16. Feeling dizzy or lightheaded
17. Situations that are hard to escape from in case of panic sensations, such as driving over a bridge or through a tunnel or being in the middle of a row in a crowded movie theater
18. Feeling an upset stomach

Social and Performance Fears

19. Interacting with certain people, such as strangers, members of the opposite sex, or authority figures
20. Having someone watch you do something, such as eat, write, or work
21. Things that could be embarrassing
22. Meeting new people
23. Public speaking

Obsessive Fears

24. Things being out of order or not just right
25. Having repulsive, horrible, or immoral thoughts or mental images
26. Throwing things away
27. Making a mistake that could cause harm to someone
28. Touching things that seem dirty or contaminated
29. Having the thought that you could do something terrible or violent

Excessive Worries

30. Thoughts of financial disaster
31. Thoughts of minor matters (such as not being on time, small repairs, and so on) turning into disasters
32. Thoughts about a loved one becoming sick or injured
33. Thoughts of problems at work, at school, or in family life becoming catastrophic
34. Thoughts about becoming sick or injured

Post-Traumatic Fears

35. Letting your guard down
36. Memories of unpleasant, stressful, or traumatic life experiences
37. Sudden noises or movements\
38. Sights, sounds, or smells that bring back bad memories
39. Situations or activities that remind you of unpleasant, stressful, or traumatic life experiences

Determine which items you circled as "moderately" or "extremely" and then read below for an explanation of your choices.

- If your answer was "moderately" or "extremely" for any of the items numbered 1 through 13, you're describing *fears of specific situations or objects*, such as Audrey's terrible fear of snakes and Michelle's fear of vomiting.
- If your answer was "moderately" or "extremely" for any of the items numbered 14 through 18, you may have a *fear of body sensations*, just as Susan was afraid of sensations that came from inside her body, such as a racing heart and dizziness.
- If your answer was "moderately" or "extremely" for any of the items numbered 19 through 23, you might suffer from *social and performance fears*. Steven had many fears like this and was very afraid that he would do or say something embarrassing or that others would see how nervous he was.
- If your answer was "moderately" or "extremely" for any of the items numbered 24 through 29, this sounds like *obsessive fears*. Many people with this kind of fear—such as Rachel, who had obsessive worries about contamination—fall into a habit of performing compulsive behaviors that are designed to prevent disasters or make themselves feel better.
- If your answer was "moderately" or "extremely" for any of the items numbered 30 through 34, *excessive worries* might be the problem. Like Samantha, you tend to think up worst-case scenarios, and you find these ideas frightening.
- Finally, if your answer was "moderately" or "extremely" for any of the items numbered 35 through 39, you might have *post-traumatic fears* that can develop after a horrific or life-threatening experience, as Andrea experienced after being assaulted.

Sometimes, taking a quiz like this can raise important questions. Here are a few that might have come up for you.

- *I said "extremely" to item 24. Does that mean I have OCD?* Not necessarily. It's important to recognize that this quiz is not meant to diagnose anxiety disorders (or any other psychiatric disorders). Diagnoses can be made only after a thorough evaluation by a professional. What it does mean, however, is that you have a certain fear that you can work on.

- *The quiz showed that I have more than one category of fear. Does that mean my problem is really severe?* Don't worry; it's pretty normal for people's fears to fit more than one category, and it doesn't necessarily mean that you're any worse off than someone who has only one category of fear. It simply means that as you design your exposure program, you'll need to pay careful attention to each category.

- *My fear isn't on the list. Does that mean that I'm really weird, or that this program can't help me?* Not at all! The list of fears out there is way longer than I could fit into this quiz. If your particular fear isn't listed there, it doesn't mean that this program is not for you. If you can find some overlap between your fear and one or more of the six categories (that is, you can determine that your fear is of a specific situation or object, body sensations, or social or performance situations, or that you have obsessive fears, excessive worries, or post-traumatic fears), you can use this program (plus a little of your own creativity) to beat it.

- *My fears were no more than "a little bit." Does that mean I shouldn't do anything about them?* If your fears are mild, you might still choose to work on them. My general rule of thumb is that if it's bad enough to bother you, it's bad enough to work on. In chapter 3, I'll show you a thinking exercise that can help you make a well-reasoned decision about what to do.

Who Is This Book For?

I wrote this book, first and foremost, for people who want to get rid of their fears. As I mentioned earlier, people who circled "moderately" or "extremely" for one or more items are likely to see a great improvement in their quality of life by following the program outlined here, although others with milder fears that are still bad enough to be bothersome will also likely find the program to be helpful.

This book is deliberately broad in its scope. As a practicing psychologist, I've read countless books on phobias, obsessive-compulsive disorder, posttraumatic stress disorder, and so on. Many of them are quite good, and I refer to them quite frequently (and will list some of my favorites for you later in this book). Yet the more I read, the more I became aware that most of these books are saying pretty much the same thing. When you get right down to it, the instructions we give to someone with social phobia are not markedly different from those we give to a person with obsessive-compulsive disorder. The instructions we give to someone with a fear of spiders are not dramatically different from what we tell an individual with posttraumatic stress disorder. Rather, these different programs are mostly variations on the same theme. The core features—exposure, eliminating avoidance and safety behaviors, addressing scary thoughts, and tracking progress—are consistent across all of these disorders. That's why this book is intended to apply to a wide range of people with fears, rather than to one specific diagnosis or type of fear. So whether your fears resemble Audrey's and Michelle's fears of specific situations or objects, Susan's fear of body sensations, Steven's social and performance fears, Rachel's obsessive fears, Samantha's excessive worries, or Andrea's post-traumatic fears, this book was written with you in mind. I emphasize the common elements that apply to a wide range of fears so that you can develop an effective program to help yourself. Of course, when differences do come up, I provide specific recommendations that are tailored to match your concerns.

You might also find this program helpful if you have a loved one whose life has been affected by excessive fear. You cannot (and should not) force people to face their fears, but you can provide support and guidance with the help of this book. In addition, the information in this book will help you understand what your loved ones are going through, why they are going through it, and what they need to do to get past it. In my clinic, I often find it extremely valuable to have a "coach," such as a friend or a family member, who can help the fearful person with his or her exposure program. People might read this book along with their loved ones, so that they can team up and work on the fears together.

Finally, mental health clinicians who work with fearful patients may benefit from reading this book. Despite the wealth of evidence supporting the use of exposure therapy, it is woefully underutilized in clinical practice. This means that most people who undergo mental health treatment for their fears receive sub-optimal treatment. One main reason for this underutilization, according to surveys of mental health professionals, is a lack of training in these procedures in graduate programs. I hope that this book can play a role in bringing many clinicians up to speed in the most effective, evidence-based interventions.

What Can I Expect in This Book?

This book focuses on exposure therapy, a powerful strategy for beating fears. Exposure therapy means facing your fears in a way that heals you, rather than traumatizes you. It's not the easiest program in the world, I admit, but it is not torture. It won't be awful, and the potential payoff is huge: a life free of excessive fears. In chapter 3, I include data from carefully controlled research studies showing just how powerful this strategy can be.

We will start with education. It's important that you be armed with as much knowledge as possible about your fear in order to beat it. So throughout the book (and especially in chapters 2, 3, and 4), I provide you with information about fear, how it works, and how to beat it. No skipping this part! In chapters 5 through 8, I guide you, step by step, as you develop your own plan for expo-sure therapy. I'll show you lots of examples of how to put your plan into practice in chapters 9 through 14. Finally, in chapters 15 through 17, we will review ways for you to monitor your progress and fine-tune the program to maximize its effectiveness.

Will It Work?

Of course, I'd be lying if I said that this (or any) program was guaranteed to work. Nothing works for everyone. Furthermore, even people who do respond well to a program sometimes find that they still struggle with certain fears. I can tell you this, however: decades of solid research, conducted by highly experienced and respected researchers, tells me that exposure therapy is the single best thing you can do to beat fear. I'll give you some statistics to prove that in chapter 3, but for now, I'll let the people from my clinic give you their take on it:

> The other day, I was watching TV and there was a snake on. It was a desert snake, going through the sand. Previously, I would have been terrified and would have had to change the channel or close my eyes. I probably would have ended up having nightmares about snakes. But this time, I was fascinated. It was kind of neat to see the patterns that the snake made in the sand. This was how I knew my life had really changed, that I could look and be interested, as opposed to being fearful. I even went back and watched a couple of YouTube videos about snakes. I'm not in love with snakes, and I probably never will be. But I'm not afraid any more. My family thinks it's the most terrific thing I've ever done. My younger sister sent me a card, saying how proud she was that I had beaten this fear that I'd been lugging around since we were kids.
>
> —*Audrey*

Exposure therapy truly changed the path of my life. I still struggle with the fear of vomit. The "stomach bug" months

are always hard for me, and the irrational thoughts sometimes creep back up. But when they do, I have the tools to
deal with them. I am wiser than my phobia. I am stronger
than my phobia. I have fun with my family. Real fun! Not
fake fun, as it was before. I feel as if I am forever changed.
I even became a school nurse substitute—a job I was sure
I could never handle prior to therapy. I have surrounded
myself with children who have tummy aches and anxiety
(the most common reasons to go to the nurse). And I love
those schoolkids. They are great. Because of exposure
therapy, I have become the trump card. I can choose to let
the anxiety beat me, or I can choose to trump it. That is
the choice I have made and the choice I hope I will continue to make in the future.

—*Michelle*

My life has changed so much. I am on my fourth and final
week of weaning off the medications I have been on since
I was eighteen. I haven't had a full blown panic attack in
more than six months. I went to New York City. I *drove* in
the city! I walked around with friends until the wee hours
of the morning. We even toasted over dinner to the fact
that I actually was strong enough now to get out, to a for-
eign place, a city no less, and enjoy my time without a care
in the world. I go to the movies all the time. I go out with
friends constantly. I couldn't be at a happier place right
now in my life. I can actually function and not be a petri-
fied person, scared of my own shadow.

—*Susan*

My life has changed dramatically since I started to face my
fears. If I encounter a social situation that makes me anxious, I make myself participate. I still feel a little bit of

anxiety, but the results have been very positive. I'm much more comfortable making conversation with people and attending social functions. I'm involved in local politics now, which requires me to speak in front of people, attend social functions, and even march in parades! It's much easier for me to talk to people, I worry less about making mistakes, and I feel freer to be myself.

—Steven

Facing my fears allowed me to get my life back. Everything came back to me—work, play, friends, cleaning normally. Everything is better. I can do so many things and not wash that it doesn't even faze me. On occasion, I'll have a blip of OCD. But it's a blip, and I turn right around and stare OCD in the face and say, "Oh, no, you don't, you're not getting into my world again. Beat it," and I go about touching the item or doing the activity.

—Rachel

I have not had an anxiety attack in more than a year. While some of the same worries occasionally pop up, they quickly come and go. My mind and body don't react to the worries in the same way, and I just don't stay afraid for extended periods of time. My son is getting ready to fly to Ecuador to visit his girlfriend in a week, and although the thought of that makes me uncomfortable, I don't shy away from thinking about it nor do I go into panic mode. I am relaxed and not as irritating to my partner. I realize that there will probably come a time when I need a tune-up—and I think I have learned a lot of the skills to develop exposures on my own.

—Samantha

There's a freedom that comes with not having to be constrained by fear. I still wish that the assault had never happened and that I had been spared all of the stress and anxiety. Sometimes I'm glad that it wasn't worse and that I wasn't hurt physically. These days, I don't get upset when I think about it. I see it mostly as a bad thing that happened that I still think of occasionally but that doesn't really affect my life on a daily basis any more.

—Andrea

I couldn't have said it better myself. The proof is in the pudding. These people are not alone. Thousands and thousands of people have overcome their fears and reclaimed their lives using exposure therapy, and *you can, too.*

Confucius is quoted as saying, "A journey of a thousand miles begins with a single step." Congratulations on having taken the first step. Now have the courage to take a few more steps in the following chapters.

What Is Fear?

Nothing in life is to be feared. It is only to be understood.

—*Marie Curie*

Remember my experience on the airplane that I described in chapter 1? What exactly was going on? My emotional state was fear. Fear is a complex, largely involuntary chain of biological, cognitive (mental), and behavioral reactions that serves an important purpose: to protect me from danger. Evolutionary theorists, beginning with Walter Cannon in 1914, have described fear as a "fight-flight-freeze" response to an external threat. As its name suggests, this response developed to make a human being (or an animal) *fight* (attack the threatening creature), *flee* (run away from the danger), or *freeze* (hold still or play dead, in hopes of not being noticed). The fight-flight-freeze response is a miracle of evolution. Without it, our species would have been wiped out long ago.

Imagine, for a moment, being one of our early ancestors out on the African savannah. This is a very dangerous place, with lots of predatory animals that are much stronger and faster than you are. Imagine further that you hear a slight rustling in the grass, and out of the corner of your eye you catch a glimpse of something large moving toward you. If you want to live to see tomorrow, you need a set of mental and behavioral responses that are so deeply ingrained, so hard-wired, that they will happen automatically and instantaneously. Without even thinking about it—in fact, maybe a split-second *before* you even realize consciously that you've seen or heard something—your attention is drawn to the location of the sight and the sound, your brain becomes extremely focused (perhaps to the exclusion of everything else, as if you have tunnel vision), and your body instinctively begins to mobilize to deal with the threat. Your heart rate speeds up, your muscles become tense, and your breathing becomes more rapid. Very quickly, and very efficiently, you are ready to attack, run away, or freeze.

Fear and the fight-flight-freeze response are basically good. They were designed to keep you alive, and, for the most part, they do a pretty darn good job of it. We run into problems, however, when the fight-flight-freeze response misfires. Think of it as being similar to a car alarm: you want the alarm to sound when someone tries to break into your car, but you don't want the alarm to go off when a strong wind blows or a bird lands on the car's roof. When your car alarm goes off too easily, it is too sensitive. Yes, it will let you know when someone is trying to steal your car, but it will also go off at the wrong times. So even though in reality there is only a strong wind, the alarm reacts as if someone is breaking into your car.

People who have excessive fears have an internal alarm system—the fight-flight-freeze response—that is too sensitive. Just as the sensitive car alarm says "car thief" when the reality is "strong wind," the sensitive internal alarm says "danger," even though the reality is much more benign. The object of your fear— whether it is flying, public speaking, dirt, the dark, or something else—is like the strong wind, and your internal alarm reacts as if it were really threatening. When your car alarm acts this way, it needs to be fixed or recalibrated. Similarly, when your internal alarm—your fight-flight-freeze response—is overly sensitive, you have to retrain it. That's what this book will teach you to do. The goal is to retrain your brain not to sound the alarm unless an actual danger is present.

We'll start by learning about fear and how it works. We will examine fear from three perspectives: biological, cognitive, and behavioral. These perspectives aren't mutually exclusive; you won't need to pick which one you agree with the most. They're all important, and they're all valid. As I'll soon explain, knowing how these three aspects of fear operate and interact with one another is key to understanding fear.

The Biological Perspective

From a biological perspective, fear can be understood in terms of the central nervous system (the brain and the spinal cord) and the peripheral nervous system (all of the nerves of the body). Let's start with the central nervous system. Fear involves lots of regions of the brain, but for our purposes we should pay particular attention to two areas: the *amygdala* and the *frontal cortex*. You can see these areas of the brain in the following picture.

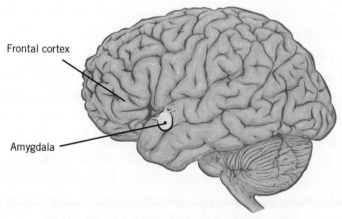

Frontal cortex

Amygdala

The amygdala and the frontal cortex of the brain.

The amygdala seems to be the primary source of our fear reactions. When we electrically stimulate a person's amygdala, he or she immediately experiences feelings of fear and signs of physical arousal. If we put someone in a brain-imaging scanner and have the person imagine really scary things, we can see the amygdala become increasingly active. On the other hand, individuals with damaged amygdalas have difficulty recognizing fearful facial expressions in others and don't seem to develop fears as readily as most people do. So it's pretty clear that the amygdala is a major driving force behind fearful reactions.

According to the late neuroscientist Paul MacLean, the amygdala and its surrounding brain region (called the *limbic system*) have been around since mammals first walked the earth (actually, some scientists think they've been around longer than that). By contrast, the cerebral cortex (which includes the frontal cortex) is a relative newcomer, evolutionarily speaking. The frontal cortex is part of what makes us distinctly human. It gives us the powers of logic and reason, helps us control our behavior, and enables us to solve complex problems. When we do that thing we call "thinking," it's mostly our frontal cortex doing the work. When people suffer damage to their frontal lobes, they often think more rigidly and concretely, become impulsive, have problems with creativity and problem solving, and fail to learn behavioral rules. So you need the frontal cortex in order to think things through, make good decisions, and help you understand what's really going on.

As you might imagine, there is a constant tug of war in your brain between your amygdala and your frontal cortex. The amygdala is in charge of sounding the fear alarm, whereas your frontal cortex is responsible for thinking about things rationally. If your brain were the starship *Enterprise* from *Star Trek*, your amygdala would be Scotty—always sounding the alarm in a panic. Your frontal cortex, on the other hand, would be Spock—cool, logical, and thoughtful. A conversation between the two parts, as imagined by comedian Eddie Murphy, might go like this:

Scotty [*in a panicked voice*]: Captain! The ship can't take much more of this! She's about to blow!

Spock [*sounding cool and calm*]: Mr. Scott, why don't you take the phasers and point them at the dylithium crystals and then use the power from the phasers to regenerate the dylithium crystals and we can get out on the impulse power.

Scotty [*still shrieking*]: Mr. Spock! It just might work!

Spock: It worked last week.

So the amygdala—Scotty—is responsible for the fear alarm. How does that signal in your brain turn into the heart-pounding, lump-in-the-throat, butterflies-in-the-stomach experience of fear? To answer that question, we need to look at the peripheral nervous system (all of the nerves of the body except the brain and the spinal cord). When the amygdala sounds the fear alarm (which happens because you have perceived a threat), assuming the frontal cortex (the voice of reason) doesn't put the brakes on, it sends a signal to another part of the brain called the hypothalamus, which in turn signals the pituitary gland, which stimulates the adrenal glands to secrete adrenaline into the bloodstream. The adrenaline then travels to all of the organs of the body and turns on the sensations known as the fight-flight-freeze response. This process—how the fear alarm makes its way from your amygdala to your entire body—is called the *hypothalamic-pituitary-adrenal axis*, or HPA axis.

More than You Probably Wanted to Know about the HPA Axis

The amygdala signals the hypothalamus, which in turn releases a substance called *corticotrophin-releasing hormone*, or CRH. Blood vessels carry CRH to the pituitary gland, which in turn releases another substance called *adrenocorticotropic hormone*, or ACTH. ACTH stimulates the adrenal glands, which sit on top of the kidneys. The adrenal glands secrete epinephrine into the bloodstream,

(Continued)

leading to sympathetic nervous system activation—what we call the "fight-flight-freeze" response.

One bit of good news is that in addition to adrenaline, the adrenal glands also produce a hormone called *cortisol*, which is sometimes called the "stress hormone." Cortisol travels back through the bloodstream to the hypothalamus, signaling it to stop producing CRH. In this manner, cortisol works a little bit like the thermometer connected to your thermostat—it tells the machine that it's getting too warm, so shut off the heat. Your body, therefore, has a natural way of stopping the sympathetic nervous system and returning to its baseline state. Fear doesn't last forever.

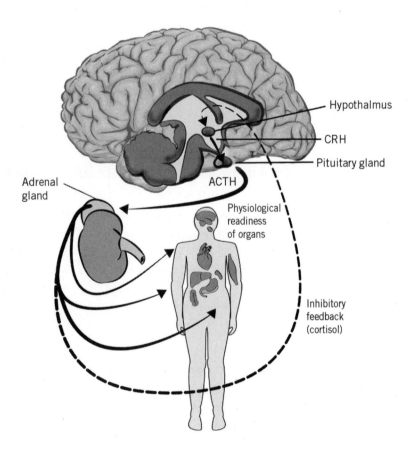

Hypothalmus

CRH

Pituitary gland

ACTH

Adrenal gland

Physiological readiness of organs

Inhibitory feedback (cortisol)

The hypothalamic-pituitary-adrenal (HPA) axis.

Now, when the adrenaline makes its way throughout your body, a number of biological changes occur that are collectively called the sympathetic nervous system. The sympathetic nervous system's job is to mobilize the body's resources under stress by inducing the "fight-flight-freeze" response. Remember, this process kept your ancestors from getting eaten. The general rule of thumb is that you need to be physically ready to run or fight.

> When I felt afraid, my heart would beat faster, and my palms got sweaty. If I heard a noise in my apartment, I would wonder if someone broke in, and I would freeze in place and listen.
>
> —*Andrea*

Preparing yourself to run or fight means sending more power to your fighting and running muscles (your thighs, for example). In the body, power means oxygen, and oxygen means blood. So, if we need to get more oxygen-rich blood to the thighs, how do we do it? One way is to increase oxygen production. Our cardiovascular system is constantly replenishing the supply of oxygen-rich blood in the body. We breathe in, taking oxygen into our lungs; that oxygen attaches itself to blood cells, and the heart pumps the blood into the body. There, our cells use up the oxygen, and the blood is returned to the lungs, where it picks up more oxygen. This system of pumping and breathing gives our bodies energy. Increasing production, therefore, means more breathing and more pumping. So, under threatening or stressful conditions, we find that our heart rate increases (and sometimes we even feel as if our hearts are pounding in our chests), and our breathing becomes more rapid (maybe even to the point of hyperventilating). These reactions have a purpose: to increase the flow of oxygen-rich blood so our thighs can help us run better.

My heart would race, my stomach would clench to the point of getting sick, I would sweat, feel cold or numb, and sleep would be impossible. When I was younger, my hands and my lips would feel funny, almost like they were swollen or something. I used to actually touch my mouth and look at my hands to be sure they hadn't swollen up; the feeling was so real.

—Samantha

My stomach was in a constant knot, filled with butterflies, from the minute I woke up in the morning until I passed out, from exhaustion, at the end of the day. I also would find it very hard to breathe. And I would cry, all the time, every day. Cry, cry, cry.

—Rachel

Another way to maximize the oxygen supply to the thighs is by diverting oxygen-rich blood away from other, less essential areas of the body. When facing imminent threat, you don't need to, say, work on digesting your breakfast. It takes energy to digest food, and right now your thighs need that energy. So your body, quite logically, shuts down the digestive system. Any food in your stomach or intestines stops being broken down and sits there like a rock, giving you an upset stomach or nausea. Your salivary glands, which are also part of the digestive system, shut down, too, causing your mouth to feel dry and your throat to feel as if something's stuck in it. Blood can also be diverted away from the extremities of your body, such as your hands, feet, or face, causing those body parts to feel numb or tingly (the technical term for that is paresthesias) or even to turn white.

Now, if there really is a saber-toothed tiger jumping out at you, you will be very glad that all of these things are happening. Your body is a survival machine, and the sympathetic nervous system works so well that you don't even need to think about it.

Sympathetic Nervous System

When the adrenal glands on top of the kidneys release adrenaline, the adrenaline makes its way through your body and a number of biological changes occur that are collectively called the sympathetic nervous system. These changes affect the following:

- Pupils
- Salivary glands
- Heart
- Bronchi of the lungs
- Liver
- Stomach
- Small intestine
- Large intestine
- Bladder

It turns on without your even knowing it (a good thing, too, because saber-toothed tigers move pretty fast). You will sprint out of there or pick up a club and clobber the tiger, burn off that adrenaline, and feel better. Of course, if there *isn't* a saber-toothed tiger, that's another story. Now you're simply standing there, with a racing heart, rapid breathing, an upset stomach, a dry mouth, and tingly fingers and toes, feeling rotten.

The Cognitive Perspective

The biological perspective isn't the only way to understand fear. Psychiatrist Aaron T. Beck pointed out that people become anxious not merely because of the feared object or situation, but also because of the particular *thoughts* or *beliefs* they have about that object or situation. For example, instead of saying, "This airplane flight scares me," it would be more accurate, according to Beck's theory (which we call *cognitive theory*), to say, "I feel scared because I am telling myself that this airplane is going to crash." It is my thought process, not the airplane itself, that is scaring me.

When our beliefs are completely rational and proportional to real danger, the system works just fine. After all, just like the biological system, the cognitive system developed to prepare you to deal with threats. Unfortunately, just as we saw with the biological system, the cognitive system can sometimes misfire. In such cases, our threat-related thoughts or beliefs tell us that an object or a situation is more dangerous than it actually is. When thought processes go wrong, they tend to do so in predictable ways, and fearful people make the same mental errors (which Beck termed *cognitive distortions*) over and over again.

One common cognitive distortion is *probability overestimation*: believing a bad outcome or event to be more likely to occur than it actually is. For example, if you had asked me, in the middle of that turbulent flight, what the probability of the plane crashing was, I might have said that there was a 25 percent chance of a crash. Of course, now that I'm off the plane and can think about it a bit more rationally, I realize how illogical my thoughts were: if there was a 25 percent chance of a plane crash, that would mean one out of every four planes crashes. There would be planes falling out of the sky all over the place! In reality, the odds of being involved in a plane crash are only about 1 in 11 million. So my belief about the likelihood of a plane crash was extremely exaggerated. In fact, if my thought process had been based on actual probabilities, I should have been much more afraid of the drive to the airport than of the flight, because the odds of dying in a car crash are a thousand times greater than those of dying in a plane crash. Come to think of it, because the leading causes of death (by a huge margin) are heart disease, stroke, and cancer, maybe I should be most afraid of the burger and fries I had at the airport while waiting for my plane!

Another common cognitive distortion is *catastrophizing*, or "making mountains out of molehills." In addition to overestimating the likelihood of a bad outcome, we tend to overestimate the significance, importance, seriousness, or magnitude of that bad outcome. A while back, I was talking to a young man who was terrified of public speaking. When I asked him what he thought might happen if he gave a speech, he said, "I'd start stuttering and blushing and sweating." "And what would be so bad about that?"

I asked. "Well, if people saw me acting that way, they'd know I was anxious." "And then?" "And then they'd laugh at me and ridicule me, and no one would respect me, and my social life would be over." This is a classic case of catastrophizing. His fearful feelings came not only from the thought that he would stutter and blush and sweat; rather, he got really scared when he thought that stuttering and blushing and sweating would be the end of the world. In reality, though, it seems pretty unlikely that it would have actually turned out that way. All of us have been embarrassed at one time or another, and most of us found that life went on after that.

In chapter 8, I'll talk more about cognitive distortions and how to deal with them. For now, though, just remember that two of the main culprits when it comes to fear are probability overestimation and catastrophizing: exaggerating the probability and the seriousness of bad outcomes.

Not only can we have errors in our mental content (our beliefs and thoughts), but we also can have errors in our mental processes (how our brains process information). Your brain is constantly taking in information through the sensory organs (such as your eyes and ears), processing that information to make sense of it, and selecting what information should be retained and what can be discarded. The cognitive processes involved are attention (selecting what to look at, listen to, and so on), interpretation (assigning meaning to ambiguous information), and memory (selectively storing information that can be retrieved and used later). Fear can result from problems in one or more of these cognitive processes, as described further on.

It's clear that people with excessive fears have biases in attention. Here's a true story: my colleagues Chris and Liz were recently walking down a hallway in my clinic. Chris is terrified of insects; Liz is not. As they walked, Chris let out a shriek, screaming, "Look at that bug!" It took a while for Liz to detect the small cricket on the carpet. "I wouldn't have even seen it if you hadn't pointed it out," said Liz. Chris, who is fearful of bugs, spotted the insect much more easily than did Liz, who is not fearful.

This phenomenon has been demonstrated in numerous studies. Psychologist Fraser Watts conducted one such study, in which he asked people with and without spider phobias to complete a version of a test called the Stroop color-naming task. In this task, the participant is shown a number of words that are printed in different colors, and the participant's job is to name the color that the word is printed in (and therefore to ignore the word itself and just focus on naming the colors as fast as possible). When the word *spider* was inserted into the word list, people with spider phobia slowed down their color-naming considerably—their brains were having a hard time disregarding the word and focusing on the color. Despite instructions to the contrary, people with spider phobias could not stop paying attention to spider-related things. Thus, fearful people seem to have an attentional bias toward threat. That's great if you're an early human on the savannah trying not to get eaten—it's definitely to your advantage to let threatening creatures and situations pull your attention away from mundane ones—but not great if you're trying to live in modern society and can't prevent yourself from watching out of the corner of your eye for spiders or can't stop paying attention to the beating of your heart.

> I would get a funny feeling in my head or my body, and it would be something so subtle, the average person wouldn't even notice it. With the disorder, I became very in tune with my body. So in tune I could almost feel my own blood through my veins. I would start to get jumpy. Then I would think, "Hmm, something might be wrong with me. . . . I could drop dead at any second!" For no reason at all, mind you. But I was convinced.
>
> —*Susan*

I grew up on a farm, and I was always fearful that snakes were around. If I was outside with the other kids building a fort or something, I might hear some rustle in the woods and would listen to see if it was a snake. It was always in the back of my mind. And of course, in my mind every noise was a snake.

—Audrey

Interpretation problems also seem to occur frequently in people with excessive fears. Psychologists Michael Eysenck, Colin MacLeod, and Andrew Mathews demonstrated this phenomenon in a study of how anxious people interpret ambiguous stimuli. These scientists read a list of words out loud to their research participants and asked them to write the words down on a piece of paper. The words on the list were called "homophones"—words that sound identical but are spelled differently, for example, *dye* and *die*, or *pane* and *pain*. The overly anxious participants were more likely to write down the threatening spellings than were the less anxious participants. So when several interpretations of an ambiguous situation are possible, fearful people tend to go for the most threatening one.

Finally, people with excessive fears can have biased memory. Unlike the memory of your computer, the memory of your brain is highly selective. When you save a document on your computer and pull it up later, you get exactly what you saved. When your brain retrieves a memory of an event, however, it engages in a complicated selection process, deciding what should be retrieved and what should not. Psychologists Adam Radomsky and Jack Rachman conducted an experiment with patients suffering from obsessive-compulsive disorder (OCD) who had a severe fear of contamination. They also included a group of patients with other anxiety-related concerns and a group of student volunteers without strong fears. They showed all of the participants fifty objects (for example, a CD or a box of crayons), twenty-five of which were rubbed with a tissue that participants were told had been found used on the hospital floor. They then tested participants' memories of the objects they had been shown. Contamination-fearful

OCD patients had a better memory for "contaminated" objects than for "clean" ones. Neither of the other two groups showed such a bias. Anxious people, therefore, are more likely to retrieve fearful memories than benign or pleasant memories. Similar results have been obtained with people who have other fears—they tend to selectively recall information that is consistent with their fears.

The result of these cognitive biases is that fearful people tend to see and hear more threats around them, read more danger into ambiguous situations or objects, and selectively recall experiences that seem threatening or dangerous. Their world is inherently scarier than is the world of someone without these fears. This process just serves to confirm their fear-related beliefs: I believe that this airplane is highly likely to crash (probability overestimation). Therefore, I listen more carefully to the sound of the engines (attentional bias), interpret the sound of the engines as whining and labored (interpretive bias), and selectively recall scary flights I've been on and plane crashes I've seen on TV (memory bias). These processing biases, in turn, serve to strengthen my belief that the plane is likely to crash.

The Behavioral Perspective

Our behavior also plays a critical role in maintaining our fears. In the 1950s, research psychologist Richard Solomon and his colleagues were doing research on fear learning in dogs. They used a principle called classical conditioning, in which two things that are presented together eventually elicit the same reaction. In this case, they would flash a light and then administer an electric shock through the metal floor of the dog's cage. The dogs, of course, would react fearfully. Eventually, the researchers didn't need to use the shock anymore; simply flashing the light was enough to elicit a fear reaction in the dogs. The scientists then turned their attention to getting the dogs to stop fearing the light. Classical conditioning research tells us that just flashing the light over and over again, without the shocks—a process called *extinction*— should eventually lead to reduced fear by showing the dog that there would be no more shocks. And that's just what happened, until the scientists added a unique twist to the procedure. Some of the dogs were given the opportunity, once the light flashed, to jump over a small fence and get away from the metal floor that had previously shocked them. When the dogs had the ability to escape from the thing that was scaring them (the light), their fears persisted indefinitely. Dogs that were blocked from jumping over the fence, on the other hand—dogs that were forced to face their fear—learned not to be afraid of the light. Therefore, avoidance and escape behaviors, even small ones, cause fear to persist.

Let's see how this applies to human fears. Suppose, for example, that you're afraid of public speaking. Just thinking about having to give a speech causes you to feel sweaty and nervous, and you're convinced that if you had to give a speech, you'd stammer, blush, or throw up, and it would be awful (if you recognized this pattern of thinking as catastrophizing, good catch!). So, quite naturally, you're highly motivated to avoid public speaking. Let's say you're able to do that. You select a job that doesn't require you to speak in front of other people. You don't volunteer to give the toast at weddings or parties, to be a reader in church, or to lead activities in your child's scout troop. What do you imagine would happen to your fear of public speaking over time? That's right, it would persist indefinitely. Just like Solomon's dogs that were able to jump over the fence whenever they saw the light flash, to get away from an electrical shock that wasn't going to happen anyway, your avoidant behavior would prevent you from learning the truth: that you could probably get through the ordeal, and nothing awful would happen. The only way to really learn the truth and beat that fear is to *stop avoiding what you are afraid of.*

Snowball Effects

So we see that fear has distinct physiological, cognitive, and behavioral elements. These various components of fear tend to influence one another, for better or for worse. An increase in the

Criteria for a Panic Attack*

A panic attack is described as a "burst" of intense fear or discomfort, with symptoms that develop suddenly. Symptoms can include the following:

Heart palpitations or increased heart rate
Sweating
Shaking
Shortness of breath
Feeling of choking
Chest pain
Nausea or upset stomach
Feeling dizzy, lightheaded, or faint
Feelings of unreality or of being detached from oneself
Fear of losing control or going "crazy"
Fear of dying
Numbness or tingling sensations
Cold or hot sensations

This information is taken from the DSM-IV-TR, American Psychiatric Association, 2000.

cognitive component of fear, for example, tends to cause an increase in the physiological and behavioral components of fear.

Let's use my experience on the airplane as an example. When I felt the plane shaking and heard the engine noise change, I interpreted those movements and sounds as being dangerous, and I began to think that the plane was likely to crash (cognitive fear

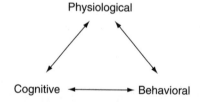

The interaction of the physiological, cognitive, and behavioral elements of fear.

response). When I said this to myself, my heart started racing, and my mouth went dry (physiological fear response). I also gripped the arm rests tightly (behavioral fear response). Thinking scared makes you feel and act scared. In fact, research has shown that an increase in any one of these three components can lead to an increase in the other two. So feeling scared makes you think and act scared; acting scared makes you think and feel scared. When the three components of fear really start to influence one another strongly, the end result is a panic attack: a discrete period of intense fear characterized by several physical and cognitive symptoms.

As we can see, a panic attack is a product of the sympathetic nervous system (physiological), with some catastrophizing (cognitive) thrown in.

Where Does Fear Come From?

Fear arises from a lot of different sources. For many people, several of these sources have to coincide in order for the fear to develop. One source is genetic. It is very clear that fears and anxiety-related problems run in families—that is, if you have one or more close biological relatives with an anxiety disorder, you are significantly more likely to have an anxiety disorder yourself. Chances are, you don't inherit fear itself; rather, you inherit a set of biological characteristics (such as particular brain processes or sensitivity of the sympathetic nervous system) that makes it easier for fears to develop.

Beyond whatever genetic or physical elements are present that set the stage for fear development, the fear has to be learned in some manner. Psychologist Jack Rachman has surveyed individuals with severe fears and found evidence of three basic "pathways" in which fear can be learned. The first of these is direct, aversive experience. If, for example, a dog bites you, you could go on to develop a fear of dogs. A more extreme example might be someone who experiences a horrific, life-threatening trauma and then develops a complex set of fears called posttraumatic stress disorder. Yet most people with significant fears don't report these kinds of experiences. I, for one, have never been in a plane crash, so direct aversive experience isn't a very good explanation for my fear reaction on the plane. I have, however, seen movie and TV depictions of plane crashes, and this is Rachman's second "pathway" to fear—vicarious (observational) learning. That is, seeing someone else have a bad experience can be sufficient. If you saw the movie *Jaws* and subsequently felt afraid to swim in the ocean, you know what I'm talking about. Finally, fear can be learned through the transmission of information. Even if you don't have the bad experience yourself or see someone else have the bad experience, merely learning about the likelihood of it happening can instill fear in some people. Take the example of a parent who is overly fearful of dogs. The parent believes that dogs are really dangerous and communicates this to his or her children through words ("Stay away from that dog, or it'll bite you!") and actions (avoiding dogs, trembling in their presence). The child can pick up on this fear through information transmission alone.

It's worth noting that our fears don't always match up with reality very well. For example, many of us have seen movie and TV depictions of gun violence, and certainly we are aware of how dangerous guns can be, yet relatively few of us have an excessive fear of guns. Conversely, lots of us fear snakes. Statistically speaking, snakes are much less likely to kill us than guns are. So, what gives? Psychologist Martin Seligman suggested that we are genetically prepared to learn to fear certain things more than others. Yes, guns are a leading cause of death now, but back in caveman days, when the basic blueprint of our brains was evolving, snakes were far more dangerous. So what we tend to fear now, according to Seligman's preparedness theory, are things that were legitimate threats to our caveman ancestors—such as snakes, spiders, high places, being trapped, or hostile strangers.

But what about the fear of flying, you might ask? After all, that's a common fear, but certainly no caveman ever set foot aboard an airplane. It helps to think about what's different between flying, which many people fear, and driving, which fewer people fear, despite it being much more dangerous. Flying on a plane involves being in a confined space, being up high, and not feeling in control of what happens—all elements that might have represented real threats to our ancestors (and therefore still trigger fear in our caveman brains).

Fear can come from many places—our genes, our learning experiences, or a combination of these. For some of us with severe fears, the cause will be pretty obvious, such as an extreme traumatic event. For the rest of us, though, we may never have a perfect answer for where our fears came from. That's okay, though. It's good to think about how your fear started (the etiology of your fear) as a first step to analyzing and understanding the fear. The method of beating fear that I discuss in this book places more emphasis on figuring out what causes the fear to persist, day in and day out (the maintenance of the fear). Therefore, even if you don't know where the fear came from, you can still create a good recovery plan by examining why the fear persists now. This book will pay close attention to factors that maintain your fears and will help you develop a plan to defeat them.

3

Why Face Fears?

To fear is one thing. To let fear grab you by the tail
and swing you around is another.

—*Katherine Paterson*

Facing fears is serious business. It's time-consuming and at
least moderately anxiety-provoking. So why do it? The short
answer is that fear and its variants (many of which are called
anxiety disorders) are painful and impairing—so potentially devastating, in fact, that many people decide that they need to do
whatever it takes to get them under control. Think carefully about
why you might want or need to beat fears. If you're like most
people with anxiety disorders, when you reflect on your situation,
you'll find the motivation it takes to sustain you through this
tough but very rewarding program.

Using a self-help approach to exposure therapy can be a powerful and effective way to overcome your fears. Although seeing
a professional therapist is certainly a good way to go, for many
people the power to beat fears is within their grasp by using this
program. If you need more help than that, this program will get

you off to a good start, and in chapter 17, I'll show you how to find a professional who can help further.

How's Your Motivation?

Fears can range from minor and annoying to terrifying and debilitating. Perhaps you're functioning reasonably well, and life isn't too bad, but you have a persistent fear that just irritates you, and you think you'd be happier if you could be rid of it. Or you might be so fearful that life has largely shut down and become intolerable. Or maybe, like a lot of folks, you're somewhere in the middle. Regardless of where you are on the severity spectrum, if your fear is bad enough that you want to do something about it, this program is for you.

> I had been afraid of snakes for more than fifty years. I thought that there was no way I could overcome it.
>
> —*Audrey*

> When exposures were first described to me, I was sure that I would actually get worse, and that really scared me. However, since I felt this was my best chance to make an improvement, I was willing to keep an open mind and work hard at whatever I needed to do. I was tired of being afraid all of the time.
>
> —*Samantha*

Are there reasons *not* to do exposure therapy? Sure. Exposure therapy is challenging. It takes time and energy. It's scary. Assuming you don't have certain serious medical or psychiatric problems, however, it's not dangerous. Yet you'll still need a pretty high level of motivation to get through the program. Therefore, I want you to think through your pros and cons of doing this program before you start. What do you have to lose? What do you stand to gain? How will your life be if you simply put this book down and accept the status quo? What might be possible if you actually have the courage to try my program?

On page 49 is a worksheet I'd like you to complete that will help you focus your thinking. I'll first show you a filled-out example below.

Reasons to keep the status quo	Reasons to face my fears
It's easier to just leave it alone. People don't expect as much from me. I have a ready excuse not to do things.	I'm tired of being afraid. It's embarrassing to be fearful. I don't want my kids to learn to be afraid from me. My work is suffering. I don't have much of a social life. I'm missing out on activities with my family.
What the future holds for me if I keep the status quo	**What the future holds for me if I face my fears**
I'll stay fearful. The longer I avoid things, the worse my fear will get. I'll become more isolated from friends and family. I might start to have performance problems at work. I'll regret missing out on an opportunity to make things better.	I'll feel better about myself. I'll be happier and less stressed out. I'll be more active with my friends and family. I won't be so irritable with people. I'll show my kids that I can be brave.

Now it's your turn. In a notebook or journal, create your own worksheet using this sample as a guide. Keep the notebook handy; you'll want to come back and refer to these answers later.

This exercise is important. I want you to think about what fear has taken from you, how it has affected your quality of life. Maybe it's caused your work or school performance to suffer. Perhaps it's affected your family and friends as well. Consider what your life will be like if you leave things as they are and really ponder whether you'd be satisfied with that. Now imagine a life

Reasons to keep the status quo	Reasons to face my fears
What the future holds for me if I keep the status quo	What the future holds for me if I face my fears

Sample worksheet to begin exposure therapy.

free of excessive fear, and think about what you stand to gain from facing your fears.

> My anxiety got so out of control, I realized I needed to take it by the throat and own it before it owned me for the rest of my life. It was definitely the best decision I ever made.
>
> —*Susan*

Anxiety Disorders

As I explained in the previous chapter, most fears fall into one or more of several categories: fears of specific situations or objects, fears of body sensations, social and performance fears, obsessive fears, excessive worries, and post-traumatic fears. These categories aren't diagnoses; rather, they're overarching groups that seem to represent general themes of fear, and I find them helpful in guiding our thinking and treatment planning. If you're like a lot of people with anxiety problems, however, you've already had some discussions with health-care professionals about fear, and diagnoses have probably come up, so it's good to know what they are. An anxiety disorder is any fear- or anxiety-based problem that is severe enough to have a significant impact on your quality of life. All mental health–related concerns are listed in the *DSM-IV-TR*. The *DSM-IV-TR* categorizes disorders into groups, such as mood disorders (which includes conditions such as major depressive disorder and bipolar disorder), psychotic disorders (which includes schizophrenia and delusional disorder), substance use disorders (which includes alcohol abuse and drug dependence), and the anxiety disorders. The anxiety disorders differ from one another in many ways but share one common feature: the presence of persistent, excessive, irrational fear. Following is a list of anxiety disorders in the *DSM-IV-TR*.

Anxiety Disorders

Disorder	*Hallmark Features*
Panic disorder	Recurrent, unexpected panic attacks and ongoing fear of future panic attacks
Agoraphobia	Avoidance of specific activities or locations due to fear of panic attacks or panic symptoms
Specific phobia	Excessive fear and avoidance of specific objects or activities
Social phobia	Excessive fear of social or performance situations that might be embarrassing or humiliating
Obsessive-compulsive disorder	Recurrent obsessive thoughts and compulsive behaviors
Generalized anxiety disorder	Excessive and uncontrollable worry about a range of life situations
Posttraumatic stress disorder	Intrusive memories, avoidance, and hyperarousal following a traumatic event
Separation anxiety disorder	Developmentally inappropriate anxiety about separating from home or caregivers

Panic disorder is characterized by panic attacks, which are discrete "bursts" of intense fear or discomfort that include some combination of the following symptoms: a racing or pounding heart, sweating, trembling, shortness of breath, choking feelings, chest pain, an upset stomach, feeling dizzy or lightheaded, feeling unreal or detached from oneself, fear of dying, fear of losing control or going crazy, numbness or tingling sensations, and chills or hot flushes. Recall from chapter 2 that the symptoms of a panic attack are essentially those of the sympathetic nervous system, with some mental catastrophizing. Panic attacks can be a feature of any anxiety disorder. In panic disorder, however, these panic attacks occur repeatedly and unexpectedly (meaning they take place in the absence of something that is perceived as particularly threatening or scary). Furthermore, people with panic disorder have a secondary reaction to their panic attacks: they worry persistently about having additional attacks, or they worry about what these attacks might mean (for example, that they will lose control, have a heart attack, or go crazy). At times, they might even go to the emergency room because of a fear that they're having a heart attack or some other medical crisis.

Another potential secondary reaction to panic attacks is when you make changes to your behavior or lifestyle because of the attacks. This behavioral complication of panic disorder is called *agoraphobia*. Although people often think that agoraphobia means a fear of open spaces (and, indeed, the literal translation from the Greek is "fear of the marketplace"), people suffering from agoraphobia actually fear being in places or situations from which it would be hard to escape or in which it would be difficult to obtain help, in the event of a panic attack. Feared places or situations could include being alone away from home, being in a crowd or standing in a line, going over bridges or through tunnels, driving on a highway, or using public transportation, such as buses or airplanes. Susan, whom you met in chapter 1, fell into a pattern of agoraphobic avoidance when she started to limit her driving, for fear that she would have a panic attack behind the wheel.

Again, the main reason the person avoids these situations is fear of having panic attacks or panic symptoms. In the case of people with agoraphobia who avoid airplanes, for example, the fear is not that the plane will crash; rather, the person is afraid that he or she will have a panic attack on the plane and will not be able to escape the situation. Some people with agoraphobia can engage in these activities only if they bring certain things with them, such as a cell phone, a bottle of pills, or a trusted companion—these anxiety-reducing tricks are called *safety behaviors*, which will be discussed in more detail in chapter 7.

Specific phobias involve an excessive and persistent fear of a particular object or situation (such as flying, heights, animals, receiving an injection, or seeing blood). People with specific phobias can become anxious simply by anticipating an encounter with these objects or situations, and their fears can escalate to the point of a panic attack. As shown in the list below, almost anything can be the target of the phobia (and I'm sure someone had fun coming up with the Greek names and then adding "-phobia" to the end; try saying hexakosioihexekontahexaphobia for a real mouthful). In reality, though, most of the phobias listed are quite rare. Most often, specific phobias tend to fall into one of five categories: animals (for example, snakes, spiders, cats, dogs), natural environment (such as storms, heights, water), blood-injection-injury (seeing blood or injuries, or receiving injections or having blood drawn), situational (for example, flying, enclosed places, or public transportation), and other (such as fears of choking or vomiting or fears of contracting illnesses). Audrey, who had a severe fear of snakes, and Michelle, who was afraid she would see someone vomit, had specific phobias.

Partial List of Phobias

Phobia	Fear of
Ablutophobia	Bathing, washing, or cleaning
Acrophobia	Heights
Agraphobia	Sexual abuse
Agyrophobia	Crossing roads

Aichmophobia	Sharp or pointed objects
Ailurophobia	Cats
Algophobia	Pain
Androphobia	Men
Anthophobia	Flowers
Anthropophobia	People or being in company
Apiphobia	Bees
Aquaphobia	Water
Arachnophobia	Spiders
Astraphobia	Thunder, lightning, and storms
Aviophobia	Flying
Bacillophobia	Microbes and bacteria
Chiroptophobia	Bats
Chorophobia	Dancing
Cibophobia	Food
Claustrophobia	Confined spaces
Coitophobia	Sexual intercourse
Coulrophobia	Clowns
Cynophobia	Dogs
Decidophobia	Making decisions
Dentophobia	Dentists and dental procedures
Emetophobia	Vomiting
Entomophobia	Insects
Equinophobia	Horses
Ergophobia	Work or functioning
Erotophobia	Sexual love or sexual questions
Erythrophobia	Pathological blushing
Gelotophobia	Being laughed at
Gephyrophobia	Bridges
Gerascophobia	Growing old
Gerontophobia	The elderly
Glossophobia	Speaking in public
Gymnophobia	Nudity
Gynophobia	Women
Halitophobia	Bad breath

(Continued)

Phobia	*Fear of*
Haptephobia	Being touched
Heliophobia	Sunlight
Hemophobia	Blood
Herpetophobia	Reptiles
Hexakosioihexekon-tahexaphobia	The number 666
Hoplophobia	Weapons
Ichthyophobia	Fish
Ligyrophobia	Loud noises
Lipophobia	Fats in food
Megalophobia	Large/oversized objects
Musophobia	Mice and/or rats
Mysophobia	Germs, contamination, or dirt
Necrophobia	Death, the dead
Neophobia	Newness, novelty
Nomophobia	Being out of mobile phone contact
Nosocomephobia	Hospitals
Nosophobia	Contracting a disease
Nyctophobia	Darkness
Ophidiophobia	Snakes
Ornithophobia	Birds
Osmophobia	Smells
Panphobia	Everything
Paraskavedekatriaphobia	Friday the thirteenth
Phagophobia	Swallowing
Pharmacophobia	Medications
Phasmophobia	Ghosts, specters, or phantasms
Phobophobia	Having a phobia
Phonophobia	Loud sounds
Pyrophobia	Fire
Radiophobia	Radioactivity or X-rays
Scoleciphobia	Worms
Scopophobia	Being looked at or stared at
Sociophobia	People or social situations

Somniphobia	Sleep
Spectrophobia	Mirrors and one's own reflections
Taphophobia	The grave, or fear of being placed in a grave while still alive
Technophobia	Technology
Tetraphobia	The number 4
Thanatophobia	Death
Tokophobia	Childbirth
Tomophobia	Surgeries/surgical operations
Traumatophobia	Having an injury
Triskaidekaphobia	The number 13
Trypanophobia	Needles or injections
Trypophobia	Geometrical objects
Xenophobia	Strangers, foreigners, or aliens
Zoophobia	Animals

The following exchange from the popular 1965 CBS-TV cartoon *A Charlie Brown Christmas* is a humorous example of how all-consuming specific phobias can be.

Lucy: Are you afraid of responsibility? If you are, then you have hypengyophobia.

Charlie Brown: I don't think that's quite it.

Lucy: How about cats? If you're afraid of cats, you have ailurophasia.

Charlie Brown: Well, sort of, but I'm not sure.

Lucy: Are you afraid of staircases? If you are, then you have climacaphobia. Maybe you have thalassophobia. This is fear of the ocean, or gephyrobia, which is the fear of crossing bridges. Or maybe you have pantophobia. Do you think you have pantophobia?

Charlie Brown: What's pantophobia?

Lucy: The fear of everything.

Charlie Brown: That's it!

Social phobia, also called *social anxiety disorder*, is an excessive fear of social or performance situations in which the person is exposed to unfamiliar people or to possible scrutiny from others. The person with social phobia isn't afraid of people per se; rather, he or she is afraid of acting in a way that will be embarrassing or humiliating (it would be a lot clearer if it were called embarrassment phobia). So, for example, someone with social phobia might be afraid that he will fall down in public while walking and that everyone will notice and laugh. Or she might fear stuttering when giving a speech, or blushing or sweating, which will cause everyone to know how anxious she is. Some people fear eating or writing in public or using a public bathroom, because of concerns that others are watching and scrutinizing and that this will lead to horrible embarrassment. Certain people with social phobias have a relatively limited range of fears—for example, someone who is only afraid of public speaking but is not afraid of other social or performance situations. Others have what is called a generalized subtype of social phobia, in which the fears include most social situations (such as initiating or maintaining conversations, dating, talking to authority figures, or going to parties).

Obsessive-compulsive disorder (OCD) is characterized by the presence of obsessions and/or compulsions. Obsessions are recurrent and intrusive thoughts, ideas, or images that come to mind over and over again and cause the person to feel anxious or uncomfortable or to have a strong sense of incompleteness or of things not being quite right. Some of the more common obsessive thoughts include fears of contamination (for example, a fear that objects are dirty or covered with germs), fears of accidentally hurting people (for example, a fear of accidentally running over a pedestrian or of accidentally causing a fire by leaving the oven on), fears of impulses (for example, a fear of suddenly being seized by an irresistible impulse to throw one's child out of a window), a fear of having personally repugnant thoughts (for example, thoughts or mental images that are blasphemous or sexually immoral), magical thoughts (for example, fears of "bad" numbers or colors, or fears that one can cause disasters merely by thinking about them), and concerns about exactness and order (for example, a need for possessions to be lined up just so or for things to be perfectly symmetrical).

Compulsions are behaviors or mental acts that the person does, more or less deliberately, to prevent disasters from occurring or in order to feel better. These compulsions tend to be done over and over again in a rigid fashion (they often need to be done "just so" or else it doesn't count, and therefore the acts have to be repeated). Some of the more common compulsions include washing and cleaning (for example, washing one's hands over and over again or scrubbing a countertop repeatedly), checking (such as circling the block to check whether one has accidentally run over a pedestrian; repeatedly checking the knobs of the oven to make sure they are off), mental compulsions (for example, repeatedly saying "good" words, phrases, or numbers to oneself; counting; or saying special prayers again and again), ordering and arranging (such as spending excessive time making sure one's clothes are lined up perfectly in the closet), and repeating (for instance, having to step through a doorway or get up from a chair over and over again because the action felt "not just right").

Generalized anxiety disorder (GAD) is characterized by persistent anxiety and worry about a number of events or activities (such as work or school performance, family stressors, finances, health, and so on). Of course, everyone feels worried from time to time; in GAD, however, the worries are both excessive (meaning they are grossly out of proportion to the actual stressor) and uncontrollable (the person has a hard time stopping the worry in order to focus on anything else). Often, the person with GAD is worrying about several stressors simultaneously. Accompanying these worries are signs of persistent physical tension, such as feelings of restlessness, fatigue, difficulty concentrating, irritability, muscle tension, and difficulty falling or staying asleep.

Posttraumatic stress disorder (PTSD) is a constellation of symptoms that emerge following a traumatic life event. Currently, the *DSM-IV-TR* defines an event as "traumatic" when it involves actual or threatened death or serious injury or a threat to the physical integrity of self or others and the person's response involved intense feelings of fear, helplessness, or horror. Some of the traumatic events most commonly associated with PTSD are rape and other types of sexual assault, combat, physical violence, seeing someone get seriously hurt or killed, severe accidents or injuries, or natural disasters. The symptoms of PTSD include reexperiencing the trauma (having intrusive memories, nightmares, flashbacks, or panic symptoms when reminded about the trauma), avoidance of trauma reminders (trying to avoid thinking about the trauma, trying to avoid doing or seeing things that remind one of the trauma), emotional numbing (decreased interest in activities, feeling detached from others, feeling emotionally restricted), and hyperarousal (for example, difficulty falling asleep, irritability, difficulty concentrating, getting startled easily). It's important to note that even though these experiences can be symptoms of PTSD, in most cases they are actually quite normal following a serious trauma, and they resolve on their own. Therefore, PTSD is diagnosed only after these symptoms have persisted for more than one month.

Separation anxiety disorder can occur in adults or in children. The hallmark of this condition is excessive fear of being separated from home or from caregivers (such as parents). People with separation anxiety disorder frequently worry about losing caregivers or are afraid that harm will come to them; in many cases, these people worry excessively that they will be lost, kidnapped, or otherwise separated from caregivers. Many individuals with separation anxiety disorder refuse to go to school, be alone, or go to sleep in their own rooms because of separation fears, or they complain of physical symptoms such as headaches or stomachaches in order to remain home with the caregiver.

How Common Are Anxiety Disorders?

The prevalence of anxiety and related disorders in the United States has been studied in several large-scale epidemiological surveys, most recently the National Comorbidity Survey Replication conducted by Ronald Kessler and his research team. As shown in the figure below, anxiety disorders are quite common: 29 percent of Americans either have or have had a diagnosable anxiety disorder. These rates are significantly higher than those of mood, substance use, or other mental health disorders. Among the anxiety disorders, social phobia and specific phobia are the most common.

What Is the Impact of Anxiety Disorders?

Anxiety disorders are not only common, but also costly to sufferers and to the economy as a whole. Researchers studying the U.S. population have estimated the total cost of anxiety disorders to be $42 billion per year in the 1990s (which, adjusting for

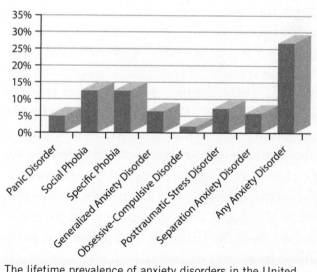

The lifetime prevalence of anxiety disorders in the United States.

inflation, would be approximately $72 billion in today's dollars). Of note, this figure is significantly greater than the estimated costs of other mental disorders such as depression or schizophrenia. Where does the money go? Most of it ($39 billion in today's dollars) is spent on nonpsychiatric medical treatment. That is, individuals with anxiety disorders have a tendency to overuse primary-care physicians, as well as specialists such as cardiologists, gastroenterologists, and emergency rooms.

You can get a sense of just how expensive that nonpsychiatric medical treatment might become when you look at the bill for an actual patient, taken from the records of an emergency room in a major city hospital. This person had chest pains and called an ambulance ($600). She was then taken to the emergency room ($1,463) and received a number of medical tests ($2,300) from an ER physician ($284). A cardiologist was sent in to consult ($447), and when it was determined that her symptoms were more likely anxiety-based, a psychiatric consult was ordered ($300). Finally, she was discharged ($130) with a diagnosis of panic disorder. Her total bill was more than $5,500 for this *single visit*. Fortunately, she was then referred for appropriate treatment of her panic disorder, where she was treated for a fraction of the cost of her one trip to the emergency room.

Anxiety disorders have also been shown to affect the family members of the sufferer. Family members of individuals with OCD and PTSD, for example, generally report levels of distress, impairment, and burden comparable to those of patients with severe mental illnesses such as schizophrenia. Marital distress is also common, and people with anxiety disorders are more likely to get divorced than are people without these disorders.

Finally, anxiety disorders can contribute to a severely diminished quality of life. Documented problems in people with anxiety disorders include financial difficulties, impaired social relationships, high rates of public financial assistance, and high rates of disability.

How Effective Is Exposure Therapy?

Once you decide that you want a life beyond fear, why choose exposure therapy? The answer is simple: it works. Period. I want to stress that this is not only my opinion; it is an indisputable fact, backed by hard science. That's what makes this program different from many others out there—everything in here, and I mean everything, has been shown in repeated, well-conducted research studies to help people beat fears. Nothing in this program is "fluff."

If I were to walk you through every study of exposure therapy that's been conducted, this book would weigh about fifty pounds (and would be pretty boring, even for a science junkie like me). Instead, I'll show you a couple of good examples of what I'm talking about and then point you toward additional resources where you can learn more.

Psychologist Lars-Göran Öst has done a lot of work on the treatment of specific phobias. Specific phobias are fears of things such as snakes and spiders, thunderstorms, blood and injections, flying, and so on. Believe it or not, Öst has refined the program to the point where he gets great results in just one session of exposure therapy! Here's an example of one of his programs. He brought twenty people with phobias (seven had injection fears, and thirteen had fears of animals, mostly spiders) into his clinic. He used a process called in vivo (or real-life) exposure, in which patients were encouraged to come progressively closer and closer to the thing they were afraid of—for example, working their way closer and closer to a spider, without retreating, until eventually they were holding the spider in their hands. This process lasted anywhere between one and three hours. After the session was over, Öst reminded the patients (as I will remind you later) to make exposure a way of life and not to fall back into avoidance. When he interviewed his patients an average of four years later, he found that a whopping 90 percent of them had noticeably less fear, avoidance, and impairment than they had before treatment—and 65 percent had completely recovered from their phobia.

Other fear-based disorders can also be addressed effectively using exposure. Because they can be a little more complex than specific phobias, however, it can take a bit longer to treat them. Psychologist David Barlow has pioneered an exposure-based treatment for panic disorder, which, as described earlier, is characterized by repeated, unexpected panic attacks and lingering fears of having another attack. In the largest study to date on this treatment, 326 people with panic disorder (many of whom also had agoraphobia) were assigned at random to one of several treatment conditions. We'll just focus on two for now. One of these groups (77 people) received therapy that emphasized *interoceptive exposure*. In this process, they were encouraged to face their fears of uncomfortable physical sensations—for example, by spinning around in a swivel chair until they felt dizzy—so that they could learn that nothing terrible was going to happen, such as throwing up or passing out. The other group (83 people) received the antidepressant imipramine, which at that time was the medication of choice for panic disorder. After the three-month period, both treatments worked well—about three-quarters of the participants in each group were classified as having a good outcome. The results got even more interesting after the treatment was over. Barlow brought the participants back for another interview six months later and found that some of the people who had previously received medication had lost their gains; their panic, anxiety, and avoidance had returned. On the other hand, people in the group that had received exposure therapy were actually doing even better six months after ending treatment. Clearly, these participants had learned something important in their therapy, and not only had they not forgotten, they were continuing to build on their progress.

Psychologist Edna Foa has used exposure therapy for obsessive-compulsive disorder, which consists of obsessive thoughts or images, as well as compulsive, ritualized behaviors. In one study, 149 patients with OCD were randomly assigned to receive various treatments; for now, we'll focus on two of these groups. One group (37 people) received *in vivo exposure*, along with response

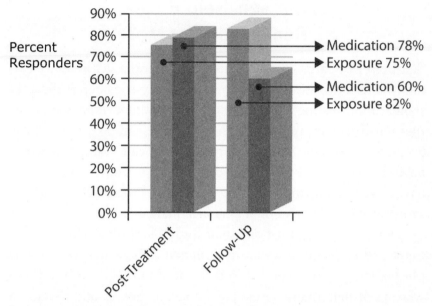

Percentage of patients in Barlow's study responding to exposure therapy versus medication for panic disorder, post-treatment and at a six-month follow-up.

prevention, or strict instructions to abstain from compulsive safety behaviors. So, for example, someone with obsessive fears of contamination and a pattern of compulsive hand washing would be instructed to touch progressively dirtier and dirtier things, while refraining from all washing or cleaning behaviors (compulsions). The main exposure treatment lasted for three weeks, with patients coming to the clinic for daily (five days per week) exposure sessions. After the three weeks of intensive treatment, patients came to the clinic for short sessions once a week for eight weeks to make sure they were keeping up with the work. The other group (47 people) received the antidepressant clomipramine, which is a well-established medication for treating OCD, during an equivalent period of time. After treatment, only 48 percent of patients taking medication were classified as having had a good response to treatment. By comparison, 86 percent of the patients receiving exposure therapy had a good response. That's a tremendous difference in effectiveness.

Can a Self-Help Program
Really Work for Me?

Self-help programs can work for many people. Although treatment with a professional therapist is widely considered the gold standard for beating fears, a wealth of scientific evidence suggests that self-directed programs such as this one can be quite helpful. Summaries of data from multiple studies, called meta-analyses, have shown that a well-designed self-help program can and does have a significant impact on the severity of the anxiety and the avoidant behaviors and on a person's quality of life.

Here's an example of one such study. Psychologist Tomas Furmark and colleagues randomly assigned 235 people with social phobia to one of several different interventions. Among these were a self-help manual based on behavior therapy and a wait-list condition, in which people were not given any treatment but were followed for assessment. After nine weeks, 62 percent of people who had used the self-help manual were considered to have shown strong improvement. By contrast, only 22 percent of people who were waiting for treatment showed a similar improvement. Impressively, results for the self-help manual group were even stronger at a follow-up one year later, with 67 percent of people showing improvement. So it turns out that people can really make a major impact on their own fears, *if* they are given the right kind of guidance.

> It took me several months to start treatment, and I wish that I had sought it out earlier. I didn't tell my family and friends about my fears; I think I was probably embarrassed. I had tried some medications but still felt afraid. I started reading about exposure therapy, and even though I was a little concerned about how much work it would involve, I decided to do it to get rid of the fear.
>
> —*Andrea*

But don't people with anxiety disorders really need to see a professional therapist? Not necessarily. These same meta-analyses examined studies in which self-directed treatment was compared to therapist-assisted treatment. Results overall did show an advantage for therapist-directed treatment, but the advantage was small. Thus, these analyses suggest that the outcomes of a good self-help book can come close to or even match those of professional therapy.

Of course, some people do need to seek help from a professional. If you have a severe medical problem that might make exposure therapy difficult or dangerous, or if you have a serious mental illness, such as schizophrenia, suicidal depression, or alcohol or drug abuse, the situation is probably too complicated to be addressed effectively by a self-help program such as this one without the addition of professional therapy. If you have any of these problems, see chapter 17 for guidelines on getting professional assistance to supplement the exercises in this book. Of course, no program will be effective for everyone, so if you don't find these methods helpful, don't worry—it doesn't mean the situation is hopeless. In chapter 17, I'll walk you through some alternative strategies that may also be beneficial.

There's no reason to think that the use of this program and seeing a professional therapist have to be mutually exclusive. In my practice, I've had very good results when the patient and I work together from a well-designed self-help program. If you're in therapy, you might find it useful to discuss this program with your therapist to get advice and support. Similarly, if you're a mental health professional, this manual can provide structure and guidance for you and your patient as you conduct exposure therapy.

I've also found (as have others) that self-administered treatments such as this one can be useful as a first step in treatment, before starting therapy. This approach, called stepped care, involves starting with the easiest and least expensive treatment option and advancing to more involved treatment only when it's needed. Often, when patients come to see me in my clinic, I recommend a good self-help program to them as a first step, with instructions to come see me again after they've given it a good try. I'm frequently pleased to see that at the next visit, the person is doing much better—sometimes so much that he or she no longer needs therapy. Other times, the patient and I decide that additional treatment is needed—but the patient who started with a self-administered treatment is usually several steps ahead of the curve by this point, ready to dive into more intensive treatment and achieve maximum benefit.

Hopefully, by now you're seeing a pattern emerge. There are lots of variations of fear-based disorders, and many variations of exposure therapy. The bottom line is that exposure therapy is an effective treatment for fear, and we have decades of solid research to prove it. Furthermore, numerous studies have demonstrated that many, perhaps most, people with fear-based disorders can obtain a great deal of benefit by working on the problem on their own using a good manual like this one. Even for people who want or need to see a professional therapist, a self-administered treatment can be a powerful addition to the process.

Are there downsides to self-administered treatment? Sure. One potential problem is that some readers might have serious psychiatric or medical illnesses of which they are unaware, and which might make it unwise for them to try self-administered treatment. If you have questions about your medical or psychiatric status, I strongly recommend that you see a professional for an assessment. Even if you don't want to receive treatment from that professional, it's important to start with a good understanding of your condition. Another potential problem is lack of follow-through. Some research shows that as many as half of all people who start self-administered treatment programs do not finish them. This problem isn't limited to self-administered treatment—professional treatment also has high dropout rates—but it's important for us to consider. I recommend starting this or any other intervention only when you're truly ready to do something about your fear (that's why I harped on motivation at the beginning of this chapter).

I was very ambivalent about trying the program. I had tried three different therapists already and was very, very afraid that the program wouldn't work—that I'd be stuck in this nightmare forever. But I knew I had a problem, that my behaviors weren't normal, and I desperately wanted to get my life back.

—*Rachel*

I knew all the cards were on the table and I finally had to face what I'd avoided for so long. Really, I would rather have just kept avoiding it. But the drive to keep my kids healthy, both mentally and physically, truly outweighed my fear of getting help. I wanted to be a better mom. I wanted to be able to go to amusement parks without thinking of the germs from puke that might be out there. I wanted to have good, honest fun with my family. It was that drive that brought me to seek treatment. It was that drive that redirected the path I was choosing in life. As corny as that may sound, it really is true. Facing my fears made me realize how much better and fuller my life and our family life could be. It was the best decision I have ever made.

—*Michelle*

So far, you've read about the various anxiety disorders and their symptoms. You are now aware of the damage these problems can do to the people who have them, as well as to their families and their larger communities. You've also learned that exposure therapy has been proven beyond a doubt to help people overcome anxiety.

Review what you wrote earlier, about choosing to either face your fears or stay with the status quo, and add to it if this chapter has given you some new issues to think about. If you decide that you're okay with the status quo, that's fine. You can always come back to this program later if you change your mind. But if you want things to be different, if you need to make a change—if you are so sick and tired of being afraid that you are willing to invest some time, energy, and discomfort now so that you can have a fear-free future, turn the page. Welcome to the program.

4

The Principles of Exposure

You gain strength, courage, and confidence by every experience in which you really stop to look fear in the face. You must do the thing which you think you cannot do.

—*Eleanor Roosevelt*

In chapter 5, you'll start planning your program of exposure therapy (facing your fears). Before we begin, though, I want to go over a few points that will help you get the most out of this process. You'll need to take each point into consideration as you design a program that's right for you. These details can make a big difference in terms of making the program more effective, more efficient, or more comfortable for you.

All at Once or Baby Steps?

One important consideration is the pacing of exposures. Most people like to use a process called *graded exposure*. This means that you start out with something that is moderately distressing but manageable. Once you begin to feel better, you move up to something that is slightly more difficult, and so on, until you are doing things that previously would have been very hard for you. You use your own fear level as a guide—feeling better is your signal to move on to the next step of the program. Because this process is preferred by most people, it's what I'll emphasize in this program.

The alternative to a graded exposure strategy is called *flooding*. Flooding means going right to the scariest exposure, instead of working up to it. In practice, graded exposure and flooding appear to work equally well, so it mostly comes down to a matter of preference. Some people like to tiptoe into the cold swimming pool, whereas other people like to do a cannonball off the side. Speaking for myself, I like to tiptoe in, but I understand why other people prefer the cannonball. The choice is based on a trade-off of comfort versus efficiency: how much discomfort are you willing to put up with in order to speed up the process? One option is generally easier for most people to tolerate, but the other option will often get the job done more quickly. In the end, everyone ends up in the pool, and things tend to work out. We'll use a graded exposure therapy approach for this program, but if flooding appeals to you (and if it's safe to do so), go for it.

At first, I tried to go too fast too soon. The level of anxiety I felt when trying to tackle all of the items on my hierarchy at once overwhelmed me into paralysis. Breaking it down into much smaller steps worked for me. It took me about seven months to get through the list, but the progress was steady. Also, even when doing the smaller steps, I'd hit an exposure that was too tough, so I'd break that exposure down into smaller steps. Maybe I'd start with getting near the item versus touching it right away. Then touching it with one finger, then more fingers, then the full hand, and so on. I just made sure I was moving forward, however small the progress was.

—*Rachel*

What Am I Exposing
Myself To?

The short answer is that you are exposing yourself to the situations, activities, or objects that scare you. The long answer is a little more complicated, because everyone's fear is a little different.

Whenever possible (and safe), the most effective and efficient way to beat your fears is to face them in real life. We call this kind of exposure *in vivo exposure*. Let's say, for example, that you're afraid of dogs. If you want to beat that fear, there is just no substitute for actually petting a dog. If you're afraid of heights, you should go to high places. If you're afraid of physical sensations such as a rapid heart rate, you should do exercises that get your heart pounding. If you're afraid of getting embarrassed in social and performance situations, you should perform those activities in a manner that carries some risk of embarrassment. If you're afraid of contamination, you should touch things that are dirty. When you face these things, you get them out in the open so that you can scrutinize them, see them for what they are, and learn that nothing terrible happens and that you can do it.

Sometimes, however, in vivo exposure is just not possible. Let's say that you're afraid of flying in an airplane. It would be very expensive if you had to buy a bunch of plane tickets in order to feel better! In such cases, we often find that *imaginal exposure* (using your imagination to envision the scary activity) can be helpful. Someone with a fear of flying could use his imagination to envision, in great detail, the act of getting on the plane, buckling in, taking off, and even experiencing scary turbulence. To make the exposure more effective, he could tell his scary story out loud and record it on a tape or digital recorder or a computer (and burn it onto a CD), and then listen to it again and again.

Instructions for Making a Repeatable Audio File

1. Start the Sound Recorder program. Usually, this is in the Accessories group of programs on your computer.
2. Click on Record and record your story using a microphone.
3. Click on Stop.
4. Select File and then Save As, then select a location to save your file.
5. Open Windows Media Player (or your preferred audio player).
6. Open your audio file by selecting File and then Open.
7. Select Play and then Repeat.
8. Click Play.

Imaginal exposure can also be helpful when the fear is a made-up scenario in your head. For example, some people worry about feared catastrophes that are unlikely to happen— such as when your spouse is late coming home from work, you worry that he or she is lying dead in a ditch somewhere. This mental image is scary, and you try to get your mind off it (which is a form of avoidance). Imaginal exposure could be used to envision a vivid scenario of your spouse lying in a ditch. Just as would happen with in vivo exposure, this imaginal exposure is expected to increase your fear level, but then you will notice yourself feeling less afraid, and the image will start to feel less real, less compelling.

How Long Should Exposures Be?

There is no hard-and-fast rule about how long to do an exposure; however, some research suggests that longer is better than shorter. Remember that exposure is meant to be a learning process. Imagine that you do a super-short exposure in which you face a fear, get anxious, and quickly retreat so that you feel better. What have you learned? You've learned that facing fear is really unpleasant.

You've also learned that retreating is a good way to feel bett.. can easily see how this plan could backfire. Behavioral scientists call this phenomenon *sensitization*—in which short exposures can actually make you *more* afraid, not less afraid. It doesn't happen all of the time, and I've met lots of people who did just fine with short exposures, but it's good to keep in mind that longer exposures are generally preferable.

Instead, it makes sense to let your own fear be a guide to how long each exposure should be. The general idea is that an exposure should start scary and end not-so-scary, so we have to come up with a good way to track your *fear level*. Let's use a numeric scale from 0 to 100, where 0 means you're totally calm and relaxed, not a care in the world, and 100 means you're in sheer terror, the worst fear you have ever experienced or could possibly imagine. When you're doing an exposure exercise, a good rule of thumb is to keep doing that exercise until your fear level decreases by 50 percent or more. That way, you are learning that fear will eventually decrease, and nothing bad will happen, even if you don't withdraw.

During exposure therapy, I'll periodically ask patients, "What's your level?" And they'll respond with a number that helps me understand how they're feeling at that moment. I'd like you to ask yourself that same question— "What's my level?" —as you conduct exposures.

Description	Fear Level
The worst terror I could imagine	100
	90
Very scary, I could panic	80
	70
	60
Moderately scary but manageable	50
	40
	30
Slightly nervous, no big deal	20
	10
Totally fine, completely calm	0

Throughout this book, I'll give you lots of examples of exposures for different kinds of fears. I want to emphasize, though, that these are just examples. The range of exposures you can do is limited only by your creativity—and you will definitely need to get creative to face your fears!

How Many and How Much?

As you go through the process of exposure, it's helpful to keep two principles in mind, which I'll call the variety principle and the repetition principle.

The Variety Principle

The variety principle advises that you need to change up your exposures and try multiple variations on the same theme. You're trying to create a convincing demonstration for your brain, so you want to make sure that the lesson you teach your brain is a broad one (for example, that situations like this are safe), rather than a narrow one (for instance, this one situation is safe, but all of the others might still be dangerous). You should also take advantage of as many exposure opportunities as possible in order to succeed in the long term. Here are some examples:

- If you have a fear of interacting with other people, you should make a point of interacting with as many different people, in as many different contexts, as possible. You might make a point of interacting not only with your coworkers but also with store cashiers, the mail carrier, and strangers on a bus. Every person you see represents a potential opportunity to face your fear.
- If you have a fear of crowded places, you should go to as many different crowded places as you can, including crowded supermarkets, shopping malls, and theaters, and experiment with different locations, different times of day, and different days of

the week. You want to try to show your brain that you can handle a wide range of crowded places, not only certain ones.

- If you have a fear of dirt and germs, touch as many "dirty" things as you can. Touch doorknobs, handrails, floors, and bathrooms at home, where you work, and all over town. Visit places that seem slightly dirty and places that seem very dirty. Mix it up as much as you can.

- If you have a fear of dogs, get to know the owners of your local pet store and meet all of the dogs there. Visit your local Humane Society (heck, volunteer a few hours of your time there while you're at it), and pet every dog you see, not only the nice and cute-looking ones. Seek out and visit all of your friends who have dogs; even offer to dog-sit when they're out.

The Repetition Principle

The repetition principle states that once is usually not enough. If you're going to face a fear, be prepared to do it again and again. Here are some examples:

- If you have a fear of snakes, your local pet store or science museum can be a great resource for contacting snakes, but it's important that you plan more than one trip. Go once and visit the snakes, and while you're there, make arrangements to come again the following week. When you come back, ask whether it would be okay for you to come a third time. More is better.

- If you have a fear of public speaking, it's probably not enough to give only one speech—that probably won't beat your fear for good. Instead, sign up to give a series of presentations at work. Or consider joining an organization such as Toastmasters, in which you'll have the opportunity to give multiple speeches at regular intervals.

- If you're afraid of having an increased heart rate, you'll need to plan to get your heart rate elevated on a regular basis, preferably daily. Consider joining a gym and commit to going every day and really working up a sweat.

- If you have excessive worries or fears related to traumatic memories, you'll want to do lots of imaginal exposure. Plan daily exposure sessions, preferably for an hour per exposure. Make sure to prioritize your exposures by setting aside enough time and making sure that family members understand that you will be busy during these periods.

What Exactly Does Exposure Do?

Hopefully, you came away from chapter 3 with the conviction that exposure therapy clearly works. *How* it works, though, is a matter of some discussion. There are four major theories about what exposure does. I'll touch on each of them in the following sections.

Habituation Theory

Ever notice what happens when you jump into cold water? It's freezing and unpleasant at first, then after a few minutes you don't notice it. What happened? Did the water warm up? No, of course not. You simply adjusted. Your brain stopped responding in the same way to the cold sensation. That process is called *habituation*, which means "getting used to it." Some people think that's what exposure therapy does: when you face something scary, your brain just gets used to it and stops responding in the same way.

> The very first time I listened to my recording, I sobbed and sobbed—and my fear level was at about a 95. After hearing it about four times, however, I realized that my mind was wandering; I was down to at least a 45 or less. It felt like kind of a miracle.
>
> —*Samantha*

When I first started doing exposures, I would get nervous in anticipation of what I was going to do. I'd have an urge to avoid the task, and I was worried that I was going to say something stupid or embarrass myself. But once I started facing the fears, I realized that the anticipation was the worst part of it. When I was actually facing the fear, it got a lot easier, and I realized that I could just be myself and talk to people.

—*Steven*

Extinction Theory

Recall from chapter 2 that some fears might develop because of classical conditioning. This is what happens when you have an aversive experience with something, such as being bitten by a dog. If the dog bite was scary enough, your brain now makes the association "dog equals bite." So now, when you see a dog, your brain anticipates the bite, and you feel afraid. We can reverse this process using *extinction*, in which repeated exposure to dogs that do not bite you creates the new association "dog does not equal bite." The extinction theory suggests that when you do exposures, the old learning is overwritten by new learning.

Some exposures were so hard that I cried while doing them, but I just kept reminding myself that I was doing it gradually and to keep trying. What really made it all work for me was when I started to see results. When I could start crossing items off my fear list, I began to see the light far, far away at the end of the tunnel. I started to feel hope, even with the teeny baby steps I was taking. Success started to breed success. Slowly, the life I had had was coming back into focus.

—*Rachel*

Self-Efficacy Theory

People who suffer from fear and avoidance often live in a world of "I can'ts." "I can't handle feeling anxious." "I can't tolerate doing things that are scary." "I can't stand thinking about this." "I can't control myself if I panic." Psychologists would describe these people as having low *self-efficacy*, or a tendency to underestimate their own capabilities. The self-efficacy theory of exposure suggests that by facing your fears, you learn to replace "I can't" with "I can." When you face a fear without avoiding or retreating, you start to realize that you are stronger, more capable, and more resilient than you thought you were.

> Initially, I found myself crying, very tearful. But then, as I was facing my fears, it turned into almost a laugh. It wasn't hysterical laughter, it was just a realization that this little animal wasn't going to hurt me, and I felt good about doing something about this fear I had.
>
> *—Audrey*

Emotional Processing Theory

The human brain loves to attach meanings to things. We're always interpreting things—giving meaning to events—as a way to try to make sense of the universe. Some people with excessive fears have a tendency to make faulty interpretations over and over again. For example, someone with social and performance fears might (erroneously) view social interactions as potentially embarrassing or threatening. In addition, he or she might (erroneously) view getting embarrassed or nervous as a sign of personal failure. Some researchers have suggested that when we face our fears, we learn a different way of processing information about what scares us. Our experiences in exposure therapy help correct our faulty way of thinking and serve as a basis for creating new meanings and interpretations—for example, the realization that social interactions can actually be rewarding and pleasant, and that ~ ings of embarrassment and anxiety are not the end of the world.

The Effectiveness of Exposure

Which of these theories is correct? My experience has been that they all are, and I can see different things happening in different patients at different times. As you go through this program of facing your fears, pay attention to what's happening. Chances are, at various times you'll find yourself getting used to situations (habituation), overwriting previously learned associations (extinction), feeling more confident in your abilities (self-efficacy), and creating new interpretations and meanings of things that were once frightening (emotional processing). In the end, they will all get you where you are trying to go—to a life free of excessive fear.

As you might recall from the previous chapter, exposure can be extremely effective. People who have faced their fears might not become completely fearless, but they can definitely see a big reduction in fear and avoidance and a huge improvement in their quality of life. In addition, unlike "old-school" psychological therapy that might have lasted for years, exposure doesn't have to be a terribly lengthy process for most people (remember the study of people with specific phobias who were able to beat their fears in only one day!). How long it takes to overcome a fear will depend on lots of factors, including how severe the fear is, how complex it is, and how willing you are to invest the time and energy into doing the exposures. I'm confident, however, that you can do it.

5

Planning Exposures

Courage is doing what you're afraid to do. There can
be no courage unless you're scared.

—*Edward Vernon Rickenbacker*

The Exposure Hierarchy

In this chapter, I'll help you put together a detailed plan for your
exposure therapy program. To start, go back to the quiz you completed in chapter 1 (if you skipped it, I recommend that you go
back and complete it). In that quiz, you classified your fears into
one or more of six different categories:

Fears of specific situations or objects
Fear of body sensations
Social and performance fears
Obsessive fears
Excessive worries
Post-traumatic fears

You might have scored high for one, two, or even all six of these categories (remember, having more than one kind of fear is normal—and it in no way diminishes your chances of success). For each category that you scored high on, you'll need to develop what we call an exposure hierarchy. An *exposure hierarchy* is a list of activities that are not objectively dangerous, but that you would normally want to avoid, due to feelings of fear or anxiety. This exposure hierarchy will become your to-do list.

It's usually best to do these exposures gradually, in a controlled and prolonged manner. To accomplish this, we need to have a way to rank the activities according to how scary they would be. We'll use the *fear level* (the 0–100 scale) I introduced in the previous chapter. As you list items on your exposure hierarchy, think of what your fear level would likely be if you were actually doing each item, and rank them accordingly.

Here's an example of what an exposure hierarchy might look like for someone who has a fear of specific situations or objects, namely, a fear of dogs:

Activity	*Fear Level (0–100)*
Being licked in the face by a large dog	90
Petting a large dog	85
Being in a room with a large dog off leash	80
Being in a room with a large dog on leash	75
Being licked in the face by a small dog	70
Petting a small dog	65
Being in a room with a small dog off leash	60
Being in a room with a small dog on leash	55
Visiting a pet shop and looking at dogs in cages	40
Watching movies of dogs	35
Looking at pictures of dogs	30

As you can see, we broke the fear down into several concrete steps and ranked the steps according to their predicted fear level. In this case, we'll start near the bottom, with something that's not too scary (looking at pictures of dogs). Once that step has been mastered (using the 50 percent reduction rule discussed in the previous chapter), it's time to move up to the next step (watching movies of dogs). When that step has been accomplished, we move up to the next step, and the next one, and so on, until the person is able to do the most difficult exposure (being licked in the face by a large dog).

Notice as well that the exposure hierarchy doesn't shy away from the scary stuff. If you happen to have a fear of dogs, you're probably thinking, "No way would I ever let a large dog lick my face! I'd freak out!" Believe it or not, that is exactly why you *must* include that item in your hierarchy. Remember, you will be working your way up the hierarchy gradually, so that by the time you get to that step, it won't seem nearly as scary as it does right now. Therefore, an important rule of the exposure hierarchy is that *you must include the scariest exposures, even if you don't feel able to do them right now.*

Here are some questions people often ask when they're starting a program like this:

How many items should I list on my exposure hierarchy? There is no hard-and-fast rule here—the idea is that you want enough steps to help you work your way up gradually, but not so many that it takes forever to complete the hierarchy. Ten items, give or take a couple, might be a good place to start, but again, this is your program, and you can use as many items as you feel you need. I've known people who did quite well with only four or five items, whereas other people have needed fifty items or more for fears that were more complex.

What kind of activities should go on the exposure hierarchy? Everyone's fear is a little different. What's scary for one person might not be scary for another. Following are some examples of exposure activities that people in my clinic have completed; perhaps they can give you a few good ideas. You'll also find a lot more examples in chapters 9 through 14.

People with *fears of specific situations or objects* have tried

- Animal-related exposures, such as
  - Holding snakes, spiders, or other animals
  - Visiting a pet store
  - Reading about, looking at pictures of, or watching movies about the feared animal
  - Drawing pictures of or singing songs about the feared animal
- Situational exposures, such as
  - Going to tall buildings and looking down over the balcony
  - Taking commercial flights
  - Spending time in confined spaces, such as closets
  - Going outside during storms
  - Being in the dark
  - Going swimming
  - Watching or listening to people vomit or pretend to vomit
  - Reading about, looking at pictures of, or watching movies about the feared situation
  - Drawing pictures of or singing songs about the feared situation
- Blood, injection, or injury-related exposures, such as
  - Watching others get injections or have blood drawn
  - Donating blood
  - Visiting a dentist
  - Watching surgeries on television
  - Reading about, looking at pictures of, or watching movies about blood, injections, or injuries
  - Drawing pictures of or singing songs about blood, injections, or injuries

Audrey's Exposure Hierarchy: Fear of Snakes

Activity	*Fear Level (0–100)*
Wrapping a snake around my shoulders, allowing it to crawl on me	99
Holding a snake in my hands	95
Letting a snake's tongue touch my hand	85
Touching a snake's head with my finger	75
Touching a snake's tail with my finger	65
Standing next to someone holding a snake	65
Putting my hand inside a snake's tank	60
Standing next to a snake tank with the lid off	50
Standing ten feet away from a snake tank with the lid on	45
Watching videos of snakes	30

Step by step, I got closer to a pet snake. I started to see that this was just a small, innocent animal. I almost felt motherly at times, seeing that there was nothing the snake could do to hurt me, and there was no reason to be afraid of that little thing. I simply realized that not every snake is out to get me. It's just another of God's creatures. I felt as if I were making progress. When I started, my throat felt tight and my muscles were clenched up. Over time, my body became more relaxed, to the point where I actually held the snake and felt fine.

—Audrey

Michelle's Exposure Hierarchy: Fear of Vomit

Activity	*Fear Level (0–100)*
Pretending to vomit	100
Watching a person pretend to vomit close up	90
Deliberately filling my mouth with saliva	85
Watching videos of people vomiting	80
Listening to someone gagging	70
Looking at photographs of people vomiting	70

Spending time with friends who had the flu	60
Looking at cartoons of people vomiting	35
Singing a song about vomiting	30
Saying, reading, and writing vomit-related words	25

I was surprised to see just how stressed out and anxious I became during even my first exposure, which was simply repeating words that had to do with vomit—*puke, vomit, barf, throw up,* and so on. I would repeat this list of words until my level of anxiety decreased to about a 3 or lower. Next, I moved on to cartoon pictures or pictures with pretend vomit. For instance, one was a carved pumpkin with the seeds spewing out of the jack-o-lantern's mouth. Even this made me stressed, which I found so silly. As I progressed, I moved on to actual pictures of vomit or of someone throwing up. This is when it all became very real. These exposures were harder to overcome, but I continued to challenge myself each day. As much as every bone in my body wanted to avoid this situation, I practiced these exposures for about thirty minutes each night. After actual pictures, I moved on to YouTube videos. I was amazed that people actually posted videos of themselves or friends throwing up! It really was gross, but I continued to watch these each day to help overcome my anxiety. When I told my friends about my therapy, they were probably as grossed out as I was because, let's face it, to dislike puke was not that unrealistic. It was hard for some people to understand that my dislike ran much deeper than most other's dislike. For one of my final treatments, I actually pretended to vomit. I made a concoction of refried beans, minestrone soup, and other food I don't like and placed it in my mouth, knelt over, and spit it out. This last exposure was when I realized I had succeeded in the treatment. It was not nearly as bothersome as some of the beginning exposures. So, all in all, my exposures involved everything surrounding my fear.

It was scary, it was gross, and it was completely necessary. Avoidance is what caused my phobia to worsen, and facing it is what helped me become stronger than my anxiety.

—*Michelle*

Making Creative Use of the Internet

The Internet is a great place to find exposure resources. You can find lots of photos and videos on sites such as Google or YouTube. You can also type your specific fear into a search engine to find resources—for example, type "vomit phobia" or "fear of spiders" into Google or another search engine, and take a look at the vast amount of resources that have been compiled.

Here are just a few that are on the Web as of this writing:

Fear of snakes: http://www.venomoussnakes.net/videos.htm
Fear of vomiting: http://www.emetophobiaresource.org/
Fear of blood draws: http://www.medicalvideos.us/play .php?vid=1436
Fear of dental procedures: http://www.youtube.com/watch?v =ZGauag5pz8s&feature=related
Fear of spiders: http://www.metacafe.com/watch/233368/ spiders/
Fear of flying: http://video.google.com/videoplay?docid=638 7749015079801615#docid=564590772272655120

People with a *fear of body sensations* have tried

- Exercises to induce dizziness, lightheadedness, or faintness, such as
  - Hyperventilating
  - Spinning in a chair

- Shaking the head back and forth rapidly
- Lowering the head between the knees for thirty seconds, then raising the head quickly to induce a "draining" sensation
- Going on rides at an amusement park
- Exercises to raise heart rate, such as
  - Running up and down stairs
  - Watching scary movies
  - Drinking caffeinated beverages
- Exercises to create a smothered feeling, such as
  - Breathing through a straw
  - Holding one's breath as long as possible
  - Lying with a heavy stack of books on one's chest
  - Wearing a tight scarf or tie
- Exercises to induce muscle tension or soreness, such as
  - Tensing all of the muscles of the body
  - Doing push-ups or sit-ups
- Exercises to induce uncomfortable digestive system feelings, such as
  - Smelling spoiled food or cigar butts to induce nausea
  - Eating to the point of feeling stuffed
  - Keeping cotton balls in one's mouth to make the mouth and the throat feel dry
  - Swallowing rapidly again and again
- Exercises to induce hot or cold sensations, such as
  - Sitting in a steamy bathroom or in a car with the heat cranked up
  - Going outside in cold weather with no coat on
- Exercises to induce feelings of unreality, such as
  - Staring at a spot on the wall or one's hand or in a mirror for several minutes
  - Starting at a light bulb or at sunlight coming through a venetian blind for several minutes
  - Wearing glasses from a 3-D movie

- Exposures to situations that are difficult to escape from, such as
  - Sitting in crowded places, such as theaters or auditoriums, away from aisles and exits
  - Going to busy places, such as supermarkets or museums
  - Driving through tunnels or over bridges
  - Driving on busy highways
  - Riding buses or subways
  - Driving in heavy traffic during rush hour
  - Using elevators or escalators
- Exposures to being away from sources of help, such as
  - Being home alone
  - Going far away from one's home or car
  - Going to unfamiliar places and deliberately getting lost

Susan's Exposure Hierarchy: Fear of Body Sensations

Activity	Fear Level (0–100)
Hyperventilating for one minute	100
Drinking caffeinated beverages	90
Breathing through a drinking straw for one minute	90
Being hot	85
Staring at a light for two minutes and then trying to read	80
Driving far from my home	75
Going to crowded places	75
Spinning in a chair	65

The hardest exposure for me was making myself hyperventilate. The first time was pretty intense and pretty scary. I had to sit there and make myself go into this fight-or-flight feeling. I got dizzy and light-headed and short of breath. It was pretty intense. Then I did it again once I "came down." And then again . . . and so on, until the sensation didn't do anything to me. The freakiest thing I did with the hyperventilation was drink a Red Bull to get my heart pumping and my blood pumping and my energy all jittery and then going out in 98 degree weather! Oh, my God . . . I would get the worst anxiety in the heat. So I was in the heat, all hopped up on what felt like liquid crack, and I had to hyperventilate. That was crazy. What a rush. But I did it. And I was fine.

—*Susan*

People with *social and performance fears* have tried

- Exposure to social interactions, such as
  - Attending parties or other social gatherings
  - Introducing oneself to strangers
  - Initiating and maintaining conversations
- Exposure to being the center of attention, such as
  - Giving speeches
  - Speaking up in classes or meetings
  - Performing music, sports, or other activities in front of others
  - Inviting others to watch one work
  - Doing things while being photographed or filmed
- Exposure to assertive situations, such as
  - Returning items to a store
  - Asking people to quiet down in a movie theater
- Exposure to having others see embarrassing behavior or signs of anxiety, such as
  - Sprinkling water on the face, hands, or armpits in order to appear sweaty, then interacting with others
  - Jogging in place to appear flushed, then interacting with others
  - Deliberately falling down in front of people
  - Deliberately making mistakes in front of people
  - Deliberately stammering while talking

Steven's Exposure Hierarchy: Fear of Interacting with People

Activity	Fear Level (0–100)
Speak for one hour in front of 75 to 100 church members	80
Attend a bar association dinner	75
Speak up at a crowded town meeting	75
Have a ten-minute-long conversation with an attractive woman	70
Have a conversation with my child's teacher	60
Call an old friend I haven't seen for several years	60
Make eye contact during a conversation	60
Initiate a conversation with another church member after the service	50
Have lunch with a colleague	50
Initiate a conversation with the parents of my child's friend	40
Make small talk with a store cashier	40

I had been feeling really awkward at church, so I started making small talk with people there. I also went to more bar association dinners and made myself talk to the people there, even though I felt anxious.

—Steven

People with *obsessive fears* have tried

- Exposure to contamination, such as
  - Touching a doorknob
  - Touching a newspaper
  - Touching someone's sweaty shirt
  - Touching toilet seats in public bathrooms
  - Touching money
  - Touching a dead animal
  - Touching household chemicals

- Making food for others with dirty hands
- Touching their children with dirty hands
- Touching someone else's saliva
- Visiting an AIDS clinic and touching things
- Touching gas pumps
- Exposures for a fear of harming others, such as
  - Holding a knife while around people
  - Reading books or watching movies about serial killers
  - Bumping (gently) into people
  - Throwing a thumbtack onto the street where cars drive
  - Driving through a crowded pedestrian area
- Exposure to making errors, such as
  - Leaving the house after turning the stove (or another appliance) on and off
  - Lighting candles and leaving the house for thirty minutes
  - Going to bed with the door unlocked if your neighborhood is reasonably safe
  - Making a deliberate mistake with paperwork
- Exposure to things being "not right," such as
  - Messing up the clothes in the closet
  - Putting things in the "wrong" order (for example, putting magazines out of chronological order)
  - Sprinkling dirt on the kitchen floor
  - Walking through doorways or going up stairs the "wrong" way
  - Eating, grooming, or brushing teeth "wrong"
- Exposures for a fear of being immoral or blasphemous, such as
  - Deliberately doing small "sins," such as littering or cursing
  - Saying or writing blasphemous things, such as "I hate God" or "I like the devil"
- Exposures for superstitious or magical fears, such as
  - Doing things a "bad" number of times
  - Stepping on sidewalk cracks
  - Praying for disasters, such as a plane crash or a tornado
  - Saying or writing "forbidden" or "bad luck" words

Rachel's Partial Exposure Hierarchy: Obsessive Fears about Contamination

Activity	Fear Level (0–100)
"Contaminating" others with mail that might have anthrax on it	90
Picking up dog feces with a plastic bag	90
Touching mail	85
Handling items in garage	85
Touching garage door	80
Touching urine	80
Touching dirty clothes to clean clothes	80
Touching household cleansers	75
Touching "contaminated" clothes	75
Putting shoes on my pillow	75
Touching shoes	70
Touching the floor	65
Touching light switches	65
Handling the TV remote control	60
Touching doorknobs	55

I initially touched the things I was afraid of, without washing. I then moved on to rubbing the feared objects all over me, carrying them around with me, rubbing them on towels and other surfaces. The hardest exposure I remember doing involved shoes. I was deathly afraid that anthrax contamination was on the bottom of our shoes. The exposure exercise that I'll always remember involved my rubbing the bottom of my shoes on my son's pillow.

I had a big list of seventy-five items, so I just did three at a time. Then the next week I added three more, and so on, until I worked my way up the list.

—*Rachel*

People with *excessive worries* have tried

- "Worst-case scenario" exposures, such as
  - Writing down a detailed story about the worst thing happening (for example, a story in which loved ones die or the house burns down)
  - Making a recording of the story and listening to it over and over
  - Holding a mental image of the worst thing happening (for example, a mental image of loved ones lying dead or the house on fire)
  - Drawing pictures of the worst thing happening to them
- "Risk" exposures, such as
  - Leaving the house with the door or the window unlocked, if my neighborhood is reasonably safe
  - Sleeping with the door unlocked, if my neighborhood is reasonably safe
  - Deliberately making small errors
  - Deliberately being late for an event

Samantha's Exposure Hierarchy: Excessive Worries about Personal and Family Safety

Activity	Fear Level (0–100)
Reading about the Mayan doomsday prophecy	100
Vividly imagining dying from a heart attack	99
Vividly imagining dying from flesh-eating bacteria	99
Reading news articles about disasters	95
Vividly imagining my son dying in a car accident	90
Vividly imagining someone breaking in and murdering me	90
Vividly imagining dying in a house fire	90
Vividly imagining dying in a train wreck	88

Activity	Fear Level (0–100)
Reading articles about nuclear war	85
Reading articles about terrorism	80
Being a passenger in a car	60
Having my son go out and not tell me where he's going or not take his cell phone with him	40

One of the most difficult fears to face was the worry about my son dying. I simply couldn't even believe I would have to face that fear—my level went through the roof just thinking about it. I described my house in detail. Then I recorded a whole scenario where I woke up in the middle of the night to an explosion, tried to get to my son (whose room is in the basement), couldn't, tried to get him out a window, failed, and watched him slip out of my hands and die.

The hardest one, though, when I was ready, was to start looking at the end-of-world things. I started with very simple exposures. Because my most recent fear centered on a Mayan doomsday prophecy, I read about the Mayans to start with (over and over, of course). I worked up to the point where I had to tape a History Channel special on the prophecy and watch it again and again. I actually got to the point of laughing (on the thirtieth viewing or so). I used to have to leave the room if anyone so much as mentioned it, and now I don't even blink.

—Samantha

People with *post-traumatic fears* have tried

- Traumatic-event exposures, such as
  - Writing down a detailed story about the traumatic event
  - Making a recording of the story and listening to it over and over

- Holding a mental image of the traumatic event
- Drawing pictures of the traumatic event
- Reading about, looking at pictures of, or watching movies about occurrences that resemble the traumatic event
- Situational exposures, such as
  - Driving or riding in a car
  - Going outside alone at night
  - Talking to people who resemble an assailant but are objectively not dangerous

Andrea's Exposure Hierarchy: Post-Traumatic Fears about Safety and Painful Memories

Activity	Fear Level (0–100)
Vividly imagining the assault	75
Sleeping with my bedroom door open	65
Sleeping with my bedroom door unlocked	60
Talking to a male neighbor	60
Watching a violent movie	50
Leaving my blinds open at night	50
Going downtown alone to meet friends	45
Showering with my bathroom door open	45
Showering with my bathroom door unlocked	40
Being alone in my apartment at night	25
Walking through a parking lot in the dark	25
Going to the laundry room	25
Talking to a male stranger at the gym	20
Using the elevator in my building	20
Walking around the corner in my apartment building	20
Walking out of my apartment backward so that I can't see whether someone is there	20

The exposure exercises involved tolerating the anxiety long enough for it to decrease and disappear. For example, I would go to a part of my apartment complex where I felt anxious and would stand there until the anxiety decreased and went away.

—*Andrea*

Maximizing the Effectiveness of the Exposure Hierarchy

How do you maximize the effectiveness of your exposure hierarchy? It's important that each task on your exposure hierarchy be a specific activity that you can do to face your fears and counteract your tendency to avoid. Therefore, keep the following principles in mind.

Action Items

Listing your feared consequences doesn't provide yo u with a clear exposure exercise to do. It is not helpful to write things such as

I'll get sick and die.
The plane will crash.
Everyone will think I'm a big loser.

Instead, try to turn those fears into exposure items that you can actually do. For example,

Instead of "I'll get sick and die," try "I will touch a can of Lysol and then make a sandwich and eat it."
Instead of "The plane will crash," try "I will fly on a small plane."
Instead of "Everyone will think I'm a big loser," try "I will deliberately fall down in a public place and scatter an armload of books."

Focus on What You Will Do

It might seem intuitively reasonable to add items such as "Don't check the locks on the door," and, indeed, it's important to abstain from these kinds of avoidance and safety behaviors (see chapter 7) as much as possible when doing exposures. Yet the exposure hierarchy should be a list of what you *will* do, not a list of what you will refrain from doing. It is not helpful to write things such as

> Stop washing my hands.
> Don't take my cell phone with me.
> Don't sit by myself in a corner at the party.

Instead, turn those items into exposure items that you can actually do. For example,

> Instead of "Stop washing my hands," try "I will touch a vial of urine."
> Instead of "Don't take my cell phone with me," try "I will go to the mall without a cell phone."
> Instead of "Don't sit by myself in a corner at the party," try "I will go to a party and mingle with people I don't know well."

Specific Is Better than Vague

Remember that the exposure hierarchy is intended to be a list of specific exercises that you will do during your program. It is important that the items on the list give you concrete, clear instructions for what to do. It is not helpful to write things such as

> Touch things that are dirty.
> Feel uncomfortable physical sensations.
> Think of disaster scenarios.

Instead, try to be clear about what you will actually do. Try to word it so that someone else reading your list would be able to understand what you're going to do.

Instead of "Touch things that are dirty," try "I will touch a spot
   of urine on toilet paper."
Instead of "Feel uncomfortable physical sensations," try "I will
   hyperventilate until I feel lightheaded."
Instead of "Think of disaster scenarios," try "I will record a
   story about someone breaking into my house and killing
   everyone; I'll and listen to the recording over and over."

Is It Safe?

A common question at this point is: "Wait a minute, couldn't
some of these things be dangerous? Wouldn't ordinary people be
reluctant to do some of these things?" It's perfectly natural to
wonder about safety. It's also important, however, to recognize
that no exposure is 100 percent safe. Life, in fact, is not 100 percent safe. We take risks all of the time; that's part of living a happy
and productive life. People with anxiety-related problems often
think that their job is to minimize all risk. Let me suggest an alternative: tolerating, even embracing, risk is one of the key ingredi-
ents of living a happy life. Think about the people you know who
are the happiest and most well-adjusted. Do they seek to minimize risk at all costs? Probably not. Rather than ask whether an
exposure exercise is safe, I encourage you instead to consider
whether it is *safe enough*.

   How do you know when something is safe enough? Every
situation might be a little different, but here are some good questions to ask:

*Does this activity kill or injure people in large numbers? Is it a
common cause of death?* The leading causes of death in the
United States, by a large margin, are cancer and heart disease
(as well as other complications of obesity and smoking).
Airplanes? Dog attacks? Sharks? Touching toilets? Not even
in the top hundred. Want to live a long life? Don't smoke, get
some exercise, and go easy on the fast food.

Do other people do these activities and survive? Think about janitors who touch toilets, dog trainers who handle dogs, flight attendants who take multiple flights every day, and so on. They seem to survive just fine.

Do I have a known medical condition that would make this exposure risky? The key word here is *known* (not merely "feared"). Some people have medical conditions that make certain exposures more risky than they would be for the average person. People with known heart disease, for example, should talk to a physician before doing exposures such as running up and down stairs. People with known deficiencies of the immune system should check with their doctors before doing exposures to dirty or contaminated objects. If you're not sure whether you have a medical condition that would magnify the risks, talk to your doctor and get the facts.

Do the benefits outweigh the risks? This is perhaps the most important question. Treatments, whether medical or behavioral, carry some risk. Here's an example from medicine. One could certainly argue that sticking a needle into your own body is risky: you could get an infection or bleed to death, or you could overdose on, or have an allergic reaction to, the medication in the syringe. Would ordinary people go around sticking needles and injecting chemicals into themselves? Certainly not, nor would I advise them to. That would be nuts. But what if the person had a serious bacterial infection? And what if that syringe contained penicillin that could save the person's life? That certainly changes the risk/benefit ratio, doesn't it? In this case, I wouldn't hesitate to recommend the shot. In fact, you could make the argument that it would be nuts *not* to get the shot. Exposure therapy is kind of like that. Think about what you stand to gain by beating this fear. That's most certainly worth taking some calculated risks. If you have trouble thinking about the risks and benefits clearly, ask a trusted friend or relative (who *doesn't* have an anxiety disorder and therefore might be able to think more realistically about risk) for a "reality check."

Why do some things—for example, plane crashes or shark attacks—seem so much more common than they actually are? Social psychologists such as Amos Tversky and Daniel Kahneman have shown us that we don't mentally calculate risk based on actual probabilities. We don't actually do the math and calculate the likelihood that something bad will happen. Instead, we rely on *heuristics*: quick and dirty rules of thumb that we use to figure situations out. Most of the time, these heuristics work just fine; however, sometimes they lead us to the wrong conclusion. One example is the *availability heuristic*, in which we make estimations based on how easily certain outcomes come to mind. The availability heuristic can be summarized as "If you can imagine it, it must be important." Media coverage can play a big role here. Things such as airplane crashes, shark attacks, or violent homicides get a lot of news coverage; therefore, they tend to stick in our heads. More routine causes of death, such as cancer and heart disease, don't make the news, even though they're more common. Yet because of the discrepancy in coverage, it's easier for many of us to imagine death by the more dramatic (yet less common) causes; therefore, we mentally inflate their likelihood. I'll talk more about this in chapter 8.

Now it's time to create your own exposure hierarchy using the sample illustration on page 101. You might find it helpful to keep it in your purse, briefcase, wallet, notebook, or any other secure place. Remember, you need to do one for every fear category that you scored high for in chapter 1. This might mean you need to make one exposure hierarchy, two hierarchies, or as many as six. You can find lots of sample hierarchies in chapters 9 through 14.

Exposure Hierarchy for My Fear	
Activity	*Fear Level (0–100)*
1.	
2.	
3.	
4.	
5.	
6.	
7.	
8.	
9.	
10.	
11.	
12.	
13.	
14.	
15.	

Sample exposure hierarchy.

6

Conducting Exposures

Just do it.
—*Nike slogan*

B y now, you have made all of the preparations you need to begin exposure therapy. You understand what fear is and where it comes from, you've mapped out your own fears, and you've constructed one or more exposure hierarchies. Now it's time to get in the pool and start the difficult but rewarding work of facing your fears.

Take a moment, right now, to remember why you're doing this. In chapter 3, you listed reasons to face your fears versus accept the status quo. Because you continued past that point, I assume that you decided that you were fed up with living in fear and that you were able to come up with good reasons to face your fears. Perhaps there are activities you want to do but can't. Your fear and avoidance may have become burdensome to you or to the people who care about you. Or maybe you're just sick and tired of feeling this way. Whatever your reasons, remind yourself of what they are.

I want to start you off with a challenge. Promise yourself that you will make this program a priority in your life. It's so easy to let the ups and downs of life interfere with your larger plans. (I, for one, really want to exercise more, but for some reason I keep coming up with other things that I "have" to do instead, so I'm going to try to take my own advice here too.) Commit, here and now, to working on your fear every day. That means seven days per week. No holidays. No breaks. Even on days when you're busy and hassled, days when you can't possibly imagine finding the time, and days when you feel terrible, you must make daily fear facing a top priority. If you're like most people reading this book, you've had these fears for a while, and they've become pretty well entrenched. It's going to take a lot of hard work and dedication to beat them. A half-hearted effort simply won't cut it.

What to Expect

Anticipation

It's natural to feel somewhat anxious before you even start an exposure. We call this anticipatory anxiety: your brain is already thinking ahead and envisioning what you're going to do. Naturally, your amygdala doesn't fully grasp that this is an exposure exercise, so it starts to rev up and sound the alarm, at least partly—and in doing so, it sends that signal through the HPA axis (see chapter 2) down to your adrenal glands, which start to release adrenaline into the bloodstream, getting you ready to fight, flee, or freeze. This is a good thing: the fact that your amygdala is paying attention and trying to protect you from harm means that everything is working. Remember, though, your job now is to work your way through that anxiety, rather than give in to it.

Starting the Exposure

When you begin an exposure exercise, two things are likely to happen. First, you'll probably experience more feelings of fear. When that adrenaline enters your bloodstream, it will make your heart rate increase, your mouth dry up, your stomach feel as if it's doing flip-flops, your palms get sweaty, and so on. Second, you'll probably feel an urge to escape, avoid, or otherwise stop the exposure. They don't call it the fight-flight-freeze response for nothing. Remember, these things are good. They're your brain and body's self-preservation system, and it's perfectly fine that they're occurring. Yet just like a car alarm that goes off in a strong wind, your self-preservation system is responding to a fear that is more imagined than real, so you need to fight that instinct to escape or avoid.

How Much Fear Am I Shooting For?

There is no hard-and-fast formula for how much fear you should experience during exposure exercises. The rule of thumb, however, is that you should try to experience as much fear as you can reasonably tolerate, no more, no less. Remember the *fear level* I introduced in chapter 4, the 0–100 scale of how uncomfortable you feel. When you start an exposure, your first question to yourself should be, "What's my level?" If the answer is a very low number (perhaps 20 or less), and you're not feeling very scared, that's a sign that you might have started too low on the exposure hierarchy, and you need to try something a little tougher. If the answer is a very high number (perhaps 80 or more), that's a sign that you may have started too high, and you need to start with something easier. This way, your own fear level will serve as a constant guide, showing you exactly how strong your exposures need to be.

Troubleshooting: Can't Get the Fear Level to Go Up

Occasionally, you try an exposure exercise, and for some reason, you just don't feel scared at all. That may mean that your exposure didn't quite hit the mark, and you need to rethink it. Ask yourself: Does this exposure really target what I'm afraid of? Am I leaving out (or avoiding) some crucial detail that would make it scary? Because everyone's fear is a little bit different, it's sometimes necessary to get very creative to gain access to your individual fear. Here are a couple of examples:

- Suppose you are afraid of public speaking. You arrange to give a speech in front of some friends, but you just don't feel anxious. Perhaps there are additional details about your fear that need to be incorporated. Maybe you're afraid of public speaking only in front of strangers or business colleagues but not in front of friends. If that's the case, you need to change your audience. Or perhaps it turns out that you are afraid not of public speaking itself, but rather fear that you might show signs of anxiety while giving a speech. In that case, try giving a speech after dabbing water on your forehead to make it look as if you're sweating, or deliberately stammer or drop your papers while giving the speech.

- Suppose you are afraid of driving. This is a simple enough exposure, right? Just get in the car and hit the road. But if your fear level isn't going up, think about what needs to be changed. Does the kind of road (country versus city versus highway) make a difference? If so, you need to make sure you're driving on the kind of road that scares you. Perhaps you're not afraid of driving in itself, but rather you fear what will happen if you feel panicky sensations while driving. If that's the case, try driving while doing body-focused exposures, such as breathing through a straw or hyperventilating. Or maybe you're afraid that while driving, you will run someone over and not know it, in which case you should consider driving closer to pedestrians or deliberately driving over bumps in the road to get your fear up—and include some imaginal exposures for good measure, such as imagining that you just ran over a whole crowd of people.

You get the idea. Any given exposure can be tweaked and modified in countless ways. If your first exposure doesn't get your fear level up, try changing the exposure to make it scarier, or combine exposure elements until you can activate your fear.

Watching Your Fear Dissolve

Now comes the good part. You're doing an exposure, your fear level is moderately (but not intolerably) high, and you are not giving in to the urge to escape or avoid. What happens? Your fear starts to dissolve. If you've been in the habit of avoiding in order to manage fear, you might be surprised by what's happening. By avoiding, you've been teaching yourself that avoidance is the only way you'll feel okay (and, conversely, that if you don't avoid, you'll just feel fearful forever). Yet here you are, doing something new and scary, and your fear level is going down, all by itself.

What's happening? We call this process *within-session habituation*. Remember that habituation simply means getting used to something—an important part of getting past a fear. We use the term *within-session* to mean that the habituation is happening within a single exposure session (the period of time you're doing the exposure) and to differentiate it from another kind of habituation called *between-session habituation* (more on that in a moment). So when you start an exposure you might feel quite anxious, and perhaps your body will go into fight-flight-freeze mode. Five minutes later, you might find that you're still anxious but not quite so bad—perhaps your body has calmed down a little. Five minutes after that, you're feeling a little bit stronger, not as scared. Five minutes later, you feel even better and might be starting to think, "I can do this! It's not so bad."

Following is a sample worksheet that you can re-create in your notebook and use to track your fear level during a single exposure session. Remember that not every exposure can or should be as long as this form indicates (a full hour). Shorter exposures are okay, too. I've marked it so that you can note your fear level every five minutes; however, if you find it helpful to use shorter or longer increments, that's fine. Just make sure you fill out the worksheet in a way that allows you to see the rise and fall of your fear level.

Exposure Session	
Exposure:_____	
Date: _____	
Time (minutes)	*Fear Level (0–100)*
5	
10	
15	
20	
25	
30	
35	
40	
45	
50	
55	
60	

Sample exposure session worksheet.

But why don't you just stay anxious forever? What's making the fear dissolve? Biologically speaking, the adrenaline that was released into your bloodstream is being reabsorbed into the cells that released them in the first place, diffused into extracellular fluid, or metabolized (eaten) by enzymes in your blood. Adrenaline can't remain in your bloodstream forever. Your amygdala is beginning to quiet down as your frontal cortex exerts more control over your thinking. Cognitively, you are starting to learn that nothing bad is happening, and that your fears were exaggerated and unnecessary.

Troubleshooting: Can't Get the Fear Level to Come Down

What if you can successfully get your fear level to go up (that is, you found an effective exposure), but then it doesn't come back down? You might be surprised to learn that failure to habituate is not that big of a deal. Sometimes, it's just a matter of time. I've known some people who habituated within a five-minute exposure session, whereas other people have to stay with an exposure for an hour or more before they feel better. Everyone's a bit different—and being a "slow habituator" doesn't mean you won't get better. You should, however, think about whether this particular exposure is too ambitious for now. You might find that if you try a slightly easier exercise (that is, one that is ranked lower on your exposure hierarchy), your fear level comes down more readily, and then you can work your way back up to the harder exposure.

> For me, watching part of a movie where someone was getting assaulted was very anxiety provoking, right at the top of my hierarchy. I found that after watching the movie, I didn't feel much better. Parts of the movie would sometimes come into my mind, and I found myself getting very angry at the perpetrators of violence in the movie. I decided that watching that scene from the movie was making things worse, and I stopped that part of the exposure, choosing instead to focus on exercises that were more manageable.
>
> —*Andrea*

Don't invest too much time worrying about within-session habituation; it's not the Holy Grail of exposure. If it happens, great, but there's a lot of research showing that it is not the most indispensable issue. Much more important, it turns out, is between-session habituation, which I'll discuss next. The presence or absence of between-session habituation is a much stronger predictor of your success.

Trying Again the Next Time

You've done an exposure exercise, you faced your fear, you didn't give in to the urge to avoid it, and your fear went down (probably). Now here comes the part where you can really measure your success: go back at another time, perhaps the following day, and try it again. Pay careful attention to your fear level. Is it just as high as it was the last time? Probably not—in which case, you are experiencing between-session habituation. We use the term *between-session* to indicate that your fear went down between the day 1 exposure and the day 2 exposure. This is a good measure (although still not perfect) of how well the process is working. When the same exposure exercise gets progressively easier and easier, this is a sign that you are getting stronger and your fear is getting weaker.

Working Your Way up the Hierarchy

As you might recall from chapter 4, your fear level should tell you when it's time to stop one exposure and go on to the next one. My rule of thumb is to stay with an exposure until your fear level decreases by 50 percent or more from its peak—so, for example, if your fear peaks at 80, you should stay with that exposure until your fear level comes down to 40 or lower. Yet this rule is not set in stone. Sometimes, the nature of a given exposure simply won't allow for prolonged exposures; short ones will probably work too. At other times, you might find that your fear level simply doesn't come down that far. If you've been at it for an hour, and your fear level is not coming down any more, it's okay to stop and move on. Many of the "rules" of exposure are really just guidelines. It's great if you can follow them all, but, ultimately, what's most important is that you just do it. So don't get too hung up on doing exposure exercises perfectly.

Beyond Normal

On the VH1 television show *The OCD Project*, I licked a shoe. And boy, did I get letters. "Are you nuts?" "What kind of crazy therapy is this?" "That's just for TV, right?" "Don't you know that's not *normal*?!"

On one hand, I can understand why people might have a strong reaction to shoe licking. It's gross. And yes, it's definitely not normal (despite what some people might think, I don't go around licking shoes in my personal life). But here's the thing: "normal" is not a good way to judge which exposures to do or not to do. Exposure therapy is not merely mimicking "normal" behavior (whatever that is)—rather, it is a series of exercises that is specifically designed to help you beat your fear. To beat fear, you sometimes have to do things that are decidedly abnormal, weird, or extreme. Remember "safe enough" from chapter 5? That should be your guide, not whether something is "normal." I licked a shoe because it was safe enough, and because the benefits (in this case, showing someone that dirt is not all that dangerous) clearly outweighed the costs (a little dirt in my mouth).

So your exposure exercises need to be significantly more scary, more abnormal than what you would anticipate encountering in real life. Just as I don't lick shoes for fun, I also don't hyperventilate while driving, I don't deliberately drop my papers when giving a speech, I don't seek out movies of people vomiting, and I don't deliberately conjure up mental images of my house burning down. Yet if I had a fear of panicking while driving, a fear of looking anxious in front of people, a fear of vomiting, or excessive worries, I would do exposures such as these.

Why do you have to push the exposures beyond normal? There are two main reasons. First, life has a way of throwing curveballs at you. You cannot possibly predict everything that will happen to you in the future, and sometimes you will be caught off guard by something that is scarier than usual. You can do all of the driving or public-speaking exposures you want, and you might do just fine and feel as if you've beaten the fear. Then one day, at some point in the future, you come down with the flu. Now you're driving while feeling lightheaded, or you're giving a speech while sweating. If your exposure exercises didn't prepare you for this—that is, if you didn't hyperventilate during your driving exposures, or you didn't dab your forehead with water before giving a speech—you're likely to become highly anxious. You might even get discouraged, feeling as if the exposure therapy didn't work, or that you're right back at square one. Those ideas aren't necessarily true, but in the long run you will be much better off having prepared for that unexpected curveball.

The second reason is what I call the *yes-buts*. Your brain is a master of the yes-but response: "Yes, I drove on the highway, but I only survived because it wasn't rush-hour traffic." "Yes, I went into the restroom, but I only survived because I didn't touch the toilet." "Yes, I touched a snake, but I only survived because I didn't let it crawl on me." "Yes, I went to a party, but I only escaped humiliation because I didn't go out on the dance floor." It's as if your brain has a built-in tendency to find ways to make exposures "not count." You, of course, are trying to get your brain to learn the truth—that none of these things were really dangerous to begin with. So you have to eliminate the "buts." That means driving in rush-hour traffic, touching the toilet, letting the snake crawl on you, and getting on the dance floor, even if you think those situations aren't "normal."

It's natural to want to minimize feelings of fear during exposures. After all, fear is uncomfortable, and every animal, from the lowly slug on up to you and me, is highly motivated to make it go away. But now you need to do something different: you need to lean into the fear as much as you can. When doing something scary, I want you to keep asking yourself, "How might I tweak this activity to make it even scarier?"

Related to this concept is the need to identify what I call *safety behaviors*. These are the little, often subtle tricks we employ to try to minimize our fear. This is such an important topic that the entire next chapter is devoted to it. For now, suffice it to say that many of these behaviors are toxic, and you need to let go of them. If you're not seeing between-session habituation, subtle safety behaviors are often to blame.

Quick Guidelines for Exposures

- *Remain in the situation until your anxiety decreases.* Usually, this means allowing a minimum of twenty minutes for each exposure. More difficult exposures may require more time.
- *Do not distract, avoid, or use safety behaviors during the exposure.* Focus on the situation as fully as possible.
- *Monitor your fear level.* After each exposure, note your fear level. Pay attention to patterns. If your level has not decreased after a number of repetitions, ask yourself whether you are using any safety behaviors or subtle forms of avoidance. If your anxiety has decreased, congratulate yourself on winning the battle.
- *Repeat the exposure frequently.* Allow enough time to do each exposure more than once during each session (three or more times is preferred). Also, repeat the exposure exercise daily until your fear level is low (for example, 20 or lower).
- *Practice daily.* Set aside a minimum of thirty minutes to one hour each day for exposure exercises, more if possible.
- *Practice exposures in different situations.* As you get more comfortable with an exposure, see if you can do it in different or more anxiety-provoking contexts.

Stick with It

The number one reason programs such as this one fail is that people don't stick with them. Life gets in the way, or they forget to do their exercises, or there's something good on TV that they just have to watch. There are few guarantees in life, but I can tell you that if you don't stick with this program, you probably won't feel better. I can also tell you that if you do stick with the program, the rewards can be tremendous. A life beyond fear is within your reach, right now.

Remember: face your fears every day. You're worth it.

Eliminating Safety Behaviors

Fear cannot take what you do not give it.
—*Christopher Coan*

What Are Safety Behaviors?

By now, I hope you agree with me that avoidance is the enemy. Through exposure exercises, you are counteracting your natural gut reaction to avoid feared objects, situations, or activities. For example, if you are afraid of dogs, you know that avoiding dogs only makes the problem worse, so you need to develop an exposure hierarchy to gradually and systematically face that fear.

Yet in many cases it's trickier than this. Avoidance can be blatant, such as simply not going anywhere near dogs, but it can also be quite subtle (although no less damaging). People with excessive fears frequently rely on certain *safety behaviors* to help them cope or make them feel safer. Another term for a safety behavior might be a crutch. It's those things you do, often little things, to help you feel safer and that make it easier for you to get through a scary situation. So, staying with our dog fear example, you might not blatantly avoid dogs—perhaps there are dogs in your neighborhood, so you can't completely avoid walking past them—but instead, you might carry a bottle of pepper spray with you, with the knowledge that you could use it to repel an attacking dog if you had to. The pepper spray makes you feel safer and makes you feel more able to walk down the street.

> When I was facing my worries about my son dying in a fire, I realized that I had to get rid of the ladder I had under his window. I put it there just in case there was a fire and the stairs were engulfed. But I had to move it, because it was only reinforcing my notion that I could completely control the safety of my son with my actions. I needed to take away my crutches. And when nothing bad happened as a result, it reinforced my newfound understanding that we can't live our lives surrounding ourselves with safety behaviors. I still get a twinge now and again when my son is visiting, and I notice that the ladder is gone. It lasts only a moment, though. It's interesting to realize that a lot of my safety behaviors are actually learned behaviors from my parents. The things I was told I should do to keep safe have never left me.
>
> —*Samantha*

People with obsessive-compulsive disorder (OCD) might be very familiar with what I'm talking about. In OCD language, we call these behaviors *compulsions*, and they are one of the hallmark symptoms of OCD. The *DSM-IV-TR* defines compulsions as

> Repetitive behaviors (e.g., hand washing, ordering, checking) or mental acts (e.g., praying, counting, repeating words silently) that the person feels driven to perform in response to an obsession, or according to rules that must be applied rigidly.

The behaviors or mental acts are aimed at preventing or reducing distress or preventing some dreaded event or situation; however, these behaviors or mental acts either are not connected in a realistic way with what they are designed to neutralize or prevent or are clearly excessive.

There are four criteria that make a behavior a compulsion. First, the behavior is repetitive. Second, it is a response to a fear (in this case, an *obsession*). Third, these behaviors are designed to prevent something bad from happening, or to make the person feel better. Fourth, they are unnecessary or excessive.

If you perform repetitive behaviors in response to your fear, does that mean you have OCD? Certainly not. As you might have guessed, the definition of compulsions in the *DSM-IV-TR* is actually descriptive of a wide range of safety behaviors that accompany many different fears, not only OCD. In fact, for virtually every fear, there are ways to avoid the fear blatantly and also ways to use safety behaviors as a more subtle form of avoidance. Here are just a few examples:

Blatant Avoidance and Safety Behaviors

Fear	Blatant Avoidance	Safety Behavior
Doctors, dentists, injections, or blood draws	Do not go to the doctor or donate blood.	Distract yourself and do not look at the needle; request extra anesthetic.
Physical symptoms such as a racing heart or dizziness	Do not exert yourself.	Keep checking your pulse; have a "safe person" with you; do relaxation or breathing exercises to stay calm.
Things being out of order or not just right	Avoid seeing anything out of order.	Arrange and rearrange things until they feel right.

(Continued)

Fear	*Blatant Avoidance*	*Safety Behavior*
Situations where it would be dangerous to lose control of yourself in the event of panic sensations, such as driving a car	Do not drive.	Stay in the right lane in case you need to pull over; drive only when you feel good.
Thoughts of catastrophes	Never think about bad things.	Check to make sure everything is safe and okay; ask others to reassure you; worry about something else.
Eating food you could choke on	Do not eat certain foods.	Have lots of water on hand in case you choke; chew your food extra thoroughly.
Having repulsive, horrible, or immoral thoughts or mental images	Try not to think about the thoughts or images.	Say prayers or do rituals after the images to feel better; remind yourself that you don't really mean it.
Memories of unpleasant, stressful, or traumatic life experiences	Try not to think about the memories.	Distract yourself with music or TV; use alcohol or drugs to numb your mind.
Being near certain animals	Do not go near animals.	Go near animals only if you have something to protect yourself with; only go near animals that are leashed or caged.

Interacting with people	Avoid social interaction.	Keep the conversation limited to "easy" topics, such as the weather; have something in your hands so that you don't have to shake hands.
Throwing things away	Do not throw things away.	Check and recheck things before throwing them away.
Situations that are hard to escape from in case of panic sensations, such as driving over a bridge or through a tunnel or being in a crowded movie theater	Do not go into these situations.	Go into these situations only with a "safe person"; stay as close to exits or escape routes as possible; carry a cell phone or a water bottle just in case.
Making a mistake that could cause harm to someone	Be sure never to make a mistake.	Double- and triple-check your actions.
Flying in an airplane	Do not fly.	Use alcohol or tranquilizers when flying; grip the armrest tightly so the plane doesn't crash.
Being in a high place	Do not go to high places.	Grip railings tightly so you don't fall; stay far away from the edge; don't look down.

(Continued)

Fear	Blatant Avoidance	Safety Behavior
Touching things that seem dirty or contaminated	Do not touch dirty things.	Wash hands repeatedly or use hand sanitizer after touching dirty things; use paper towels or your sleeve to minimize contact.
Public speaking	Do not give speeches.	Speak only about familiar topics; stay behind the podium; don't make eye contact with the audience.

What's Wrong with Safety Behaviors?

You might be asking, "Wait, isn't it normal to want to feel better when I'm anxious? Doesn't everyone do little things to take his or her mind off their anxiety?" Sure, it's normal, perfectly understandable, and even adaptive for some people in some situations. I know lots of people, for example, who don't like to look at the needle when they're getting an injection. Certainly, many people will wash their hands if they think they've touched something dirty. And who doesn't feel a little better carrying a cell phone when they go out? Remember, though, that what's "normal" isn't necessarily what will help you overcome your fear. If you have just a little bit of fear and simply need to live with it, fine. Do all of the safety behaviors you want, if you find them helpful.

Yet if, like most people reading this book, you have more than a little fear—if your fear is getting the better of you—you need to take some extra steps in order to beat it. After all, we're here to beat this fear, not merely live with it, right?

Safety behaviors are a problem for the same reason that blatant avoidance is a problem. These behaviors, these "crutches," might help you feel better in the short term, but they keep you stuck in the long term. Let's stay with the "crutch" metaphor for just a second. If you have a broken leg, you might need to use crutches. Yet what would happen if you continued to use crutches, even without a broken leg, indefinitely? Over time, your leg muscles would start to waste away from disuse. Eventually, your natural ability to walk without crutches would become less and less. You very well might think, "Hey, I use crutches because I need crutches." In reality, though, *you need crutches because you use crutches.* Because they make you feel better, you become addicted to them.

> I had to stop washing my hands or my kids' hands unless I saw dirt on them. I stopped wiping tables down or using Purell. It was very hard but *so* empowering to realize what I already knew—my thoughts were at times irrational. But it also went against everything I was taught in my career as a nurse. So in that sense, I was living a double life. I had to wash my hands while I was at work, of course. And we tell our patients good hand washing is a must. So why did I need to stop? I realized that I needed to stop because the theory behind my actions was not normal. I was washing not for good, healthy reasons but only because of a fear of throwing up.
>
> —*Michelle*

Part of the problem with these safety behaviors is that they teach your brain the wrong message. During exposure, you want your brain to learn a message of *unconditional safety*: for example, "This situation is safe." When you use a safety behavior, on the other hand, your brain learns a message of *conditional safety*: "This situation is safe as long as criteria A, B, and C are satisfied."

There's an old joke that goes something like this: A guy is standing on a street corner in New York City. He's stomping his feet, clapping his hands, yelling, whistling, making a lot of noise. Another man walks up to him and asks, "Why are you making all this racket?" "I'm doing it to keep the alligators away," the guy replies. "Huh? There are no alligators here." The guy says, "See? It's working." The joke here, of course, is that even if the man wasn't making a racket, he wouldn't have been attacked by an alligator, because there simply are no alligators on the streets of New York. The reality is one of unconditional safety: he's safe from alligators, whether he makes noise or not. What makes the joke funny is that instead of recognizing the unconditional safety, this guy has taught himself an inaccurate lesson of conditional safety: he believes he is safe only because of his behavior. The fact that he's not being attacked by alligators only serves to strengthen his belief in conditional safety; the absence of disaster just reinforces his belief that his behaviors are necessary.

> If I had to go to some kind of social function, I'd try to go with someone I knew, like my brother or my wife, and I'd make sure to sit next to them so I wouldn't have to make as much small talk with people I didn't know well. Most of the time I'd have to have a couple of drinks to calm myself down.
>
> —*Steven*

Let's take someone with significant social interaction fears as a more realistic example of this lesson on unconditional safety versus conditional safety. Someone with social fears might be convinced to go to a party. If, however, while at the party, he remains in a corner with a close friend (safety behavior), in the long run he will not overcome his fears. When the party ends without horrendous embarrassment, his brain learns that parties are okay as long as he sticks with close friends (conditional safety). He does not learn that parties are okay in general, whether he sticks close to friends or not (unconditional safety). He hasn't learned the right lesson. He hasn't learned to view the situation realistically. Another example would be someone who has an obsessive fear of contamination. Having learned that avoidance is the enemy, she makes a point of touching some things that seem dirty or germy. If, after touching those things, she pulls out a bottle of hand sanitizer and sterilizes her hands, she's not going to beat the fear. When she doesn't catch some terrible disease, her brain will simply learn that she's safe as long as she cleans her hands (conditional safety), instead of learning that it's reasonably safe to touch dirty things (unconditional safety).

I had to eliminate hand washing, abnormal cleaning, avoiding items (walking around them or not touching them), and asking people whether they thought something was contaminated. Not doing the behaviors felt unnatural, excruciatingly hard sometimes. I also stopped asking people to wash their hands after touching something I thought was contaminated. I invited them, too, to slowly return to what they remembered as being normal. It was sometimes hard to know I had agreed to no longer ask people to wash at certain times, but it also began to be a relief. It was one less thing I felt I needed to be responsible for. It started to be very freeing.

—*Rachel*

I worked on not checking the doors in my apartment, checking to see what was causing a noise, making sure the blinds were closed so no one could look in. I also worked on keeping the bedroom door open at night (my safety behavior was to have it locked). It was hard and scary to eliminate some of the safety behaviors, but it did get easier with time.

—*Andrea*

I had to get over needing to drink or take a Xanax to go to the movies. I had to stop calling my aunt so much, too. I used to call her every day to ask whether I was dying over something. Poor woman, now that I think back, I must have driven my family insane. I also stopped clenching my teeth. Whenever I'd get a headache, I'd clench really hard. Stupid me, it causes a worse headache!!! I also stopped saying no (because I was scared) when something fun came along. I just threw myself out there. Guess what? I lived.

—Susan

You can see how sneaky and subtle these crutches can be, but I can't emphasize their importance strongly enough. In my clinical experience, when exposure therapy doesn't work, most of the time it's because of safety behaviors that we failed to eliminate. In order to beat fear, you must let go of your crutches, as the following scene from a 1994 episode of *Seinfeld* humorously shows.

Jerry Seinfeld: If every instinct you have is wrong, then the opposite would have to be right.

George Costanza: Yes, I will do the opposite. I used to sit here and do nothing, and regret it for the rest of the day, so now I will do the opposite, and I will do something!

The Myths of Distraction and Relaxation

If you're like a lot of people reading this book, this isn't the first time you've read about beating fear and anxiety. Perhaps you've even seen a professional counselor about it, or you've listened to audiotapes that promise to show you how to rid yourself of anxiety using distraction or relaxation exercises. Maybe they told you to read a book or watch TV to get your mind off unpleasant worries, thoughts, or memories. Perhaps these strategies worked well, perhaps not so well (although I suspect that if they had really solved the problem, you wouldn't be reading this book in the first place). I'm not a fan of these strategies, because they don't really address the fear in a meaningful way. Instead, they just tend to pile more safety behaviors on top of what you're already doing—which is not only unhelpful but can even make the problem worse. I'll explain why.

The Myth of Distraction

Perhaps someone has told you that when you feel afraid, you should try to distract yourself. I've heard of counselors who advised people to focus on something external, such as a picture on the wall or the scenery. Other counselors have advised people to start going over their grocery-shopping lists in their heads. I get the rationale: when you're distracted, you don't feel quite as anxious, and you are potentially able to get through more scary situations.

But is distraction a good idea? Does it help exposure therapy or hurt it? Psychologist Jonathan Grayson and colleagues tested it out with a group of patients who had an obsessive fear of contamination. These researchers instructed some of the patients to touch something dirty (in vivo exposure) and to focus their attention on what they were doing. The other patients were also instructed to touch something dirty but to play video games at the same time. When the patients came back the next day and touched the dirty object again, the group who had focused their attention on the exposure had significantly less anxiety than did the group who had been distracted by the video game.

Now, I should acknowledge that not all researchers have obtained the same results, and there are some very respectable researchers and clinicians who suggest that distracting yourself during exposure exercises is okay or even desirable. Yet my sense is that overall it's not a great idea, and that's why I'm not recommending that you do it, at least at first (although we will revisit this issue in chapter 17, where I'll talk about alternative strategies). Distracting yourself during an exposure exercise might make you feel better in the short term, but my experience has been that it may prevent you from fully engaging in the exposure. Like all safety behaviors, it risks teaching your brain a message of conditional safety: "I'm okay as long as I can distract myself." In the long run, that doesn't help.

A particularly unhelpful variant of distraction is called *thought stopping*. Perhaps someone has recommended this strategy to you. The basic idea is that when you start thinking of something scary or upsetting, you're supposed to yell, "Stop!" out loud. Over time, the yell becomes a whisper, and eventually you simply think, "Stop!" to yourself. Some people have suggested adding actions, such as snapping the wrist with a rubber band whenever a scary thought comes to mind. Although the idea might seem intuitively appealing (it must, because a lot of people still use this strategy), most people ultimately find that thought stopping is unhelpful at best and harmful at worst. It's a safety behavior, and like all safety behaviors, it prevents your brain from learning the message of unconditional safety. Yet thought stopping can also be harmful because it's asking your brain to do something it's simply not wired to do. The brain just doesn't do a very good job of not thinking about things. In fact, sometimes your efforts to stop thinking about something can have the exact opposite effect (see the sidebar on page 125).

One sneaky (and still unhelpful) way to distract yourself is by worrying about something else. Psychologists Thomas Borkovec and Lizabeth Roemer surveyed people with excessive worries (in this case, people who had generalized anxiety disorder) about their reasons for worrying. These people were significantly more likely than were people without excessive worries to agree with the statement "Worrying about most of the things I worry about is a way to distract myself from worrying about even more emotional things, things that I don't want to think about." That is, because situation A is really scary, I'm going to focus on worrying about situation B, which is somewhat less scary. The idea that my husband might be late because he's lying dead in a ditch

More than You Probably Wanted to Know about Thought Stopping

Try this experiment. For thirty seconds, try not to think about a white bear. Did it work? Probably not. I can't do it, either.

Social psychologist Daniel Wegner has done a lot of research showing that most people simply cannot force themselves not to think about something (which he terms *thought suppression*). When they try, they tend to experience a rebound effect, in which they actually start thinking about it more. The theory goes like this: in order not to think about something, you have to remember what you're not thinking about—and then, of course, you are thinking about it! It's enough to tie your brain in knots.

My colleagues and I have studied the rebound effect in people with obsessive-compulsive disorder (OCD). We found a particularly nasty pattern, in which people with OCD tend to (1) believe that controlling their thoughts is both possible and necessary, (2) use thought suppression a lot in their daily lives, (3) fail miserably at attempts to suppress their thoughts, and (4) interpret their failure to suppress thoughts as further evidence that something is really wrong or dangerous.

Clinical practice, however, has been slow to catch up with the evidence. Psychiatrist Robert Goisman surveyed 231 people with anxiety disorders about what kind of treatments they had received. Only 28 percent had ever received exposure therapy. By contrast, 48 percent had received thought stopping, and 44 percent had received distraction instructions. That's right—people with anxiety disorders are more likely to receive unhelpful treatments than helpful ones.

somewhere is too scary to think about, so instead I'm going to become preoccupied with whether the kitchen is clean enough. This "worry skipping," as I call it—jumping from one worry to the next before you get too worked up—is just one more way of distracting yourself, which ultimately undercuts your efforts to face your fears.

The Myth of Relaxation

The idea of using relaxation exercises to combat fear and anxiety was first pioneered by physician Edmund Jacobson in his 1929 book *Progressive Relaxation: A Physiological and Clinical Investigation of Muscular States and Their Significance in Psychology and Medical Practice*. The general idea is to systematically relax the muscles of the body, one section at a time, by tensing and then relaxing the muscles. Often, these relaxation exercises will be accompanied by breathing retraining instructions, which encourage slow abdominal breathing. Relaxation-based therapies for fear and anxiety became especially popular in the 1960s, although they are still commonly used today. I've used these exercises myself, and they feel great. For some people, they might be a very nice way to reduce general feelings of anxiety and tension (I'll discuss this issue more in chapter 17).

For now, let's consider whether it makes sense to add relaxation to exposure exercises. In the early days of behavior therapy, psychiatrist Joseph Wolpe pioneered a treatment called *systematic desensitization*. In this treatment, patients would use imaginal exposure (remember from chapter 4 that this is using your imagination to envision a scary situation, object, or activity), while simultaneously doing progressive relaxation exercises. People got better, and systematic desensitization caught on. Over time, other researchers tried experimenting with variations on the procedure. They found that the treatment worked equally well with or without the relaxation exercises. The important ingredient, it turns out, was the exposure. The relaxation exercises didn't add to the overall effects.

In some cases, relaxation and breathing exercises can actually get in the way of exposure. There's a great example of this in a research study by psychologist Brad Schmidt, who was examining the outcome of exposure-based therapy for people with panic disorder. These people were doing lots of exposure to body sensations (exercises such as hyperventilating, spinning in a chair, and so on), and they were also doing in vivo exposures to situations that were hard to escape from (for example, going to crowded places, driving on highways, and so on). As I mentioned in chapter 3, this is a very effective treatment for panic disorder. In addition to the exposure, these people were assigned at random (for example, with a coin flip) to receive additional instructions in slow, relaxing breathing exercises or to receive no such instructions. Which group do you think did better? If you subscribe to the "more stuff is better" theory, you'd predict that the group who got the additional instructions for relaxed breathing would do better than the group who didn't. In actuality, however, at a one-year follow-up evaluation, only 37 percent of the people who got the additional breathing instructions had recovered from panic disorder, compared to 57 percent of those who received only the exposure-based therapy without any breathing instructions!

Why on earth would adding some feel-good relaxation exercises actually make the outcomes worse? By now, you probably get the picture: they might feel nice, but they can backfire when they teach your brain the wrong message. Remember, during exposure you're trying to teach your brain unconditional safety (in other words, "I'm okay because this situation isn't that dangerous"). When you add relaxation exercises to the exposure, your brain could instead reach a conclusion of conditional safety (that is, "I'm okay because I'm doing this relaxation exercise"). When the relaxation exercise doesn't work (which happens quite often), you then have that much more to worry about ("Oh, no! I can't relax! What's wrong with me?").

Acceptance as an Alternative

So, if you're not supposed to relax, and you're not supposed to distract yourself, what should you do? One helpful alternative is to practice acceptance. This is a concept borrowed from Zen Buddhism and adapted during the last few years by psychologists Marsha Linehan, Steven Hayes, and Jon Kabat-Zinn. Acceptance doesn't mean giving up, or believing that things will never get better. Rather, it means accepting that your feelings of fear and anxiety, your fight-flight-freeze response, are perfectly normal and okay. It means noticing those emotions and sensations without feeling as if you always have to do something about them. The drive to feel better now is part of the problem, not the solution. It leads us to rely on avoidance, safety behaviors, and all kinds of things that mess us up.

Steven Hayes compares this process to the old Chinese finger trap—it's a tube made of straw, and you insert a finger into each end of the tube. When you try to pull your fingers out (struggle against the tube), what happens? The tube gets tighter and won't let your fingers loose. The only way to escape from the trap is first to push your fingers *in*, and then the tube loosens enough that you can slide your fingers out. When you struggle against fear—when you try to control it with safety behaviors, distraction, relaxation, alcohol, or whatever—it's like trying to pull your fingers out of the Chinese finger trap. The fear tightens around you, feels worse, and doesn't let go. The more productive alternative is to *push into the fear*—to actually try to make yourself feel more anxious, not less—so that the fear will loosen its grip on you. Trying to feel better makes us feel worse, and trying to feel worse can actually make us feel better.

Psychologists Georg Eifert and Michelle Heffner illustrated this principle nicely with a research study of people who had a fear of body sensations. They asked these patients to breathe air that had been enriched with 10 percent carbon dioxide (it's harmless but can make you feel dizzy and make your heart flutter, so it's a way of exposing yourself to the physical sensations). Half of the participants were taught a relaxing breathing exercise (just as a lot of self-help books and counselors would recommend), and half were instructed to push into their symptoms, to accept that what they were feeling was okay. The participants who received acceptance instructions felt significantly less anxious over time and had fewer worried thoughts and avoidant behaviors than did the participants who were trying to control their symptoms with relaxation.

If Relaxation Gets in the Way of Exposure, What about Medications?

Certainly, some people need medications, and there's no question that some medications can be helpful for anxiety disorders. I'll discuss the specifics in chapter 17.

Most research suggests that exposure therapy works equally well with or without medications, but there is one potential exception to this rule that you should know about. Psychologist Henny Westra surveyed forty-three people who were receiving exposure-based treatment for panic disorder about their use of a particular class of medications called benzodiazepines. Benzodiazepines are tranquilizing medications that produce a fairly rapid relaxation response. People who did not take benzodiazepines showed an 82 percent reduction in panic attacks during the course of treatment. People who were taking benzodiazepines on a regular schedule—for example, three times a day at the same time every day—had a virtually identical reduction, 80 percent. Yet people who took benzodiazepines on an "as-needed" (also called "p.r.n.") basis had only a 62 percent reduction in panic attacks.

Why would taking p.r.n. benzodiazepines result in a poorer treatment outcome? One explanation is that for some people, these medications were serving as a crutch. They were learning conditional safety ("I'm okay as long as I have my pills"), rather than unconditional safety ("I'm okay because these sensations and situations aren't dangerous").

Therefore, the take-home message of this chapter is: Don't relax. Don't distract. Don't try to feel better. Don't use crutches. Instead, push into the fear. I know it sounds weird. Try it and see for yourself.

Take out your notebook, and create a list of your safety behaviors following the sample on page 130. If your exposure hierarchy

---

My "Don't" List

During and after exposure, I will not do the following things that distract me:
1.
2.
3.

During and after exposure, I will not do the following things that increase my sense of safety:
1.
2.
3.

During and after exposure, I will not do the following things to relax or feel better:
1.
2.
3.

During and after exposure, I will not bring the following things or people with me:
1.
2.
3.

Sample list of safety behaviors.

is your "to do" list, this is your "don't" list. Using the four sentences provided as your guide, write down all of your crutches, even the very minor ones.

Once you've identified your safety behaviors, your job is to watch out for them and make sure that they don't creep back into your exposures.

When I discussed exposures, I suggested using a gradual approach (baby steps), rather than trying to do it all at once. When it comes to getting rid of safety behaviors, however, my advice to you is a bit different: I want you to try your best to go "cold turkey"—to stop all of your safety behaviors right away. Why? Think about what safety behaviors do: they prevent your brain from learning the right lesson during an exposure exercise. So if you continue to allow yourself to perform safety behaviors, even partial ones, during an exposure exercise, you're not getting the most out of the exercise. I'd rather have you put a lot of effort into stopping the safety behaviors, even if that means you have to take the exposures more slowly.

Remember, as with everything else I'm telling you, don't get too hung up on doing this perfectly 100 percent of the time. If you're like most people, you'll slip up and use some safety behaviors once in a while. No big deal. Do your best, be aware of the need to lay off the safety behaviors, and you'll be fine.

8

Addressing Scary Thoughts, Examining the Evidence

Fear: False Evidence Appearing Real.

—*Author unknown*

Remember what I explained about the cognitive perspective in chapter 2? I'll go into much more detail about it in this chapter, because understanding your thoughts and what they do will go a long way toward helping you figure out and conquer your fear. The Stoic philosopher Epictetus (CE 55–135) is quoted as saying, "Man is disturbed not by things, but rather by the view he takes of them." Think about the implications of that statement for a moment. When it comes to fear, Epictetus was saying that you don't feel afraid because of flying, snakes, public speaking, contamination, or whatever. Rather, you feel afraid because of your *perspective* on these things. If you're a fearful flyer, it's not the flight that's causing your fear reaction; it's your *thoughts and ideas* about the flight.

Let's look at how this principle plays out. In the illustration that follows, you'll see some familiar scenarios in which people feel fearful. In the first column is the situation—flying in an airplane, having a worried thought (such as worrying that a loved one will arrive at his or her destination safely), or giving a speech. Imagine your own feared situations; these are the things you listed in your exposure hierarchy in chapter 5. On the right is our old friend fear. In the middle is something new: your thoughts, ideas, and beliefs about the situation; the words you say to yourself in your head. This part is crucial. What you make of the situation—the meaning you attach to it—is what determines, in large part, how you feel about it.

Like everything else about fear, the cognitive system usually does a good job of keeping us safe from harm. The ability to size up a situation quickly and decide whether it's dangerous is important, healthy, and key for our survival, but what happens when this system

Familiar scenarios in which people feel fearful.

makes errors? Psychiatrist Aaron Beck refers to these thinking errors as *cognitive distortions.* Everyone has them from time to time; it's a natural part of being human. Yet when people are struggling with fears, their cognitive distortions usually lead them to conclude that their feared situations are more dangerous, more threatening than they actually are. To complicate matters further, we have the tendency to make the same kind of cognitive distortions again and again, so that our fears become more firmly entrenched over time.

The solution to these cognitive distortions is to examine the evidence. If a distorted perception of reality leads to feelings of fear, then a realistic view of the evidence can result in reduced fear. When you see things as they really are, they tend to get much less scary. Examining the evidence means detaching, at least for a moment, from how you *feel*, and focusing on what you *know*. As Detective Joe Friday said on the old TV show *Dragnet*, "Just the facts." There are several ways to do this. Try them and see which ones are most helpful for you. In this chapter I'll give you some examples, but you'll need to fine-tune them through trial and error to make them work for you.

Tackling your scary thoughts by examining evidence is a powerful strategy when used in addition to exposure. It's not a substitute for exposure exercises, though—you still have to face the fear. But if you feel stuck, try adding these strategies before, during, or after exposure.

Following are some of the most common cognitive distortions and how you can examine the evidence in order to defeat them.

Probability Overestimation

The basic idea behind probability overestimation is that you believe a bad outcome or event to be more likely than it actually is. Some examples I've heard include

- "The plane is going to crash!"
- "I'm going to throw up!"

- "That dog's going to bite me!"
- "Someone's going to break into my house!"
- "I'm going to catch a disease!"

Do these things happen in real life? Of course, they do. My aim here is not to suggest that they don't happen or even that there can't be a kernel of truth to these thoughts. Rather, my point is that these bad events are often much rarer than we make them out to be.

You might ask, "Who cares? Even if the chance is one in a million, that's still unacceptable!" But think about that for a moment. There are risks all around us, some of which are much more likely than others. Part of healthy living means adjusting your fear reaction to the actual probability of risk. I was once talking to someone who had a terrible fear of flying. He told me that he was extremely afraid that the plane would crash, and that the only way he could get on a plane was to take high doses of benzodiazepine (tranquilizer) medication before the flight. Statistically speaking, you're far more likely to be harmed by taking high doses of benzodiazepines (especially if you mix them with alcohol, which he did, or drive a car with benzodiazepines in your system, which he did) than by riding in an airplane. His fear reaction was so skewed and distorted that he was terribly afraid of something that was unlikely to harm him but was surprisingly unafraid of things that were much more dangerous!

When people struggle with fear, they often have a hard time recalibrating their fear to the actual risk. I'll show you how to do it by examining the evidence.

An Evidence-Examining Strategy for Beating Probability Overestimation: Do the Math

If probability estimation comes from faulty math, then the solution can be found in applying correct math. Probability is calculated as:

$$\frac{\text{Number of times the bad event occurs}}{\text{Number of times the bad event could have possibly occurred}}$$

Let's take flying as an example. The probability of a fatal plane crash, according to National Transportation Safety Board statistics for 1990–2009, is:

$$\frac{\text{Number of fatal plane crashes}}{\text{Total number of flights}} = \frac{42}{191,355,969} = 0.00002\%$$

In English: There were 42 fatal accidents (including the terrorist attacks of September 11, 2001) on scheduled U.S. air carriers between 1990 and 2009. During that same time period, there were more than 191 million flights. Therefore, the probability of any given flight being involved in a fatal accident is two hundred-thousandths of 1 percent, or about 1 out of every 4.5 million flights.

Even if you don't know the exact numbers, you can do some similar calculations by reviewing the evidence from your own life. Ask yourself two basic questions:

"What evidence do I have that this is going to happen?"
"What evidence do I have that this is *not* going to happen?"

Let's take the example of someone who worries that he or she will be bitten by a dog. The person's responses to the questions might go something like this:

"What evidence do I have that this is going to happen?" I was bitten by a dog once that looked kind of like this one. Other than that, I don't really have any evidence—I just feel scared.

"What evidence do I have that this is not *going to happen?"* The dog isn't actually doing anything menacing. Most of the dogs I've met didn't bite me. I know this dog's owner, and I'm certain he wouldn't own a dangerous dog. Come to think of it, most of the evidence suggests the dog is not going to bite me.

This same logic can be applied to lots of fears. Here are some examples:

If you think	*Ask yourself*
"I'm going to throw up!"	"How many times have I been in similar situations and not thrown up?"
"I'm going to have a heart attack!"	"What evidence do I have for this thought? Do I have a real cardiac illness? Have I had a heart attack before? What would my doctor say about it?"
"Someone's going to break into my house!"	"How long have I been living here? How many break-ins have I had during that time?"
"I'm going to catch a disease!"	"How many people have done what I'm doing? Of those, how many have actually caught a disease from it?"

As you can see, it's the same basic principle each time. Even if you don't know the exact numbers (for example, I didn't know the actual number of plane crashes until I looked it up), you can probably make a rough guess by thinking about the evidence. Often, the things you fear are really unlikely to happen, and it's important to remind yourself of that fact.

For some time after my house was broken into, I overestimated the likelihood of that happening again. I also worried more about getting attacked in other places, such as while walking to my car or to a restaurant at night—even if it was a pretty safe area. I made lists of the evidence for and against some of my beliefs, in an effort to determine which ones were true and which ones were only distortions influenced by my fear. I also remember looking up statistics and calling my friends to see whether they viewed things the same way I did.

—Andrea

When I first went into a room with a caged snake, I was very fearful that it was going to get out of the cage and attack me. But that seemed to dissipate. The more I watched the snake, the more I realized it was a small, harmless creature, and even if it did get out, nothing was going to happen.

—Audrey

Catastrophizing

Catastrophizing (a great word, attributed to psychologist Albert Ellis) refers to making mountains out of molehills. As its name suggests, catastrophizing is a way of making things seem like catastrophes, as if they were the end of the world, even when they aren't. Here are some examples:

- "If I faint or throw up, it will be devastating!"
- "If I start feeling anxious, I'll get more and more scared until I just can't stand it!"
- "If I make a mistake in front of others, I'll die of embarrassment!"
- "If something bad happened to my family, I'd never be able to cope!"

Part of catastrophizing is underestimating your ability to deal with things that are unpleasant or unfortunate. You can see the common themes in these statements—if X (the bad event) were to happen, it would be awful, horrible, and devastating; I would feel terrible forever; it would be the end of life as I know it; I would never be able to cope, heal myself, or go on.

When I was monitoring my body sensations and my thoughts, I often wrote down in big letters I AM CATASTROPHIZING! Then

I jotted down what was really happening to my body and why. For example, I had a headache, and I started to panic. So, I wrote: Headache. What I think: Scared it is a brain aneurysm. I AM CATASTROPHIZING. What's really happening: It is just a headache. I had no sleep last night, I am staring at a computer screen, and I drank too much last night. I am okay.

—*Susan*

This is not to say that these events aren't unpleasant. I know, for example, that I wouldn't like to make a mistake in front of other people nor would I like to faint or throw up. So I'm not trying to convince you that these events are hunky-dory. But I would like to introduce the possibility that perhaps they are not as awful as they might seem at first. If these bad things were to happen to me, I would probably feel very bad, but then something else would happen: resilience would kick in. I would probably pick up the pieces and get on with my life. You probably would, too.

An Evidence-Examining Strategy to Beat Catastrophizing: The Downward Arrow

When you catch yourself catastrophizing, try another evidence-examining strategy that therapists call the "downward arrow." Ask yourself, "What if that actually happened? How would things actually turn out? Would it be the end of the world? Would I really feel awful forever? What would I do to cope? What does the evidence tell me?" The downward arrow is a good way to make those catastrophic predictions more explicit so that you can examine them more critically. It's a series of "if-then" questions: If that happened, how bad would it actually be? And if that happened, what then? And how bad would that be?

There are two ways that the downward arrow tends to turn out, as shown in the illustration on page 140. The first, which we'll call the "Not the End of the World Scenario," is that you start to realize that your feared consequences are not as awful, not as catastrophic, as you had previously thought. This scenario

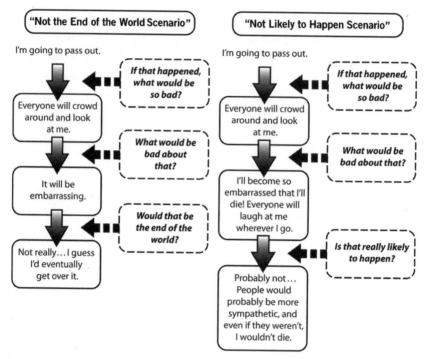

An example of someone catastrophizing an unpleasant situation.

is depicted on the left, in which this person comes to realize that even if he felt embarrassed, it wouldn't be the end of the world and he would eventually move on with his life. The second possibility, as depicted on the right, we'll call the "Not Likely to Happen Scenario." In this example, the person does come up with some truly terrible outcomes—dying, being ridiculed for life—but realizes that these things simply aren't that likely to occur.

A side note: it's important to distinguish between probability overestimation and catastrophizing. Probability overestimation refers to thinking that something is *likely*. Catastrophizing is thinking that something is *awful*. Of course, in many cases people do both at the same time, such as:

"That dog is going to bite me (probability overestimation), and I'll bleed to death (catastrophizing)"
"I'm going to faint (probability overestimation), and it will be the most humiliating thing ever (catastrophizing)"

Here are some more downward arrow examples:

If you think	*Ask yourself*
"If I faint or throw up, it will be devastating!"	"If I fainted or threw up, what would happen to me? Would it be the end of the world, or would it just be unpleasant?"
"If I start feeling anxious, I'll get more and more scared until I just can't stand it!"	"When I've been scared in the past, how long did it actually last? Was I scared forever? Or did my fear eventually subside?"
"If I make a mistake in front of others, I'll die of embarrassment!"	"Have I ever heard of someone dying of embarrassment? Am I exaggerating the severity of being embarrassed?"
"If something bad happened to my family, I'd never be able to cope!"	"If something bad did happen to my family, what would I do to cope? What would my plan be? Do I have the ability to heal from bad experiences and move on with life?"

You can see the central themes of "de-catastrophizing" here. Actually think through what would happen. Ask yourself whether it would really be the end of the world. Remind yourself that you can cope with a lot of bad events. Ask yourself whether these terrible, imagined outcomes are really going to happen. Again, we're not wishing for these bad things to happen; we're simply thinking about them more realistically, without exaggerating their awfulness.

Black-or-White Thinking

When we engage in black-or-white thinking, we're thinking only about the extremes, without considering the middle ground. Things are either perfect or they're terrible. People are either wonderful or evil. With the black-or-white thinker, it's all or nothing. Of course, this thinking style ends up being so rigid that everything ends up being in the "bad" category. I've heard people say things like this:

- "If the situation isn't 100 percent safe, it's dangerous!"
- "If I don't do a perfect job, I'll be a failure!"
- "If things aren't 'just right,' they're all wrong!"
- "If I feel anxious, I must be weak!"

People who think this way tend to filter a lot of things out. They focus only on opposite ends of a spectrum—"If it's not A, it must be Z"—and fail to recognize that there are usually many more possibilities than that. They don't grasp the fact that there is such a thing as partway (and that *partway*—such as partway safe, partway successful, partway correct, and so on) can be perfectly acceptable.

> I realized that I was being a perfectionist, thinking in black or white. I felt as if every word that came out of my mouth had to be just right, and if it wasn't, I felt as if I had completely messed up and embarrassed myself. I started to be able to put things into perspective and realized that I could be myself and joke around, and that I didn't have to measure my words so carefully. And if what I said wasn't perfect, it wasn't the end of the world.
>
> —*Steven*

An Evidence-Examining Strategy for Beating Black-or-White Thinking: Scaling

The solution to black-or-white thinking is to remind yourself of all of the shades of gray. Are there really only two possible answers? Or are these extremes of a spectrum? "Scaling," actually putting a number to your estimates, is a great way to counteract black-or-white thinking. For example, instead of calling something "bad," try putting a percentage on how "bad" it is. Is it 50 percent bad? 60 percent bad? 80 percent bad? If you find yourself going to the extreme—telling yourself that it's 100 percent bad—ask yourself whether that's really accurate. Not many things in this world are 100 percent bad. The flip side of scaling is to ask yourself what number would be acceptable to you. If you've determined that a situation is X percent "bad," how low does that number need to be in order to be okay? Do you need it to be no more than 40 percent bad? No more than 30 percent bad? No more than 20 percent bad? Again, if you find yourself insisting on 0 percent badness, remind yourself that very few things in this world are 0 percent bad (or 100 percent good).

Here are some examples:

If you think	*Ask yourself*
"If the situation isn't 100 percent safe, it's dangerous!"	"Is anything in this world 100 percent safe? Does being happy mean accepting a certain degree of risk?"
"If I don't do a perfect job, I'll be a failure!"	"Is it possible to do a 'good enough' job? Would I think that someone else was a total failure if he or she made a mistake?"
"If things aren't 'just right,' they're all wrong!"	"Am I exaggerating how perfect things need to be? If something wasn't just right, would that really mean that everything was completely wrong? Could I get by if things were just mostly right?"
"If I feel anxious, I must be weak!"	"Is anxiety really a sign of weakness? Or is it a normal human emotion? Do other people feel anxious? Are they weak because of it?"

The general idea here is that we try to tone down the language of our thoughts, so that we're not always pitting two extremes against each other. If it's not A, it might be Z—but it might also be B, C, D, E, F, and so on. There are lots of possibilities, not only two. We run into trouble when we start to believe that there is one and only one acceptable set of circumstances.

> I realized that even though my environment is not 100 percent safe, it is usually "safe enough," and I don't have to be on my guard all the time.
>
> *—Andrea*

Intolerance of Uncertainty

Life is full of uncertainty. Bizarre, random events happen. Bad things happen to good people. The world is full of all kinds of bad things that could happen—to you, to me, to anyone. Most of us take this fact for granted every day, but some people struggle against it. They feel as if they need things to be known, clear, and predictable at all times. For them, it's terrible if they don't know what's going to happen next. Here are some examples:

- "I have to be certain of my decisions!"
- "I need to be prepared for everything that could possibly go wrong!"
- "It would be terrible if something unexpected happened!"
- "I need to know exactly what's going to happen in order to feel okay!"

Two common themes run through these examples. The first is that "I can and should be certain of things at all times." This, of course, is not possible. No one is 100 percent certain all of the time—which leads to the second theme: "If I can't be 100 percent certain, it's terrible, awful, and intolerable." This, too, is likely unrealistic. Think about the people you know who are happiest.

How do they respond to uncertainty? Do they run from it? Do they try to be 100 percent certain all of the time? Probably not. In most cases, people who are happiest tend to be the ones who can tolerate uncertainty, who can get on with the business of life even when they don't have all of the answers.

> Battling and overcoming OCD, for me, was learning to live with uncertainty. I began to overcome this first by simply allowing my brain to entertain an awful outcome. Before, I would shut terrible outcomes out of my mind by doing a compulsive act. Now I allowed a picture of an awful outcome to be there. At first, my mind would react with a "no no no no"; then that turned into, "Well, maybe not"; then, "Well, hopefully not," and through repeating the thought over and over and over (versus avoiding it), I finally got to, "Oh, who cares? . . . This thought is so boring, I'm having trouble even remembering it." So, it wasn't that I'd gotten to "certainty"; rather, I'd gotten to be comfortable with uncertainty.
>
> —*Rachel*

An Evidence-Examining Strategy for Beating Intolerance of Uncertainty: Embracing the Unknown

Part of overcoming fear and worry is learning to tolerate uncertainty, even to embrace it. Often, when we try something new or go into a situation without having all of the answers, we feel uncomfortable. That's perfectly normal. The trick here is not to run away from that discomfort but rather to prove to yourself that it's okay. Here are some examples:

If you think	*Remind yourself*
"I have to be certain of my decisions!"	"I don't need to be certain; I just need to take my best guess and move forward."

(Continued)

"I need to be prepared for everything that could possibly go wrong!"	"No one can prepare for everything. I need to be reasonably prepared for the most likely things."
"It would be terrible if something unexpected happened!"	"Surprises are part of life. No one has a crystal ball. I know from experience that if something unexpected happens, I can deal with it."
"I need to know exactly what's going to happen in order to feel okay!"	"I can feel okay even if I can't predict the future. Time will tell how things turn out."

The trick, then, is learning not to minimize uncertainty but to *tolerate* it—to remind yourself that it's not possible to predict everything that's going to happen, and that you can cope with not having all the answers.

The Need for Control

Just as life is not 100 percent predictable, it's also not 100 percent controllable. We run into trouble when we lose sight of this fact. Some people seem to operate under the belief that in order to be okay, they must be able to control external events such as the behavior of other people. Others hold the belief that the secret to happiness is to gain absolute control over their thoughts, mental images, or feelings. Yet believing that absolute control is possible, desirable, or even necessary is a great way to sign up for a lifetime of fear and worry. Here are some examples I've heard:

- "I have to make sure the situation is safe!"
- "If I think bad thoughts, it makes me a bad person!"
- "I'd better relax . . . or else!"
- "I can't face my fears until I get these thoughts under control!"

In my mind, every place a child played could be infested with the stomach bug. In turn, I would try to control that. I would let my kids play in those places, but I would watch them like a hawk and squirt Purell in their hands every chance I was able to.

—Michelle

People who think this way are setting themselves up for failure. None of us has that degree of control, so when we insist on a level of control that is simply not possible, life starts to feel that much more out of control. Again, think about people you know who are happy. Do they need to control things all of the time? Probably not. Similarly, none of our minds—and I include myself here—are spotless. The human mind thinks up all kinds of strange things—scary things, disgusting things, violent things—that are perfectly normal and nothing to worry about. People who are happiest are the ones who can tolerate unpleasant thoughts and images, rather than trying to control them or make them go away. Remember the discussion about thought suppression in the last chapter? The more we try *not* to think of something, the more we usually think of it.

An Evidence-Examining Strategy for Beating the Need for Control: Surrendering

We're trained to think of surrendering as a bad thing. In our language, it usually means admitting defeat and letting someone else claim victory. There is another way to look at it, however. If attempting to control the inherently uncontrollable simply leads to increasing misery, then the solution is to lessen your perceived need for control and to stop trying so hard. Here are some examples:

If you think	*Remind yourself*
"I have to make sure the situation is safe!"	"I'm not the world's lifeguard. It's not all my responsibility to make sure things are safe, and besides, I can never guarantee safety."

(Continued)

"I have to make sure nothing happens to my loved ones!"	"There's no way I can prevent every bad thing from happening. Part of caring for my loved ones involves letting them live their lives, not over-preparing for every possible threat."
"If I think bad thoughts, it makes me a bad person!"	"Everyone thinks weird thoughts from time to time. What I do, not what I think, defines what kind of person I am."
"I'd better relax . . . or else!"	"Or else what? My experience tells me that I can be just fine whether or not I feel comfortable."
"I can't face my fears until I get these thoughts under control!"	"No one has perfect control over his or her thoughts. Regardless of whether I feel as if I'm in control of my thoughts, I can still face my fears—and that might help me feel a bit better about the thoughts."

I had the automatic thoughts "I should be able to protect my son all the time. If something bad happens to him, I'm a bad mother, and my life will be over." I asked myself, What's the evidence for and against this thought? Is this a thinking error? And I realized several things: All parents make mistakes. I can only do so much to prevent catastrophe. And if something bad happened to my son, my life would not be over. Just real-izing these facts allowed a large weight to lift from my soul.

—*Samantha*

I put that last example in there on purpose. It's awfully easy to get hung up on this stage of the process and to believe that you *must* get your thoughts under control before you can start facing your fears. It's true that thinking more rationally can help you feel better, which in turn can make you feel more able to face your fears. But remember our discussion in chapter 2 about the interaction of thoughts, physiology, and behavior. They all influence one another. Therefore, just as changing your thoughts can help change your behavior, so, too, can changing your behavior help change your thoughts. Facing your fears behaviorally serves as a kind of experiment that helps you test whether your thoughts are accurate. When you face a fear, you're checking out whether your assumptions are true, testing whether things really turn out the way you had feared. Therefore, if you feel as if you're having trouble getting your thoughts under control, step back, remind yourself that controlling thoughts is very difficult, and try doing something instead.

The Myth of Positive Thinking

Some people miss the point of challenging these negative, automatic ways of thinking. I've heard people say things like, "Look on the bright side!" or "Just think positively!" Even singer-songwriter Bobby McFerrin had a hit in the 1980s with a song called "Don't Worry, Be Happy."

Call me a humbug if you want, but I don't believe in positive thinking. The aim of the exercises in this book is not to replace unrealistically negative thoughts with unrealistically positive thoughts. Trying to convince yourself that everything is fine and that nothing bad can happen is likely to be an exercise in futility. So just as I don't want you to lie to yourself in a negative way (cognitive distortions), I also don't want you to lie to yourself in a positive way (Don't worry, be happy). As I mentioned earlier, bad things do happen, and there's no escaping this fact. The trick is to think about them realistically, rather than positively. The truth is usually not nearly as scary as your imagination. The common theme throughout this entire exercise is to ask yourself: *What's the truth here? What's the evidence?* You're aiming for realistic thinking, not positive thinking.

Thought-Tracking Form

Date/Time	Triggering Event	Thought	Fear Level (0–100)	Cognitive Distortions (check all that apply)	Evidence Examination	Fear Level (0–100)
9/14, 2 p.m.	Son's football game	He'll get hurt or paralyzed. It's my responsibility to make sure nothing happens to him.	60	☒ Probability Overestimation ☐ Catastrophizing ☐ Black-or-White Thinking ☐ Intolerance of Uncertainty ☒ Need for Control	He hasn't been seriously injured before, and he knows what he's doing. I don't have to try to control what happens.	30
9/16, 4 p.m.	Felt a flutter in my chest	I'm having a heart attack!	70	☒ Probability Overestimation ☐ Catastrophizing ☐ Black-or-White Thinking ☐ Intolerance of Uncertainty ☐ Need for Control	I don't have a heart condition. I've felt this way many times, and it's never been a heart attack. It's probably just anxiety.	40
9/18, 12 p.m.	Lunch with coworkers	I'm just going to embarrass myself if I speak up, and then everyone will laugh at me.	50	☒ Probability Overestimation ☒ Catastrophizing ☐ Black-or-White Thinking ☐ Intolerance of Uncertainty ☐ Need for Control	I have no reason to believe that I'm going to embarrass myself. And even if I did, so what? It wouldn't be the end of the world.	20
9/19, 9 a.m.	Going to the mall	How will I guarantee my safety? It's terrible not to know what's going to happen!	65	☐ Probability Overestimation ☐ Catastrophizing ☒ Black-or-White Thinking ☒ Intolerance of Uncertainty ☐ Need for Control	No situation is 100 percent safe or 100 percent dangerous. There's no way I can completely know the future, and I don't need to.	40

Date/Time	Triggering Event	Thought	Fear Level (0–100)	Cognitive Distortions (check all that apply)	Evidence Examination	Fear Level (0–100)
9/21 3 p.m.	Flying in an airplane	The plane's going to crash! I need to know what every noise means so I can be vigilant for signs of trouble!	60	☒ Probability Overestimation ☒ Catastrophizing ☐ Black-or-White Thinking ☐ Intolerance of Uncertainty ☒ Need for Control	The odds of being in a plane crash are very low. I don't need to know what every sound means, and I'm certainly not going to stop a plane crash.	35
9/25 5 p.m.	Planning an exposure exercise	If I allow myself to get anxious, I'll just get more and more anxious forever! I have to achieve a state of relaxation!	40	☐ Probability Overestimation ☒ Catastrophizing ☐ Black-or-White Thinking ☐ Intolerance of Uncertainty ☒ Need for Control	No one is anxious forever. I'll probably feel anxious for a while, and then I'll feel better. I would prefer to be relaxed, but I don't require it.	20
				☐ Probability Overestimation ☐ Catastrophizing ☐ Black-or-White Thinking ☐ Intolerance of Uncertainty ☐ Need for Control		
				☐ Probability Overestimation ☐ Catastrophizing ☐ Black-or-White Thinking ☐ Intolerance of Uncertainty ☐ Need for Control		

A sample thought-tracking form.

Quick Guidelines for Addressing Scary Thoughts

- *Thoughts are what scare you.* We get scared of things because of how we think about them, the things we say to ourselves about them, and the meanings we give them in our minds.
- *Not all thoughts are accurate.* Some ways of thinking are irrational, distorted, or just plain wrong. Don't believe everything you think.
- *Examine the evidence.* Ask yourself: What evidence do I have to support this thought or belief? What evidence do I have that *doesn't* support it?
- *Do the math.* If you're thinking that a bad outcome is really likely, take the time to figure out just how likely that outcome is.
- *Turn mountains back into molehills.* If you're telling yourself something is going to be the end of the world, ask yourself honestly what would really happen, and remind yourself that you could probably cope with it.
- *See shades of gray.* Recognize that very few things in this world are black or white, all or nothing.
- *Tolerate uncertainty.* Accept that you can't predict the future and you don't need all of the answers in order to be okay.
- *Give up the need for control.* Remind yourself that you can't control the world. Sometimes, you can't even control your own thoughts and feelings. And that's fine.
- *Don't think positive.* Think realistic. See the whole picture for what it is.

Challenging Your Thoughts

In this section, you'll find two sample worksheets to help you monitor and challenge your fearful thought patterns. The first one is completed and shows how someone might deal with a variety of fears. After you've reviewed the example, you can create a blank one in your notebook following the sample illustration. Your job is to complete it the next time you feel fearful. As you go through the worksheet, ask yourself the following questions:

- What is the *triggering event?* That is, what is the situation, the activity, or the experience that is leading me to feel fearful?
- What are my *thoughts?* What am I saying to myself about the triggering event? What do I think is going to happen?
- What is my *fear level?* Thinking this way, how anxious do I feel right now, from 0 to 100?
- What kind of *cognitive distortions* are present in my thinking? Am I overestimating the probability of an unlikely outcome? Am I catastrophizing? Am I thinking in black or white? Am I intolerant of uncertainty? Am I putting a premium on control?
- What does the *evidence* tell me? The aim here is to engage in realistic, rather than simply "positive," thinking. What's the most realistic, rational way to think about this? How can I look at the whole situation, not only at a selected, scary part of the situation?
- What is my *fear level* now? Did thinking rationally help me feel a bit better?

PART II

Facing the Different Kinds of Fear

9

Beating Fears of Specific Situations or Objects

There is no terror in the bang, only in the anticipation of it.

—*Alfred Hitchcock*

I n this and the upcoming five chapters, I will explain in more detail how to tailor exposure for different kinds of fear. I don't want to get too hung up on diagnoses—after all, what's most important is not what label you assign to your fear, but rather how well you understand what you're afraid of and why (from an emotional, cognitive, and behavioral perspective) that fear persists. The types of fears I discuss in this book are only loosely related to the *DSM-IV-TR* diagnoses, and there's lots of overlap. For example, fear of body sensations occurs frequently in people with panic disorder; however, it can also show up in people with hypochondriasis, social phobia, and generalized anxiety disorder.

Even if you have not been given a particular diagnosis, if you're experiencing a specific kind of fear that is common with that diagnosis, then you're likely to find the chapter on that kind of fear helpful. If you have a fear of panic-like body sensations, you may or may not have panic disorder, but the chapter on fear of panic-like body sensations will probably apply to you anyway. The chapter will provide you with the exposure tips you need to beat that fear, regardless of what *DSM-IV-TR* diagnosis might be assigned to you.

"Self-diagnosing" can be a tricky business, and it's often easy to mistakenly believe you have a disorder that you really don't or to fail to recognize a disorder that you actually do have. So please bear in mind that if you want a truly accurate diagnosis, you need to talk to a trained mental health professional who knows about these conditions.

You've already met Audrey, who was paralyzed by her fear of snakes, and Michelle, who was terribly afraid that she might vomit. Although these fears might seem quite different, they can both be classified as a fear of specific situations or objects. There are countless variations of this kind of fear. Here are just a few:

- A seven-year-old boy is terrified of thunderstorms, cries uncontrollably when there is a storm, and is afraid to go outside whenever the weather is cloudy or rainy. He's started to have temper tantrums in the mornings before school when the weather is bad because of his reluctance to leave the house.
- A forty-two-year-old businessman is afraid to fly in an airplane. Previously, he had managed to make it through flights by drinking alcohol or taking tranquilizing medications; however, his fear is getting worse, and he has started to make excuses for missing important business trips, which is causing problems in his job performance.
- A twenty-eight-year-old woman can't stand the sight of blood or needles. Whenever she sees blood, she feels dizzy

and lightheaded. At times, she has even fainted at th
of blood. She hasn't been to the doctor in years and ha.
even put off getting pregnant because of her fear of medical
procedures.

- A seventeen-year-old girl has become so afraid of spiders
that she's reluctant to even walk across her own lawn. She
won't enter the basement of her home and always feels as
if she has to scan the room for spiders or their webs. She
fears that if she came across a spider accidentally, she would
become so panicked that she would lose control of herself.
Even the sight of her younger brother's toy spider is enough
to send her running from the room.

- A sixty-three-year-old man is deathly afraid of enclosed
spaces. Whenever he finds himself in a small space without
an easy exit, he feels as if he's trapped. He worries that he
might suffocate. All he can think of is that he must get out
right now. He hasn't visited his son and grandchildren in
their apartment, which is on the twentieth floor of a high-
rise building, because he can't stand the idea of being
trapped in the elevator. Sometimes even being in a small
room bothers him, and he has to keep a door or a window
open in order to tolerate it.

The name for these types of fear, according to the *DSM-IV-
TR*, is *specific phobia*. The criteria for specific phobias in the *DSM-
IV-TR* are:

1. Severe, persistent, and excessive fear of a specific object or
   situation (such as flying, heights, animals, receiving an
   injection, seeing blood). We're not talking about mild fears
   or fears that come and go. Rather, people with specific
   phobias feel a strong sense of fear that stays with them for
   a long time. The fear can be triggered not only by the situation or the object but also by the anticipation of encountering these things. Someone with a fear of flying doesn't
   have to be on a plane to feel afraid—simply knowing that

a flight is coming up, simply imagining being on the plane, can be just as scary.

2. Exposure to the feared object or situation almost always triggers an immediate anxiety response, which may take the form of a panic attack. Panic attacks are the bursts of fear that characterize the fight-flight-freeze response, in which the amygdala sounds the alarm and leads to the release of adrenaline into the bloodstream. The adrenaline, in turn, produces a host of physical reactions, including an increased heart rate, sweating, muscle tension, an upset stomach, and so on. Of course, not everyone with a specific phobia experiences panic attacks, and the fear reaction can be milder. Fear reactions can look somewhat different in children than in adults and might include behaviors such as tantrums or crying.

3. For the most part, people with specific phobias know that their fears are overblown or exaggerated, at least on some level. Of course, as I discussed in chapter 8, when they are confronted with the feared situation or object or anticipate being confronted with the feared situation or object, they can still have cognitive distortions, such as probability overestimation and catastrophizing. Children might not have as much insight as adults do and might truly believe that the fear is justified.

4. The feared object or situation is avoided or else is endured with intense anxiety or distress. Avoidance is a major reason that these fears persist. Avoidance can be blatant (for example, not traveling on airplanes) or more subtle, in the form of safety behaviors (such as flying only after having an alcoholic drink or two).

5. The fear or avoidance interferes significantly with the person's functioning or causes severe distress. This item comes up frequently in the *DSM-IV-TR*. In order for a fear to be considered a phobia, it has to be more than simply unpleasant. As you saw in each of the previous examples, people

with specific phobias have inadvertently allowed their fears to hijack aspects of their lives. These fears and the avoidance that goes with them have started to affect the sufferers' social lives, work and school performance, family life, or leisure activities.

6. In children, the fear has lasted for at least six months. This criterion was added because in children, many fears can come and go. Often, fears go away on their own without any intervention. It's only when these fears persist that there may be a need to address them directly.

Variations of Fears of Specific Situations or Objects

Virtually any object or situation can, in theory, be feared and avoided and therefore can be the target of a specific phobia. Yet surveys of people with severe phobias suggest that most of them fall into one of these categories:

- *Animal Type*: Snakes and spiders top the list here; however, phobias of dogs, cats, insects, and birds are not uncommon.
- *Natural Environment Type*: This category refers to phobias of heights, storms, water, and other aspects of the natural environment.
- *Blood-Injection-Injury Type*: These fears include the sight of blood and injuries, as well as medical procedures such as injections, blood draws, or dental visits. One distinctive characteristic of this type of fear is that many sufferers faint in the presence of the feared situation or object.
- *Situational Type*: Situational phobias include fears of flying in airplanes, riding in elevators, or being in enclosed spaces or in other situations that are not part of the natural environment.

- *Other Type*: Other fears, such as of situations that might lead to choking or vomiting, fears of loud sounds, and fears of costumed characters such as clowns can also be specific phobias.

Common Cognitive Distortions in Fears of Specific Situations or Objects

Probability overestimation is common among people with fears of specific situations or objects. Probability overestimation refers to the tendency to believe that a feared outcome is more likely than it actually is. Therefore, many (though not all) people who are afraid of flying think, at least when anxious, that a plane crash is highly likely. Many people who are afraid of snakes or spiders believe that they are about to be bitten. When these feared outcomes don't happen, they tend to discount this evidence, often attributing their survival to safety behaviors or thinking that they "got lucky this time." If you're working on this kind of fear, it's important to do the math and examine the evidence. How many times has the bad outcome occurred? How many times has it *not* occurred?

People with fears of specific situations or objects also tend to catastrophize. That is, they tend to think that if they come into contact with the feared situation or object, the results will be terrible, awful, or intolerable. So, for example, someone with a fear of dogs might not only fear being bitten but may also tell himself that the bite would be especially vicious and nasty and might possibly kill him. Someone with a fear of vomiting not only worries that she will throw up but also believes that throwing up would be an excruciating experience from which she would never recover. The downward arrow can be helpful here. Think through the worst-case scenario. Is that really how things are likely to turn out? If the worst-case scenario came true, would it be the end of the world?

Avoidance and Safety Behaviors in Fears of Specific Situations or Objects

As the *DSM-IV-TR* criteria for specific phobias indicate, sufferers tend to stay away from the things they fear—a tendency that can be counteracted with exposure. The tricky part is identifying the more subtle safety behaviors that are easy to miss. Because it's not always possible to completely avoid feared situations or objects, people with phobias often have to come up with all kinds of tricks to help them feel safer or more comfortable when they can't avoid things. We reviewed some of these behaviors in chapter 7, but it's worth going into more detail here.

It would be impossible to list every possible safety behavior for this category of fear; however, two common themes tend to be present: first, these safety behaviors often give the person the illusion of making feared outcomes less likely (therefore, we can think of these behaviors as a reaction to probability overestimation). So, someone with a fear of flying might grip the armrests to reduce the (already low) likelihood of a plane crash, as if doing so could keep the plane up in the air. Someone with a fear of heights might stay far away from balconies to reduce the (already low) likelihood of falling. Someone with a fear of dogs might only go near dogs that are on a leash, to reduce the (already low) likelihood of being bitten.

The other common theme of these safety behaviors is that they often serve to minimize the impact or severity of the feared outcomes (therefore, we can think of these behaviors as a reaction to catastrophizing). Someone with a fear of vomiting, for example, might avoid eating in public places—not to minimize the likelihood of vomiting, but rather to reduce the perceived risk of humiliation in the event of vomiting. Someone with a fear of receiving an injection might avoid looking at the needle to minimize his or her fear reaction and likelihood of fainting.

Overcoming a Fear

Psychologist Ronald Kleinknecht surveyed members of the American Tarantula Society, a group of spider enthusiasts. Approximately half of the members surveyed reported that they had once been fearful of tarantulas but had overcome their fears. How did they do it? The most frequently reported way of overcoming fear was by learning more about tarantulas—reading articles and books or taking classes that taught them that tarantulas were not as dangerous as they had thought. The next most common ways they overcame fear were by observing tarantulas and actually handling them.

Exposure Tips for Fears of Specific Situations or Objects

As with any fear, fears of specific situations or objects should be confronted using gradual and systematic exposure, as described in chapters 5 and 6. Because fears of specific situations or objects are often less complex than are the other fears described in this book, some people mistakenly think that their exposure program can be "easy" and make the error of conducting exposures that are too brief, too mild, or too infrequent. Don't be fooled, though—even these relatively straightforward fears usually still require intense work in order to beat them. Make sure that you set up your program so that you can do exposure exercises often and for a prolonged period of time, and that your exposures will be in the "target zone" of moderate-to-high fear levels.

Exposure programs for fears of specific situations or objects often require that you do a good deal of planning to gain access to the necessary triggers. If you have a fear of flying, for example, you'll probably need to plan several trips to the airport (if that's part of your exposure hierarchy) and more than one flight, if possible. People with a fear of spiders or snakes might need to make some calls to their local zoo or science museum (I've often found staff members of these institutions to be quite understanding of phobias and very willing to help). People with a fear of heights need to do some reconnaissance to find high buildings, balconies, and so on, to visit.

Be sure to eliminate safety behaviors from your exposure program. Remember, the aim here is to allow yourself to feel anxious, not to try to make yourself feel better. Seek out things that are scary, and notice how your anxiety subsides with time.

Many people with a fear of blood, injections, or injuries tend to faint when exposed to their feared situations. Usually, this is not dangerous (as long as you don't fall and hit your head); however, fainting poses a unique challenge for exposure. After all, you can't benefit from the exposure if you're unconscious! In chapter 17, I'll introduce you to a supplementary strategy called *applied tension* that is designed to help keep people with blood-injection–injury fears from fainting.

You've already seen Audrey's and Michelle's exposure hierarchies in chapter 5. Here are some more examples to stimulate your thinking. You can borrow these items as you see fit; however, most people will need to get creative and come up with items that are specific to their concerns.

Notice that these hierarchies tend to start at the low-to-moderate fear level. That's just about right. Most people won't benefit much from starting with very-low-level exposures (but again, you'll need to try it out and see what works for you).

Exposure Hierarchy: Fear of Blood, Injections, and Injuries

Activity	Fear Level (0–100)
Getting an injection	95
Letting a nurse hold an uncapped hypodermic needle against my arm	80
Letting a nurse swab my arm with alcohol	75
Sitting next to someone getting an injection	70
Smelling rubbing alcohol	65

Watching a video of someone getting an injection	60
Holding an uncapped hypodermic needle against my arm	55
Holding a capped hypodermic needle against my arm	40
Holding a hypodermic needle with the cap off	35
Holding a hypodermic needle with the cap on	30

Exposure Hierarchy: Fear of Spiders

Activity	*Fear Level (0–100)*
Holding a spider	100
Touching a spider being held by someone else	90
Standing next to someone holding a spider	80
Putting my hand inside the spider tank	70
Watching videos of spiders moving	65
Being near a caged spider	65
Looking at close-up pictures of spiders' faces	55
Looking at photographs of spiders	50
Looking at drawings of spiders	40
Reading about spiders	35

Exposure Hierarchy: Fear of Flying

Activity	*Fear Level (0–100)*
Flying in bad weather	85
Flying in calm weather	75
Sitting in a plane on the ground	65
Waiting for a flight in the airport	60
Buying a plane ticket	55
Visiting an airport	55
Watching videos of airplanes	40
Playing computer flight-simulation games	40
Vividly imagining a turbulent flight	30
Vividly imagining a calm flight	25

Exposure Hierarchy: Fear of Enclosed Spaces

Activity	Fear Level (0–100)
Stopping an elevator between floors	95
Getting into the trunk of a car (with a helper outside to let me out)	95
Getting in a small closet	85
Riding in a crowded elevator	80
Riding in an empty elevator	75
Wrapping myself tightly in blankets	70
Wearing tight-fitting clothing	60
Sitting in a small office with the door locked (with a helper outside to let me out)	55
Sitting in a small office with the door closed	45
Sitting in a small office with the door ajar	35

Exposure Hierarchy: Fear of Heights

Activity	Fear Level (0–100)
Riding a roller coaster	95
Riding a Ferris wheel	90
Looking over a tall cliff	90
Looking over the open observation deck of a tall building	85
Looking out the window of a tall building	75
Looking over the edge of a second-story balcony	65
Driving on a high bridge	60
Climbing a tall ladder	55
Looking out of a second-story window	50
Climbing a stepladder	30

10

Beating Fears of Body Sensations

Never worry about your heart till it stops beating.
—*E. B. White*

Unlike fears of specific situations or objects, fears of body sensations are directed inward. The person's fear is triggered by physical sensations inside his or her own body. Susan, who developed debilitating panic attacks, had this kind of fear, and there are many other variations. Here are a few more:

- A twenty-four-year-old woman began to experience panic attacks after her college graduation. Whenever she felt her heart racing or noticed a palpitation, she jumped to the conclusion that she was having a heart attack. This thought, in turn, made her even more anxious. She couldn't predict when the next panic attack was going to come and always felt nervous and preoccupied, as if she had to keep monitoring her body for signs of an impending panic attack.

- A fifty-five-year-old woman has become increasingly iso-
lated due to her fear that she will faint. She doesn't experience outright panic attacks; however, she does often feel
dizzy or lightheaded and worries that she is about to faint.
She avoids going to crowded places such as the mall, where
fainting would be embarrassing. She also avoids driving on
the highway or over long distances, because she is afraid of
fainting behind the wheel and causing an accident.

- A forty-year-old man can't get past the worry that he might
have cancer. Whenever he has a headache, an upset stomach, or any other unusual bodily sensation, he assumes it's
a tumor. He has gone to his doctor repeatedly and has had
every test in the book, but his doctor has been unable to
reassure him. He has begun to seek second, third, and
fourth opinions from other doctors. He's also been checking
his body for lumps, irregular moles, or other possible signs
of cancer several times per day.

Some (but not all) people with this kind of fear are diagnosed
with *panic disorder*. The criteria for panic disorder in *DSM-IV-TR*
are:

1. Recurrent, unexpected panic attacks. You can see a definition of panic attacks (which can be an aspect of virtually any fear-based problem) in chapter 2. The words
   recurrent and unexpected are worth noting here. First,
   panic disorder can be diagnosed only when the attacks
   happen repeatedly, not just once. Second, the word
   unexpected is potentially misleading. Sometimes panic
   attacks can appear to be completely spontaneous, taking
   the person by surprise. At other times, however, they
   are predictable—such as when entering a crowded
   place. A more accurate way to think about panic disorder is that the panic attacks are not caused by a specific
   phobia or by something that most people would find
   frightening.

2. The attacks are followed by an ongoing concern about having additional attacks and worries that one will lose control, have a medical disaster, "go crazy," or experience a significant change in behavior due to fear. This part is really key to the diagnosis of panic disorder, and it's what most clearly distinguishes panic disorder from other anxiety disorders. People who suffer from panic disorder are afraid of their panic attacks. They are often preoccupied with worry about when the next attack will occur and always feel as if they have to pay close attention to their bodies so that they can detect an oncoming attack.

3. The panic attacks are not due to drugs, medications, or a physical illness. Several drugs can cause panic attacks, as can some medical conditions. In people with panic disorder, it's not uncommon to find that the first panic attack had a physical cause—for example, many people have told me that they experienced their first panic attack when they had the flu, or when they first tried drugs such as marijuana—however, subsequent panic attacks were psychologically driven. Excessive use of caffeine or other stimulating drugs can also cause body sensations (such as rapid heartbeat, sweating, or feeling jittery) in some people; we want to make sure that this isn't the sole cause of the panic attacks.

The behavioral avoidance associated with a fear of body sensations is called *agoraphobia*. Not everyone with panic disorder has agoraphobia, and not everyone with agoraphobia has panic disorder; however, the two appear to be closely related in most people. The *DSM-IV-TR* criteria for agoraphobia are:

1. Fear of being in places or situations from which escape might be difficult (or embarrassing) or in which help may not be available, in the event of having a panic attack. Agoraphobic fears typically involve characteristic clusters of situations that include being outside the home alone; being

in a crowd or standing in a line; being on a bridge; and traveling in a bus, a train, or an automobile. The crucial part here is that the person with agoraphobia is afraid of situations in which escape might be difficult (as in a long highway tunnel) or embarrassing (for example, having to get up and leave in the middle of worship services), or in which help might be unavailable (such as being far away from home), in the event of body sensations.

2. The person avoids these situations or requires the presence of another person in order to enter the situation. This criterion highlights the behavioral avoidance that is characteristic of agoraphobia. It's noteworthy that a common safety behavior is mentioned here: the need to have someone with you in a frightening situation. Often, people with agoraphobia can enter these situations only when accompanied by a trusted "safe person" who can help them escape, if necessary. Other safety behaviors might include carrying a cell phone, a bottle of pills, or a paper bag to breathe into.

An often-overlooked variation of the fear of body sensations is called *hypochondriasis*. Although *DSM-IV-TR* does not classify hypochondriasis as an anxiety disorder, in my opinion that's where it belongs (and indeed, some of my colleagues have abandoned the name hypochondriasis altogether in favor of the term *health anxiety*, which seems more accurate to me). The *DSM-IV-TR* criteria for hypochondriasis (health anxiety) are:

1. Persistent fears of having, or a belief that one has, a serious disease. This fear is based on misinterpreting physical sensations or symptoms. The concept of "misinterpretation" is key here. Just as we see in people with panic disorder, people with health anxiety tend to misunderstand what is happening in their own bodies and to attribute physical sensations to imaged serious illnesses.

2. Even if the person receives appropriate medical evaluation and reassurance, the fear does not subside. Many people

with health anxiety seek multiple medical opinions and often undergo numerous unnecessary medical tests. Yet hearing doctors tell them they're not sick doesn't seem to make them feel better, at least not for long. The doubts and worries creep back in: "What if the last doctor missed something?" "What if the test was wrong?"

3. These fears and preoccupations impair the person's functioning. As we've seen in other *DSM-IV-TR* diagnoses, hypochondriasis is diagnosed only when the fears and preoccupations, and the behaviors that go along with them, are serious enough to intrude on a person's ability to function. For example, some people with health anxiety miss work to go to unnecessary doctor's appointments or spend too much money on unnecessary medical tests.

4. The duration of the fear or preoccupation is at least six months. It's fairly common for people to have short-term worries about their health. Hypochondriasis is diagnosed only when these worries persist for a long time.

Variations of the Fear of Body Sensations

People can have all kinds of fearful reactions to body sensations. Some of these reactions fit well with the *DSM-IV-TR* criteria for disorders, whereas others don't. Here are some examples:

- *Acute fear of medical catastrophe*: This fear is characterized by a sense of imminent disaster. A heart palpitation is thought to forecast a heart attack. An upset stomach means you are about to vomit. A lightheaded or dizzy feeling means you're going to faint. These catastrophes are all pretty unlikely to occur, but in the person's mind, they can feel as if they're imminent.

- *Chronic preoccupation with illness*: Sometimes, fear of body sensations doesn't take the form of acute attacks. Instead, the person is just chronically worried, nervous, and tense about what he notices in his body and is afraid that these sensations are signs of a serious illness. So, for example, a headache is interpreted as a symptom of meningitis. An upset stomach isn't merely an upset stomach, it's stomach cancer. Again, these illnesses are rather unlikely, but the person tends to overlook more benign explanations and instead to focus on possible worst-case scenarios. People with this kind of fear often do a lot of research in the library or online, looking up diseases. They often seek medical opinion after opinion, a pattern sometimes referred to as "doctor shopping."

- *Fear of choking*: Some people have a very specific fear of choking while eating or drinking. It's not necessarily that they believe they have a serious illness; rather, when eating or drinking, they feel as if something is "wrong" with the sensations in their mouths and throats and worry that this means they are about to choke. When people start to restrict their diet due to choking fears (for example, consuming only liquids or very soft foods), this avoidance can become dangerous.

- *Fear of fear*: As described in the *DSM-IV-TR* criteria for panic disorder, people with this problem worry about having additional attacks or worry that having a panic attack will lead them to lose control, have a heart attack, or go crazy. These people are afraid of fear itself—or, more precisely, they are afraid of what will happen if they experience fear.

Common Cognitive Distortions in Fear of Body Sensations

It's clear that probability overestimation is a big issue in people with a fear of body sensations. For most of us, medical events such as heart attacks, fainting, or vomiting are pretty unlikely. Yet people who have a fear of body sensations frequently fool themselves into believing that these events are not only likely, but also imminent. As with many other kinds of fears, the fact that these events don't happen doesn't have much impact on these people's thinking. This is largely because of the safety behaviors that are so prevalent in these fears, which I'll discuss further on. So when the person doesn't have a heart attack, throw up, or choke, he or she tends to conclude that this is because of the safety behaviors ("I didn't choke because I chewed my food extra thoroughly"), rather than because of the objective safety of the situation ("I didn't choke because choking is a low-probability event"). This is why it's so important to conduct exposures without safety behaviors— so that you can convince your brain of the unconditional safety of the situation.

Catastrophizing also shows up a lot in people who have a fear of nonlethal things such as fainting. They are concerned, in part, with the feared consequences of fainting, which they worry will be horrible and devastating. Many people worry that fainting would not be merely inconvenient and unpleasant; it would be socially humiliating to the extent that they would never be able to show their faces in public again. Catastrophizing is also a factor

---

An Exaggerated Fear of Body Sensations

It's long been known that inhaling small concentrations of carbon dioxide (CO_2) reliably causes a range of body sensations, including a racing heart, dizziness, and lightheadedness. Psychiatrist Kees Verburg and colleagues asked people with panic disorder and people with generalized anxiety disorder to inhale a mixture of 35 percent CO_2 and 65 percent oxygen. People in both groups showed a similar increase in body sensations. The people with panic disorder, however, showed a much higher increase of fear level (a 45-point increase on a 0–100 scale) than did the people with generalized anxiety disorder (only a 15-point increase), demonstrating that people with panic disorder are unique in their excessively fearful reaction to body sensations.

for people who have a preoccupation with chronic illnesses. They rarely worry that they have a mild disease; rather, they tend to jump immediately to the worst possible scenario.

Many people who have a fear of body sensations cannot tolerate uncertainty. It's particularly noticeable among those who are preoccupied with chronic illnesses. I've heard a lot of people say things like, "I'd almost rather get a diagnosis of cancer than have to live with not knowing whether I have cancer." When you step back and think about that statement, it's clear how irrational it is. Cancer is objectively bad. Uncertainty isn't.

I also mentioned in chapter 2 that people with all kinds of anxiety disorders can be characterized by an attentional bias toward threat cues—a tendency to be hypervigilant for signs of danger. In people with a fear of body sensations, that hypervigilance is directed inward, toward the person's own body. These individuals pay close attention to their heart rates, their breathing, the feelings in their stomachs, any physical sensations that might be a sign of an impending panic attack or medical catastrophe. As with all hypervigilance, of course, the problem is that the more you pay attention to something, the more likely you are to notice a bodily sensation that frightens you (even if it's not objectively dangerous). If you pay close enough attention to your heartbeat, for a prolonged period of time, eventually you will notice it speeding up, slowing down, or skipping a beat—giving your fear something to seize on.

Avoidance and Safety Behaviors in Fear of Body Sensations

Agoraphobia, by definition, is a form of avoidant behavior. When people are afraid of their body sensations, they tend to avoid three main categories of situations. First, they tend to stay away from situations in which they believe panic attacks would be potentially harmful. Having a panic attack in one's home is bad enough. Having one in public (and perhaps, as the person fears, throwing up, fainting, losing control of one's bodily functions, and so on) would be significantly worse because of the predicted embarrassment and humiliation. So public places, such as shopping malls, movie theaters, or churches, are often avoided. Similarly, many people worry that panic symptoms will lead them to lose control of their motor functions. It follows, therefore, that having a panic attack while driving would have disastrous consequences (even though in reality people experiencing panic attacks don't lose control of their motor functions). So the person stops driving or at least avoids certain "high-risk" driving situations, such as highways. The second category of avoided situations is those from which escape would be difficult. A crowded rock concert, for example, might be avoided not because of a fear of embarrassment but rather because it's physically difficult to get out in case of a panic attack or a medical emergency. If these people have to go to a crowded place, such as a theater or a place of worship, they may try to sit close to the exit or on the aisle so that they can escape easily. The third category of avoided situations consists of those in which it would be difficult to get help in the event of panic or medical catastrophe. Some people with agoraphobia, for example, avoid going far from home or into places where they could get lost, in case of a medical crisis. I've even known people who, before going somewhere, had to map out every hospital along the route, just in case. All of these are safety behaviors that can undermine the success of exposure and keep you trapped in fear.

People with a fear of body sensations are also masters of subtle safety behaviors. Once, I was leading a therapy group for people with panic disorder. We were all seated around a large table, and I asked the participants to go through their pockets and purses and to take out everything that made them feel safer. I was amazed at the pile of stuff that ended up on the table! There were bottles of pills, cell phones, paper bags, a rosary, a rabbit's foot, an mp3 player cued to relaxing music, a book of self-affirmations, and more. Everyone was carrying at least one object.

A subtle, tricky form of safety behavior in panic disorder is overbreathing. Many people with panic disorder are worried that they will suffocate, and they persistently feel as if they're not getting enough oxygen. So, sometimes without even realizing it, they start breathing a bit more rapidly or more deeply. Sometimes it will sound as if they are sighing or gulping air. The result of this overbreathing is that they are mildly hyperventilating. They might not notice any effects of this at first; however, over time, they might start to feel typical hyperventilation effects such as dizziness, lightheadedness, and nausea. Because the overbreathing is subtle, the people might not even know why they're experiencing these symptoms. So their minds jump to a scary conclusion (such as some medical disaster), which in turn increases their fear sensations, and off they go into a panic cycle.

Exposure Tips for Fear of Body Sensations

The centerpiece of an exposure program for a fear of body sensations is interoceptive exposure. The word *interoceptive* means "coming from inside the body," so interoceptive exposure is a program of exposure to bodily sensations. The idea behind interoceptive exposure is not to try to make yourself have a panic attack; rather, as with all exposures, the aim is to gradually retrain your brain not to have an alarm reaction to those sensations when they occur naturally. There are countless ways to arouse feared body sensations, several of which are described in chapter 5. The key to success is determining what physical sensations you're afraid of and then targeting those sensations using interoceptive exposure. Afraid of lightheadedness? Try hyperventilating. Afraid of dizziness? Try spinning in a swivel chair. Afraid of a racing heart? Try running up and down the stairs.

When agoraphobia or similar avoidant patterns are present, in vivo (real-world) exposures will also be important. As described previously, people with agoraphobia will often limit their activities due to their fear of body sensations, staying away from situations or activities in which escape is blocked, help is unavailable, or a panic attack would be perceived as particularly dangerous or embarrassing. These are precisely the situations and the activities that must be targeted with in vivo exposure. Set up a program that will gradually bring you back into these situations. Go to the mall. Sit in the middle of the row in church or at the movies. Drive on the highway. You can work up to these things a bit at a time, as long as you keep moving in the right direction.

As you work your way up the exposure hierarchy, try mixing interoceptive and in vivo exposures. That is, in the midst of real-world exposures, try to increase the feared body sensations. When you go to the movies, have a double cappuccino beforehand to make your heart rate increase. When you go to the shopping mall, step inside the restroom and spin around a few times to make yourself feel dizzy before going back into the crowd. While driving on the highway, try taking very deep breaths in order to bring on a sensation of lightheadedness. Prove to yourself and to your brain that these things aren't dangerous and that they don't make you panic, lose control, or die.

Because safety behaviors are so pervasive in people with a fear of body sensations, it's crucial to eliminate these behaviors from your exposure program. As tempting as it might be to bring a "safe person" or a cell phone with you during in vivo exposures, try to do without. If you absolutely must bring them with you the first time, fine, but get them out of the process as quickly as you can. Remember, an exposure conducted with safety behaviors is not nearly as effective as one conducted without them. You might be in the habit of carrying "antipanic" tools such as medications or a paper bag to breathe into. Try leaving them at home when you're doing exposures. They probably cause more problems than they solve. Allow yourself to be anxious, and watch how your anxiety subsides with time, without your having to force it down.

It will also be important to watch for probability overestimation, catastrophizing, and intolerance of uncertainty. Do the math and recognize how unlikely your feared consequences really are. Use a downward arrow to help yourself see that many of the feared consequences would not be the end of the world, and others are truly unlikely to happen. Embrace the unknown, and recognize that there is no such thing as absolute certainty. Refer back to chapter 8 for more suggestions on challenging scary thoughts.

Chapter 5 shows the exposure hierarchy for Susan, who had panic disorder. Some of her hierarchy items might apply to you; if so, feel free to use them. Here are some more examples of exposure hierarchies to help you get creative.

Exposure Hierarchy: Acute Fear of Medical Catastrophe

Activity	Fear Level (0–100)
Hyperventilating for one minute far away from home	90
Spinning for one minute far away from home	85
Breathing through a straw for one minute far away from home	80
Drinking coffee far away from home	70
Running up and down stairs for two minutes far away from home	65
Hyperventilating for one minute at home	50
Spinning for one minute at home	45
Breathing through a straw for one minute at home	40
Running up and down stairs for two minutes at home	30
Drinking coffee at home	30

Exposure Hierarchy: Chronic Preoccupation with Illness

Activity	Fear Level (0–100)
Writing my own obituary	90

Hyperventilating to make myself feel
   lightheaded   75

Activity	Fear Level
Hyperventilating to make myself feel lightheaded	75
Spinning to make myself feel dizzy	75
Vividly imagining having brain cancer	70
Visiting a cancer clinic	65
Reading obituaries of people my own age	55
Visiting a cemetery	50
Watching a documentary about cancer	40
Reading newspaper articles about people who developed brain cancer	35
Visiting a sick person at a hospital	30

Exposure Hierarchy: Fear of Choking

Activity	Fear Level (0–100)
Eating a steak sandwich in a restaurant alone	90
Eating chicken in a restaurant alone	85
Eating soup in a restaurant alone	75
Eating a steak sandwich in a restaurant with others	60
Eating chicken in a restaurant with others	55
Eating soup in a restaurant with others	50
Holding a tongue depressor on the back of my tongue	40
Gargling mouthwash	35
Holding cotton balls in my mouth	30
Wearing a tight scarf or necktie around my throat	20

Exposure Hierarchy: Fear of Fear

Activity	Fear Level (0–100)
Riding a roller coaster	100
Being up front at a crowded rock concert	90
Taking over-the-counter cough medicine	70
Holding my breath as long as possible	65

Staring at a light until my vision
    becomes blurry   55
Walking through a crowded shopping
    mall   45
Watching a scary movie   40
Sitting in the middle of the row at a
    movie theater   40
Getting into an argument with someone   30
Reading a suspenseful book   25

11

Beating Social and Performance Fears

According to most studies, people's number-one fear is public speaking. Number two is death. Death is number two. Does that sound right? This means to the average person, if you go to a funeral, you're beter off in the casket than doing the eulogy.

—*Jerry Seinfeld*

You've met Steven, the attorney who developed a debilitating fear of public speaking and interacting with others. Steven suffered from social and performance fears, which are among the most common fears. Social and performance fears can come in many forms. Here are a few:

- A fifteen-year-old boy is painfully shy when meeting new people. Many consider him to be a "loner," because he rarely reaches out to others. In groups of people, he stares at the floor and barely mumbles a few words. He has few friends, and dating is completely out of the question.

- A forty-seven-year-old businesswoman has recently been promoted to a new job that requires public speaking. She's considering quitting, because she finds the idea of speaking in front of others so aversive. When she has to give a speech, she begins to sweat and blush and is certain that everyone can see how nervous she is.
- A nineteen-year-old college student is at risk of failing out of school. He studies hard and knows the material well enough. Yet whenever he has to take a test, he falls apart. He becomes nervous and worried, and his mind seems to go blank.
- A fifty-year-old man finds himself unable to use public restrooms. Whenever there is someone else in the restroom—or if he even thinks that someone might enter the restroom— he can't urinate. He's sure everyone can tell that he's not going, and he becomes even more anxious. As a result, he's unable to travel long distances from home unless he has access to a private restroom.

Some of these social and performance fears are listed in the *DSM-IV-TR* as *social phobia* (also called social anxiety disorder). The criteria for social phobia in the *DSM-IV-TR* are:

1. Severe and persistent fear of social or performance situations in which the person fears that he or she will act in a way (or show anxiety symptoms) that will be humiliating or embarrassing. Individuals with social and performance fears aren't afraid of people; rather, they're afraid that their own behavior will lead them to be humiliated or embarrassed. For example, they might worry that when interacting with others, they will make a mistake that will cause others to laugh at them. At times, they are worried that others will see their physical signs of anxiety, such as blushing, sweating, or trembling. They fear that others will be able to tell how anxious they are and will think badly of them.

2. Exposure to the feared social situation almost always triggers a strong anxiety reaction. Social and performance fears might take the form of panic attacks, or they might be milder. You'll recall that panic attacks reflect the physical consequences of the fight-flight-freeze response—an increased heart rate, muscle tension, sweating, and other symptoms. As we saw with the diagnosis of specific phobia, *DSM-IV-TR* also notes that children's reactions can be a bit different and aren't always immediately recognizable as fear. Instead, children may express fear by crying, tantrums, freezing, or shrinking from unfamiliar people.

3. The person avoids the feared social or performance situations. As with most other types of fear, social phobia is characterized by avoidant behavior. Even when blatant avoidance is impossible, people with social phobia often resort to subtle safety behaviors to make feared situations seem more tolerable.

4. The social fear or avoidance interferes with the person's functioning or causes severe distress. As we have seen elsewhere in the *DSM-IV-TR*, social phobia can be diagnosed only when the fear and the avoidant behaviors are severe enough to cause noticeable impairment in one's ability to function.

5. In children, the fear has lasted at least six months. Because fears can come and go during childhood, social phobia isn't diagnosed in children unless the fear and the avoidance persist over time.

Variations of Social and Performance Fears

Social and performance fears can show up in a variety of guises. Sometimes, social and performance fears are a component of other, complex fears. For example, we've seen examples previously in this book of people with a fear of body sensations who worry, in part, that their panic attacks or other bodily reactions will prove embarrassing or humiliating. There are even trickier variations of social and performance fears, as well. I vividly recall trying to treat a man with a severe choking fear. We weren't making tremendous progress until I learned that his fear only seemed to show up when he was eating in public. On further questioning, he told me that he wasn't afraid of choking itself; rather, he was afraid that others would *see* him choking and that he would become embarrassed. Once we reconceptualized his fear as a social and performance fear, we were able to come up with more effective exposures that targeted what he was really afraid of. Most people with social and performance fears, however, find that they are concerned with one or more of the following:

- *Social interaction*: Some people find interacting with others quite painful. In many cases, fear is triggered by certain aspects of social interactions, such as starting a conversation, maintaining a conversation, talking to authority figures, or talking to people who are attractive or romantically desirable.
- *Public speaking*: A fear of public speaking is very common. Even people who aren't shy in conversation can become terrified when they have to speak in front of others. They might be fearful of speaking up in meetings or in class or of giving formal presentations.
- *Assertiveness*: Some people experience great difficulty standing up for themselves. They have a hard time saying no to unreasonable requests or asking others to change their behavior. As a result of these fears, they often act passively or get pushed around.
- *Performance anxiety*: For many, the idea of being watched while doing something triggers a great deal of fear. They might have little problem interacting with people, as long as they don't have to do anything in front of others. Yet they might be terrified by the idea of having a supervisor watch

them work, playing sports in front of spectators, eating in public, writing in public, or using a public restroom.

Common Cognitive Distortions in Social and Performance Fears

Catastrophizing is a common theme in the thoughts of people with social and performance fears. They tend to worry about what will happen when others watch them, pay attention to them, or see their outward signs of anxiety. A man with a fear of public speaking, for example, might worry that if others see him blush, they will think that he's weak, stupid, or crazy. He then worries that he'll be a laughingstock, and his social and professional life will be ruined (which is most likely untrue). The downward arrow strategy, however, will help him recognize that even if people see him blush, it probably wouldn't be a disaster.

People with social and performance fears also tend to have an attentional bias toward threat. In many cases, this bias is similar to that of people with a fear of body sensations: it's directed inward. Just as a person who has a fear of body sensations might repeatedly monitor her heart rate for signs of an impending heart attack, someone with social and performance fears might always pay attention to whether his face is getting hot so that he can be vigilant for blushing and sweating. As with any attentional bias, this kind of hypervigilance can lead to a breakdown in functioning. You've only got so much attentional capacity in your brain, so if you pay more attention to one thing, you have to pay less attention to something else. Imagine trying to focus on a conversation or think about the topic of your speech, while simultaneously monitoring your appearance, skin temperature, signs of trembling, and so on. Diverting your attention away from the actual situation and toward yourself will make it much more difficult to make the situation go smoothly.

Social-Performance Situations

Whenever we are in a social-performance situation, there are a number of social cues that we could pay attention to. Do fearful people pay excessive attention to negative cues? Psychologists Kathy Veljaca and Ronald Rapee asked people with high or low levels of social anxiety to give a five-minute speech in front of three audience members. The audience members were coached to give positive cues (e.g., smiles) and negative cues (e.g., frowns) during the speech. The participants giving the speech were instructed to press one button every time they saw a positive cue and to press another button whenever they saw a negative cue. People with high levels of social anxiety were more likely to detect the negative social cues, while people with low levels of social anxiety were more likely to detect the positive social cues. So people with social and performance fears tend to focus their attention on negative feedback from others, while ignoring positive feedback.

Avoidance and Safety Behaviors in Social and Performance Fears

When people fear a social or performance situation, they tend to avoid that situation. Someone with a fear of public speaking might do everything in his power to avoid having to give a speech—even if that means failing a class or turning down a job. People with a fear of social interactions might avoid talking to people they don't know well and may stay away from situations in which they would have to mingle with others, such as parties. People who fear being assertive might choose to let others take advantage of them, rather than speak up.

Of course, it's not always possible to avoid every social or performance situation. That's where subtle safety behaviors come in. These are the "tricks" that we use to make seemingly intolerable situations feel tolerable. At a party, a woman might gravitate toward the corner of the room or stick close to people she already knows, to minimize the likelihood of having to meet new people. A man might make sure to always have a drink and a plate of food in his hand, so that he won't have to shake hands with others or his hands won't tremble. A student giving a speech in class might make sure to grip the podium tightly and rush through the presentation.

Exposure Tips for Social and Performance Fears

Part of exposure for social and performance tips is relatively straightforward: you must put yourself gradually into the situations that you tend to fear and avoid. If you're afraid of public speaking, for example, you should seek out opportunities to speak in front of others. If you're afraid of social interactions, you should find new ways and places to meet people. Choose to become anxious, and watch how your fear level goes down when you do.

A couple of additional components to exposure are likely to make it more effective. First, make sure that you include exposures to the specific behaviors or outward signs of anxiety that you fear will be embarrassing or humiliating. Are you afraid that people will notice you sweating? Try dabbing your forehead with water before giving a speech or moistening your palms with water before shaking hands. Are you afraid that others will see you blush? Then make yourself blush by jogging in place for a few moments before entering the party. Are you worried that people will see you tremble or make a mistake? Do these things on purpose while others are watching you. Prove to your brain that even if people see these things, nothing terrible will happen. It's scary, but liberating.

The second additional component is crucial for many people. Make sure that you actually can produce the right skills to make social and performance situations go well. This requires some serious self-reflection: is your fear due, in part, to a lack of skill? Some people are naturally good conversationalists. Some people are good public speakers. Others aren't. If you feel that you need to brush up on your skills, seek out opportunities to do so. Organizations such as Toastmasters (www.toastmasters.org) are designed to help people learn and practice public-speaking skills in a nonthreatening environment, or consider signing up for a public speaking class at a local college or adult education program. Have trusted friends or family members give you feedback about your conversational skills, including nonverbal behaviors such as your eye contact, how fast or how slow you talk, the loudness or softness of your speech, your facial expression, and your body posture. Practice social interactions, focusing on the skills you need to improve most.

In addition to Steven's exposure hierarchy (chapter 5), here are some more exposure hierarchies for social and performance fears that might give you inspiration.

Exposure Hierarchy: Fear of Social Interaction

Activity	Fear Level (0–100)
Mingling at a party with water dabbed on my forehead	90
Mingling at a party	85
Talking to an attractive person of the opposite sex	80
Starting a conversation with a stranger	70
Telling a joke to a stranger on the bus	65
Starting a conversation with someone I've met only once or twice	65
Making prolonged eye contact with someone	55
Asking a salesperson a question about an item in a store	50
Asking a stranger what time it is	45
Saying hello to passersby on the street	40

Exposure Hierarchy: Fear of Public Speaking

Activity	*Fear Level (0–100)*
Giving a speech in front of a large audience and deliberately stuttering	100
Giving a speech in front of a large audience	90
Giving a speech in front of a small audience and dropping my papers	80
Giving a speech in front of a small audience	70
Deliberately giving the wrong answer when called on in class	65
Speaking up in a class meeting	60
Answering a question in class	55
Calling in to a live radio talk show	50
Calling across a crowded shopping mall to a friend	40
Humming on the bus	35

Exposure Hierarchy: Fear of Assertiveness

Activity	*Fear Level (0–100)*
Asking someone to quiet down at the movies	85
Telling someone when he or she has hurt my feelings	80
Sending an order back at a restaurant	70
Refusing a request	65
Returning an item to a store	60
Calling a customer service line with a complaint	50
Disagreeing with someone's opinion	45
Asking a neighbor for a favor	35
Asking a restaurant server to change the TV channel	30

Asking a barber or a hairdresser to make
  changes to my hair   25

Exposure Hierarchy: Performance Anxiety

Activity	*Fear Level (0–100)*
Auditioning for a community theater	95
Playing a musical instrument in front of others	90
Singing in a karaoke bar	90
Playing sports in a public area	80
Being videotaped while working	75
Using a public restroom with others near me	70
Having someone watch me work	65
Eating in a restaurant	60
Writing on a blackboard in front of a class	50
Writing a check in public	45

12

Beating Obsessive Fears

Doubts are more cruel than the worst of truths.
—*Molière*

Obsessive fears come from inside our heads. They might take the form of scary or repulsive thoughts, or they might resemble phobias in some respects. You've met Rachel, who was troubled by worries that she would touch something that was contaminated. Here are some more examples:

- A thirty-two-year-old man worries excessively that he will contract HIV by touching something that has blood on it. He avoids using public restrooms, touching doorknobs, or even touching things that are red. If he accidentally comes into contact with one of these things, he washes his hands over and over until his skin is cracked and bleeding.
- A fifty-five-year-old woman has become afraid to drive for fear that she will accidentally run over a pedestrian. Even

though she knows rationally that she hasn't hit anyone, the thought in her mind becomes so compelling that she feels as if she must circle the block to make sure no one has been hurt.

- A twenty-eight-year-old new mother is plagued by ideas that she will harm her baby. Even though she loves her baby and has never harmed anyone, she is bothered by a mental image of throwing the baby out the window or against the wall. As a result, she must say a special prayer for protection before she will hold the baby.

- A ten-year-old boy has become obsessed with odd and even numbers. Whenever he does something an odd number of times, he feels that something terrible will happen, even though he's not sure what that is. As a result, he has to repeat actions such as turning on a light switch until he has done them the "right" number of times.

- A forty-year-old man needs everything around him to be arranged "just right." He spends hours each day lining up the clothes and shoes in his closet, making sure they are arranged perfectly. He believes that if he can't have everything arranged perfectly, he will feel awful and will not be able to cope.

- A sixty-two-year-old woman is fearful of throwing things away. Old newspapers, clothes that no longer fit, and even old food containers are stacked in her house, creating clutter that prevents her from moving around comfortably. She's embarrassed to have people over, and her family is increasingly worried about her.

The *DSM-IV-TR* identifies these kinds of fears as *obsessive-compulsive disorder* (OCD). The criteria for OCD are:

1. Obsessions
   - Recurrent and persistent thoughts, impulses, or images that feel intrusive and inappropriate, and that cause the person severe anxiety or distress. Obsessions come from

inside the mind, taking the form of scary thoughts, impulses, or mental images. Everyone has strange thoughts from time to time; however, in OCD, these thoughts happen over and over again and are upsetting.

- The obsessions are not simply excessive worries about real-life problems. Excessive worries about real-life problems are characteristic of generalized anxiety disorder, which will be discussed in the next chapter.

- The person attempts to get rid of or "neutralize" the thoughts with some sort of behavior or mental act. The concept of "neutralizing" is key to understanding OCD. The person feels as if he or she must "do something" about the obsessive thoughts, which leads to the compulsions as described further on.

- The person recognizes that these scary thoughts come from inside his or her own mind. People with OCD aren't delusional and haven't lost touch with reality. They simply can't stop the thoughts from coming.

2. Compulsions

- Compulsions are repetitive behaviors or mental acts that people feel as if they must perform in response to an obsession or according to rigid rules. The central feature of compulsions is that they are performed in direct response to obsessive fears. Compulsions can be either outward behaviors or mental acts that no one can observe. For examples of the latter, some people might count to themselves, say a silent prayer, or think "good" thoughts to neutralize their obsessions.

- The compulsions are aimed at making the person feel better or preventing a feared event; however, these behaviors either are not connected realistically with what they are designed to prevent or are clearly excessive. So the idea here is that compulsions are designed to make the person feel better or to prevent something bad from happening. Yet they're clearly out of proportion to the actual threat, or they don't logically connect to the threat at all.

3. At least in adults, people with OCD understand that their fears are irrational. That doesn't stop them from having the fears, however.

4. The obsessions or the compulsions impair the person's functioning, take up a large amount of time, or cause severe distress. Lots of people have uncomfortable thoughts or engage in superstitious behaviors. That doesn't necessarily mean that they have OCD. OCD is diagnosed only when these behaviors take up a lot of the person's time or significantly interfere with the person's ability to function.

Variations of Obsessive Fears

Surveys of people with OCD show that obsessive fears usually fall into one of several categories (and most people with OCD have more than one of these):

- *Contamination and washing*: Many people are afraid of coming into contact with things that are dirty or "germy." They may worry that they will contract or spread a disease, or they may simply be afraid they won't be able to cope with feeling dirty. There is some overlap with hypochondriasis (health anxiety) here, and some people with this kind of obsessive fear might also experience fear of body sensations.

- *Fear of harming others*: Some people worry that they will harm others by accident. Others fear that they will be suddenly seized with an urge to commit a harmful act.

- *Repugnant thoughts*: Some people are bothered by thoughts that they find personally or morally repugnant. For example, they may have bothersome sexual thoughts, violent mental images, or thoughts that they consider blasphemous or sacrilegious.

- *Magical fears*: Some people with OCD become preoccupied with certain numbers, letters, colors, or words. They believe that some of these are "bad" and others are "good." Often, if they accidentally encounter a "bad" item—for example, doing things a "bad" number of times—they feel as if they must offset the experience with a "good" item, such as repeating the action until it has been performed a "good" number of times.

- *Fear of disorder or inexactness*: People with a fear of disorder or inexactness feel as if things need to be "just right" or else they are completely unacceptable. They might insist that their belongings are lined up just right or placed perfectly symmetrically. Others might worry excessively that they will make a mistake of some kind and feel a need to keep checking or redoing their work just in case.

- *Hoarding*: Many researchers (I'm one of them) are increasingly concluding that hoarding might be distinct from OCD. Nevertheless, for our purposes, it's reasonable to think of hoarding as including an obsessive fear of discarding objects. People who have a problem with hoarding save items that others might consider worthless, often to the point of creating clutter that makes it hard to live comfortably in their own homes. I should note that overcoming the condition of hoarding can require more than exposure therapy; for more information about hoarding, I'll refer you to my book *Buried in Treasures: Help for Compulsive Saving, Acquiring, and Hoarding*.

Common Cognitive Distortions in Obsessive Fears

A wide range of cognitive distortions can show up in people with obsessive fears. One common distortion is probability overestimation, which is present in many fear-based problems. People with obsessive fears often worry that bad outcomes are more likely to happen than they actually are. For example, the risk of contracting HIV from a public toilet is infinitesimally small—so small that most people would consider it a near impossibility. Yet for some people with an obsessive fear of contamination, every time they use a public restroom they are convinced that they are at high risk for contracting the virus.

Intolerance of uncertainty can also be a major issue for people with obsessive fears. Some people feel that if they can't be absolutely certain about what's going to happen, it's as bad as (or perhaps even worse than) if a bad outcome occurred. For these folks, uncertainty is at the core of what they're afraid of. For example, a person with a fear of accidentally harming someone might be 99.99 percent certain that she hasn't run over anyone with her car; however, she finds the 0.01 percent of doubt to be absolutely intolerable.

Black-or-white thinking shows up a lot in obsessive fears. For people with these fears, the world tends to get divided into extreme categories: clean vs. dirty, safe vs. dangerous, perfect vs. horrible. This way of categorizing the world usually involves setting very high standards before something can be considered acceptable. So, for example, if something isn't 100 percent perfect, it's considered to be all wrong.

Finally, people with obsessive fears often have a strong need for control. They think that if they don't have perfect control over their thoughts, it means that they are crazy, evil, or dangerous. In many cases, their thinking is characterized by what researchers call *thought-action fusion*, in which a thought about a harmful or immoral action is viewed as being just as harmful or immoral as the action itself. So they try hard to suppress or otherwise control those thoughts, which in turn makes the thoughts get even worse (see chapter 7 for a detailed description of how this happens). They may also feel an excessive need to control events happening around them, worrying that if they can't have everything "just so," it will be completely intolerable.

Obsessive Thoughts and OCD

People with obsessive fears are bothered by intrusive, unacceptable thoughts or impulses. They often worry that these thoughts mean that they are crazy, evil, or dangerous. Psychologists S. Jack Rachman and Padmal de Silva surveyed 124 healthy people with no history of OCD or other anxiety disorders about their experiences with intrusive thoughts or impulses. More than 80 percent of them reported having these kinds of thoughts at least some of the time. The researchers wrote down the intrusive thoughts of healthy participants, as well as the intrusive thoughts reported by patients with OCD. They then asked a panel of experts to see whether they could guess which thoughts were from healthy people and which were from people with OCD. The experts failed miserably—only half of the OCD patients' responses were judged to have actually come from OCD patients, and a quarter of the healthy participants' responses were erroneously thought to have come from OCD patients! The take-home message here is that most people have weird thoughts or impulses at least some of the time, and for the most part, there's nothing particularly unusual about the thoughts that people with OCD have. The key distinction is that people with OCD overreact to their thoughts, thinking that they mean more than they actually do, and feel compelled to try to do something about their thoughts.

Avoidance and Safety Behaviors in Obsessive Fears

Two main kinds of avoidant behavior tend to accompany obsessive fears. The first of these is passive avoidance, which is defined as the things you don't do, the places you won't go, the things you won't touch, and so on. Someone with a fear of contamination, for example, might not want to use a public bathroom or touch a doorknob. Someone with a hoarding problem might not be able to throw things away. Essentially, the person avoids doing these things in an effort to minimize his or her feelings of anxiety.

The other kind of avoidance is a safety behavior called a compulsion. As you saw in the *DSM-IV-TR* criteria for OCD, compulsions are behaviors that the person does again and again in an effort to feel better or to try to prevent something bad from happening. So, people who worry that they will accidentally harm others by leaving the stove on might feel compelled to check and recheck the knobs on the stove before they leave the house. People with a fear of disorder or inexactness might spend inordinate amounts of time lining up their possessions, making sure they are placed just so.

Exposure Tips for Obsessive Fears

In exposure for obsessive fears, it's important to tackle both of the forms of avoidance I just described (passive avoidance and compulsions). Passive avoidance (for example, not touching a doorknob) should be confronted by engaging in as much of the feared activity as possible (such as touching as many doorknobs as you can find). Compulsions need to be eliminated as rapidly and completely as possible. Like all safety behaviors, the presence of compulsions can really undermine your exposure efforts (and risk reinforcing your brain's existing belief that the compulsions are a good way to make yourself feel better). So it's important, as you work your way up your exposure hierarchy, to make every effort to stop washing, checking, repeating, and so on. In the case of people with OCD, I often find that it's most helpful when we go beyond "normal." For example, I will usually recommend that someone with washing compulsions stop washing altogether for three full days, or that people with checking compulsions never go back to check their doors or their stoves, even if they really aren't certain about whether things are safe. This might seem drastic, but it makes sense when you recognize how much damage compulsions can do to their exposure progress. Remember that the risks we're talking about here are quite low (people go camping all of the time and don't wash for three days or longer, and they all seem to survive just fine).

For people with hoarding-related fears, much of the exposure will involve sorting possessions and letting them go (by discarding, recycling, selling, or giving them away). This will likely require some advance preparation. You'll need to make sure that you have a supply of garbage bags, boxes, storage bins, and pens to make things go smoothly.

Rachel, who was terrified of contracting and spreading the anthrax virus, shared her exposure hierarchy with us. Here are some more examples of exposure hierarchies for people with obsessive fears:

Exposure Hierarchy: Contamination and Washing

Activity	Fear Level (0–100)
Touching blood	100
Touching urine	95
Touching a public toilet	90
Touching my bed and all of my "clean" clothes with unclean hands	85
Touching the doorknob in a public bathroom	75
Serving food with unclean hands	70
Touching something red	60
Touching the bottom of a shoe	55
Touching the floor	55
Touching a doorknob	45

Exposure Hierarchy: Fear of Harming Others

Activity	Fear Level (0–100)
Carrying a pocketknife in a crowded place	90
Chopping food in the presence of others	85
Dropping thumbtacks onto the sidewalk	80
Bumping into someone in a crowded place	75
Driving in a crowded pedestrian area	60
Driving over speed bumps	55
Leaving the house for thirty minutes while a candle is burning	50

Leaving the house for ten minutes while
   the oven is on   45
Leaving the house with the front door unlocked,
   if my neighborhood is reasonably safe   40
Turning the stove on and off and then leave the house   40

Exposure Hierarchy: Repugnant Thoughts

Activity	Fear Level (0–100)
Deliberately thinking "I hate God"	95
Vividly imagining hurting a loved one	90
Writing "I am a child molester" over and over	85
Looking at pictures of nude men or women	75
Wishing for a loved one to die	65
Watching a movie about the devil	60
Trying to make planes crash by using my mind	60
Watching a "slasher" movie	55
Thinking "I am a murderer" over and over	55
Reading biographies of serial killers	50

Exposure Hierarchy: Magical Fears

Activity	Fear Level (0–100)
Vividly imagining "bad" people and wishing to become like them	85
Writing a "forbidden" word or number on my arm in permanent ink	85
Writing "forbidden" words over and over again	80
Saying a prayer wishing for people to die	75
Breaking a mirror	70
Stepping on sidewalk cracks and wishing for people to be harmed	60
Wearing clothes that have a "bad" number, such as 666, written on them	55
Crossing through a doorway while thinking a "bad" thought	50
Doing things the "wrong" number of times	45
Wearing clothes that are a "bad" color	35

Exposure Hierarchy: Fear of Disorder or Inexactness

Activity	Fear Level (0–100)
Deliberately making a mistake on a test	75
Rearranging the clothes in my closet and drawers so they are in disarray	65
Rearranging the food in my kitchen so that it is in disarray	65
Eating, drinking, and brushing my teeth the "wrong" way	60
Tossing some waste paper on the floor and leaving it there	55
Messing up the items on my desk and leaving them that way	50
Wearing mismatched socks	50
Rearranging my furniture so that nothing is lined up right	45
Making the pictures on the wall crooked	40
Deliberately misspelling something on a form	40

Exposure Hierarchy: Hoarding

Activity	Fear Level (0–100)
Allowing others to handle my things and help discard them	85
Discarding information that I might need someday	80
Deliberately "wasting" something	75
Discarding things that I feel a sense of attachment to	70
Discarding things that might still be useful	65
Discarding old newspapers	60
Discarding old clothes	60
Finding a great bargain and then not buying anything	55
Handling items at a yard sale without buying them	50
Driving by a yard sale without stopping	45

13

Beating Excessive Worries

You can never worry your way to enlightenment.
—*Terri Guillemets*

E xcessive worries are a bit like obsessive fears, in the sense that both of them can reflect a fear reaction to one's own thoughts. People with excessive worries have scary thoughts or images that pop into their heads; these thoughts, in turn, make them feel anxious. They then respond to these anxious feelings with even more worrying, as if that will somehow make them feel better.

Samantha, who was preoccupied with worries about her son's safety and about the end of the world, is a good example of someone with this kind of fear. Here are a few more:

- A sixty-year-old woman can't stop worrying about her children and grandchildren. Even though they are perfectly healthy, she constantly worries that they will get sick or get into an accident. She has trouble sleeping, because her mind runs through scary scenarios as she lies in bed. She frequently calls her children, even late at night, to make sure they are all right.

- A twelve-year-old boy, who is earning good grades, worries excessively about his performance at school. When a test comes up, he feels sick to his stomach, worrying that he won't get an A. He also worries about whether he will succeed in school sports and whether he has enough friends. At times, he tells his parents he's worried that a robber will break into the house.

- A forty-two-year-old man describes himself as a worrywart. He seems to worry about nearly everything: he worries that the economy will collapse and he will lose his savings; he worries that he will get fired from his job, even though he gets good performance reviews; he worries about being late to social events; and he worries whenever his wife is late coming home by even ten minutes. He has become increasingly irritable toward his family, "snapping" at them. His wife and children feel as if they are walking on eggshells around him.

When people have these kinds of excessive worries about life situations or problems, they might meet criteria for *generalized anxiety disorder* (GAD). According to the *DSM-IV-TR*, the criteria for GAD are

1. Excessive worry, occurring on most days and persisting for at least six months, about a number of events or activities. In GAD, the worry is usually not limited to only one problem. Instead, people with GAD seem to worry about a range of things, such as finances, work or school performance, social competence and status, or their own health or that of their family members. Certainly, all of these issues can be stressful, and we all worry about them from time to time. In people with GAD, however, these worries happen a lot (on more days than not) and persist for a long time (at least six months).

2. People with GAD often describe their worries as "uncontrollable," popping into their heads even when they don't mean to think about them, and they then have a hard time redirecting their attention to other things.

3. The anxiety and worry are associated with at least three of these symptoms:

   - Feeling restless or keyed up
   - Fatigue
   - Difficulty concentrating
   - Irritability
   - Muscle tension
   - Difficulty falling or staying asleep, or restless sleep

   As I discussed in chapter 2, these are all classic signs of the sympathetic nervous system (the fight-flight-freeze response). When the brain perceives a threat, the body mobilizes to deal with the threat. The problem here is that the "threat" is a thought, and by worrying, the brain keeps sending that threat signal to the adrenal glands, which secrete adrenaline into the bloodstream. So, instead of having a "burst" of adrenaline that will protect them from danger, people with GAD have the equivalent of a "slow drip." Their bodies chronically produce just enough adrenaline to make them miserable.

4. The anxiety, worry, or physical symptoms impair the person's functioning or cause severe distress. This is crucial for GAD and other diagnoses in the *DSM-IV-TR*. To be considered diagnosable, the person's worry and anxiety need to be bad enough that they have a noticeable impact on his or her quality of life.

5. The anxiety and worry are not due to drugs, medications, or a physical illness. Lots of drugs and medical conditions can cause symptoms that resemble those of GAD. That's why a good medical evaluation is an important first step in determining what's going on.

Variations of Excessive Worries

People worry for many different reasons, and their worrying can take several forms:

- *Worry-skipping*: Some people avoid thinking about topic A by worrying about topic B. It goes like this: A scary thought or mental image pops into the person's head, perhaps an image of a loved one being seriously injured or sick. The person thinks about this for a while, until he or she starts to feel too anxious. So the person "skips" to a different worry, maybe something that's slightly less scary, such as whether he or she will get to work on time.

- *Worrying to reduce uncertainty*: Some people seem to use worry as a way of trying to resolve uncertainty. To these people, not having all of the answers or not being able to predict what's going to happen feels intolerable. So they worry about a topic as a (usually unsuccessful) means of trying to become more certain.

- *Worry about worry*: Remember "fear of fear," which I mentioned in regard to a fear of body sensations? Worry about worry is a bit like that. As we know, everyone worries from time to time; however, some people seem to overreact to their worries. They might think that if they allow themselves to worry, they'll never be able to stop, or they might even fear that worrying will cause them to become sick, have a heart attack, or suffer other dire consequences.

Common Cognitive Distortions in Excessive Worries

You can clearly see the theme of probability overestimation in the previous examples of people with excessive worries. These people often try to predict the future, usually greatly overestimating the likelihood of bad (but improbable) outcomes. It's not that these bad outcomes are impossible—certainly, bad things do happen. Yet the person with excessive worries feels as if these events are imminent. Take, for example, the woman who worries that her children and grandchildren have gotten sick or have had an accident. Are these things possible? Of course, they are. But on any given evening, the odds of their having a serious medical issue are low.

Catastrophizing also plays a big role in excessive worries. Part of the reason some people feel a need to worry about things is because they tell themselves that if a bad event were to occur, it would be terrible, awful, or intolerable. So the boy who worries about his school performance is worried not only that he will fail a test (probability overestimation) but also that if he does fail a test the results will be disastrous and will follow him for the rest of his life (catastrophizing).

Intolerance of uncertainty can also be a factor in worrying. As I mentioned previously, some people use worrying as an attempt to make themselves feel more certain about what's going to happen. It doesn't really work (after all, thinking about something doesn't provide you with any new information that could make you more certain), but some people persist in worrying due to a belief that somehow, if they just worry long enough and hard enough, an answer will come to them.

We see a lot of black-or-white thinking in people who have excessive worries. They can often seem like perfectionists, feeling as if they need to do tasks 100 percent perfectly. Getting a "B" on a test is unacceptable to some worriers—for them, it's as bad as if they had failed the test.

Finally, people with excessive worries have a great need for control. Sometimes, this need is directed toward the external world—for example, needing to remind everyone to be safe, or insisting that no one stress them out or give them bad news. Often, the need for control is directed inward, toward the worry itself. Many people feel that it's important to be in control of their minds at all times; they think that if unwanted worries come to mind, it must mean that they are out of control, defective, or crazy. A variation of this that shows up in a lot of people with excessive worries is a belief that worrying will somehow give them control over things. Someone might mistakenly assume that worrying about a bad event will make that event less likely to occur (for example, worrying about my family members' health will keep them from getting sick, or worrying about a problem will help me find the right solution to that problem).

You might have noticed that some of these worry-related beliefs are in direct conflict with one another. For example, people who have excessive worries might believe, on one hand, that worrying will make them more prepared, help them solve problems, or even prevent bad things from happening. At the same time, however, they might also believe that worrying will give them a heart attack or make them go crazy. Many people with excessive worries are trapped between these two sets of conflicting beliefs.

Avoidance and Safety Behaviors in Excessive Worries

Even though avoidance isn't listed in the *DSM-IV-TR* criteria for GAD, people with excessive worries do a lot of things to try to minimize their feelings of anxiety. One common pattern is a tendency to avoid things that might be stressful or unpleasant. I've known several families that seem to live by the motto "Don't upset Mom (or Dad)." Because some people with excessive worries underestimate their ability to cope with anxiety, they stay away from uncomfortable conversations, newspaper articles, or TV shows. They convey a message to the people around them that they are fragile and therefore should never be allowed to become upset.

Some people with excessive worries use thought suppression as a safety behavior. Because they find anxiety to be highly unpleasant, whenever an anxiety-provoking thought comes to mind, they try to make the thought go away by mentally distracting themselves, thinking about something else, or finding busywork to do. As I described in chapter 7, however, thought suppression is a losing game for most people. Whenever we try not to think about something, we simply tend to think about it even more.

Finally, for some people, worrying itself can be a safety behavior. That is, people assume that if they worry about something enough, they will become more certain, will solve a problem, or will be prepared for the worst-case scenario. Of course, these assumptions are all false: excessive worrying does not actually make people more certain, solve problems, or prepare people to deal effectively with threats. In some cases, worrying can also be used as a form of thought suppression, as in the worry-skipping example described earlier. So, if people start to think about something unpleasant, they might try to distract themselves from that thought by worrying about something else that is slightly less threatening.

Exposure Tips for Excessive Worries

Exposure can be a useful way to beat excessive worries. I should note, however, that most therapists augment worry exposure with other strategies that I describe in chapter 17. In particular, I recommend paying attention to

- *Problem-solving skills*: Many people use excessive worrying as a form of pseudo-problem solving. For them, worrying means that they're dealing with whatever problem they are facing. The problem is, excessive worrying rarely leads to a good solution to problems. It turns out that a lot of worriers have difficulty solving problems in a healthy way, which is why they rely on worrying—even if it's not really solving problems, it's a way of "going through the motions" as if they were solving a problem. In chapter 17, I'll give you some tips on how to practice healthy, productive problem solving. Take a close look at that section and try it out. Even though it might seem awkward at first, I think you'll find that it beats the heck out of worrying.

- *Relaxation*: As you know by now, I don't routinely recommend using relaxation exercises for dealing with acute fears. All too often, they become just another safety behavior or "crutch" that gets in the way of recovery. Yet because people with excessive worries also tend to have a lot of chronic physical tension (that "slow drip" of adrenaline), they often find that adding relaxation exercises to their program can help them feel better.

Now on to the exposure itself. In the case of excessive worrying, it can be tricky to design a program, because in many cases worries are both the fear and the safety behavior. The person has a fear reaction to a mental thought or image and then tries to deal with that fear by worrying harder. The basic idea in exposure is that we want to confront and experience the scary thoughts and feelings, without avoiding them or trying to distract ourselves. Often, people with excessive worries have gotten so hung up on trying to calm themselves down that the idea of choosing to become anxious seems very weird and unsettling. Yet as you've seen throughout this book, that's exactly what will help. Here are some tips that can help you get the most out of the program:

- *Set aside a specific worry time*: The idea of scheduling your worrying might sound weird, but that's exactly what I recommend. Pick a time of day—perhaps a half hour or so—during which you will do nothing but worry. Write it in your calendar if that helps. During the rest of the day, if a worry pops into your mind, jot it down on a piece of paper so that you can remember to include it during your worry time. Some people find that doing this helps them feel less of a need to worry during the day.
- *Focus*: Worry-skipping is part of the problem in excessive worries. So, during your worry time, the key is to worry about one thing and worry about it hard. If your mind starts to wander or dwell on other worries, gently remind yourself

to keep focusing on the worry at hand. When you're really done worrying about one topic, you can move on to the next one.

A Sample Imaginal Exposure Script for Excessive Worry

My daughter is dying of cancer. She's lying in a hospital bed, wasting away. She looks thin and pale. Her breathing is raspy and labored. I'm by her side, holding her hand and feeling so guilty because I know it's all my fault that she's dying. I knew that our house was too close to the power lines, and I knew that living close to power lines would put my family at risk, but I chose not to do enough research. I chose not to move the family away from there. Now for the rest of my life I'll have to live with the knowledge that I didn't do enough to protect my family. She's dying, and it's my fault.

Target the parts of the worry you'd rather not think about. This is hard for many people but important. Often, we tend to worry around the periphery of an issue, without getting to the core (which we find more unpleasant). So, for example, someone might worry excessively about whether his child has been in an accident—and yet shy away from thinking about the specifics. What kind of accident? What kind of injuries might the child have sustained? What would that look like? What would life be like then? These are the more painful aspects of the worry that many people would rather avoid—but it's important to confront them so that they stop controlling you.

Treating People with Generalized Anxiety Disorder

Psychologists Lizabeth Roemer and Susan Orsillo treated people with GAD using a form of therapy based on the concept of acceptance: stopping their efforts to try to control their thoughts and feelings.

(Continued)

They encouraged patients to experience their worried thoughts and anxious emotions fully, without trying to change them in some way. They also emphasized having patients put renewed energy into doing things that were truly important to them, rather than putting all of their efforts into emotional control. At the end of treatment, more than three-quarters of the patients no longer met the diagnostic criteria for GAD, a very strong response. Thus, learning to accept anxious thoughts and feelings and redirecting your efforts toward living well can be good strategies for beating excessive worries.

Samantha's exposure hierarchy, as shown in chapter 5, is a good example of a worry exposure hierarchy. Here are some more that might help with your planning, although you will most likely need to tailor these to your personal concerns.

Exposure Hierarchy: Worst-Case Scenario

Activity	Fear Level (0–100)
Writing a eulogy for my child as if he or she had died	100
Vividly imagining my child dying in a car accident	95
Vividly imagining my child dying from a disease	90
Vividly imagining that my child has a disease	80
Vividly imagining dying from a disease	75
Vividly imagining that I have a disease	70
Downloading the sound of a car crash and listening to it over and over	60
Looking at pictures of car accidents on the Internet	55
Watching TV documentaries about diseases	45
Reading articles about diseases	40

Exposure Hierarchy: Taking Risks

Activity	Fear Level (0–100)
Leaving the front door unlocked while I'm sleeping, if my neighborhood is reasonably safe	90
Deliberately making a social blunder that could be embarrassing	85
Deliberately making a mistake at work	80
Asking family members to go out without me and not tell me where they're going	75
Leaving the front door unlocked when I go out, if my neighborhood is reasonably safe	65
Inviting people over without cleaning up first	60
Deliberately making a mistake on a test	50
Leaving the front door unlocked while I'm home, if my neighborhood is reasonably safe	45
Deliberately being late for an event	40
Driving with a nearly empty gas tank	35

14

Beating Post-Traumatic Fears

Each one has to find his peace from within. And peace to be real must be unaffected by outside circumstances.

—*Mahatma Gandhi*

Traumatic events happen to lots of people. Most of the time, we're able to get on with our lives. Some people, however, develop persistent fears after experiencing a trauma. Andrea, who was sexually assaulted and whom you met earlier in this book, is an example of someone with this kind of problem. Here are a few more:

- A twenty-two-year-old soldier has just returned from active duty overseas, where he witnessed people being killed in combat. Now he has recurrent nightmares in which he relives his combat experiences. He feels jumpy all of the time and feels as if he has to keep looking over his shoulder.

If a war documentary comes on TV, he feels panicked and has to change the channel.

- A thirty-eight-year-old woman was badly injured in a car accident. Even though her physical injuries have healed, she's now fearful of driving or even being a passenger in a car. When she has to drive somewhere, she grips the wheel tightly, her heart races, and she feels as if she's about to lose control of the car. She has begun to lose interest in her usual activities and often feels emotionally numb.

- A forty-six-year-old man who was sexually abused as a child feels chronically nervous and tense. He keeps having moments in which he feels as if the abuse is happening to him again in the present—he can see the face of his abuser and hear the man's words echoing in his head. He gets particularly anxious whenever he sees anyone who even remotely resembles the person who abused him all of those years ago. He feels as if no one understands him, and he has withdrawn from his family and friends.

Some people who experience these lingering fears after a trauma have *posttraumatic stress disorder* (PTSD). The criteria for PTSD in the *DSM-IV-TR* are:

1. The person has been exposed to a traumatic event or events that involved actual or threatened death, serious injury, or threat to the physical integrity of self or others, and the person's reaction was one of fear, helplessness, or horror. There's some controversy on this issue, but right now a "trauma" is defined in the *DSM-IV-TR* as an event that is life-threatening or a threat to physical integrity. This means that events such as rape or assault, combat, accidents or injuries, or natural disasters could meet this definition, whereas other stressful life events, such as being fired or getting divorced, probably don't. That's not to say, however, that people can't develop fearful reactions following

non-life-threatening stressful events. They can and do, and the exercises in this chapter may still apply to them.

2. Persistently reexperiencing the traumatic event, such as
   • Having recurrent, intrusive, distressing memories of the event
   • Having recurrent nightmares about the event
   • Acting or feeling as if the event were happening again
   • Feeling intensely distressed, or experiencing physical signs of anxiety, when reminded of an aspect of the traumatic event

These items all center around the theme of "reexperiencing." The idea is that people with PTSD feel as if they constantly have to deal with the traumatic event in some way, whether it's through painful memories, nightmares or flashbacks, or feeling panicky when something reminds them of the trauma.

3. Persistent avoidance of trauma reminders or a general sense of numbing, such as
   • Efforts to avoid thoughts, feelings, or conversations related to the trauma
   • Efforts to avoid activities, places, or people that remind the person of the trauma
   • An inability to recall an important aspect of the trauma
   • Severe loss of interest or participation in significant activities
   • Feeling detached or estranged from other people
   • A restricted range of emotion
   • A sense of a foreshortened future (for example, the person does not expect to have a normal life span)

Some of these criteria refer directly to behavioral avoidance. People with PTSD often go to great lengths to avoid thinking about what has happened to them. They can be reluctant to talk about it, try hard to keep their mind off it, and avoid situations that might remind them about it. Other criteria refer to a more general "numbing" of responsiveness to the world. Many people with PTSD lose interest in doing things, feel cut off from other people, and feel numb or dead inside.

4. Persistent symptoms of physical arousal, such as
    • Difficulty falling or staying asleep
    • Irritability or angry outbursts
    • Problems in concentrating
    • Being overly alert
    • An exaggerated startle response

These criteria are rather similar to some of the symptoms of GAD described in the previous chapter. As is the case with GAD, these symptoms represent a persistent "turning on" of the sympathetic nervous system (the fight-flight-freeze response). The adrenal glands are constantly secreting adrenaline into the bloodstream, as if to prepare the body for imminent danger— even though that danger might be little more than a memory.

5. These symptoms have lasted more than one month. It's important to recognize that many of the reactions described previously are actually quite normal following a serious trauma. In most cases, these reactions decrease over time and eventually disappear. Therefore, PTSD can be diagnosed only when the symptoms persist.
6. The symptoms impair the person's functioning or cause severe distress. As with other diagnoses, PTSD is diagnosed when the person's fear and other reactions are severe enough to cause his or her ability to function to suffer in some way.

Variations of Post-Traumatic Fears

Traumatic events can give rise to a variety of fears. These can be classified broadly into two categories:

1. *Externally directed fears*: Part of the complex array of post-traumatic fears is an anxious apprehension about the environment. People with PTSD are often described as "hypervigilant," meaning they constantly scan their surroundings for signs of danger. They might take extra safety precautions, such as not letting anyone sit behind them or checking and rechecking the locks on their doors. They might start to withdraw from normal activities due to safety fears.

2. *Fear of memories*: Other fears are inwardly directed. Traumatic memories are painful and unpleasant, and most of us would rather not dwell on them. Yet for some people with post-traumatic fears, the memories are so disturbing that they go to great lengths to try to avoid them. If memories of past traumas enter their minds, they might try to suppress the thoughts or distract themselves. They might even try to "numb" the unpleasant memories with alcohol or drugs. We've already seen what happens when people try not to think about something, however; they just tend to think about it more. This is what happens in PTSD: the memories that someone is trying to suppress pop into consciousness when the person doesn't want them to. This can take the form of intrusive recollections or flashback experiences or can even happen while people are sleeping, in the form of nightmares.

Common Cognitive Distortions in Post-Traumatic Fears

Externally directed fears are often associated with probability overestimation. Because certain people have experienced traumatic events, they assume that it's highly likely that something else terrible will happen to them. Although it's fairly rare for people to be violently attacked on the street, for someone with post-traumatic fears, the risk might seem much higher. People with post-traumatic fears often say things like "The world is a very dangerous place." We know that there are dangers in the world, but for people with post-traumatic fears, their sense of risk has been inflated by their unfortunate experiences. Here's where it's essential to do the math. The fact that the traumatic event occurred does not necessarily mean that it's highly likely to occur again. Of course, we always should take *reasonable* precautions—but those precautions should be based on a realistic appraisal of actual risk, not on one's memories or fears.

Catastrophizing also seems to play a role in post-traumatic fears, particularly for people who have a fear of memories. They often worry that they are unable to cope with feeling anxious, sometimes even going so far as to call themselves "damaged" or "defective." When they think this way, they're underestimating their own resilience and ability to manage things that are diffi-cult. The downward arrow helps here—recognize that even when you feel anxious or uncomfortable, you can still recover and survive.

We also see lots of black-or-white thinking in people who have post-traumatic fears. For some, the traumatic experiences have shattered their way of thinking about themselves and the world, leaving them with an overly pessimistic, all-or-nothing way of thinking. One person might have the belief that "If I can't be 100 percent safe all of the time, then I'm never safe." Someone else might think, "If I'm not strong and capable every minute of the day, then I'm incompetent and broken." Others might think, "If I couldn't prevent this bad thing from happening, then I'm a victim and always will be a victim." The solution is scaling—understanding that there are shades of gray, not only black or white. We are all somewhere between safe and unsafe, between strong and weak. That's life, and it's fine.

The need for control is also a big deal for many people who have post-traumatic fears. In particular, people with fears of memories get hung up on the idea that they need to somehow remove the memories from their consciousness or somehow reduce the memories' frequency or intensity. Their need to control their memories can be so powerful that they might resort to unhelpful behaviors, such as alcohol or drug misuse, in their efforts to gain control. When they fail to control their memories (as they almost always do), they take this as further evidence that they are somehow damaged or weak. Try to let go of that need for control. Recognize that no one, no matter how healthy, can control his or her thoughts all of the time. Furthermore, control of your thoughts and feelings is not crucial for your recovery and happiness. People who come to terms with trauma in a healthy way don't do so by suppressing their thoughts and memories. Instead, they face the reality, put it in its proper context, and move forward with their lives.

Avoidance and Safety Behaviors in Post-Traumatic Fears

As you saw in the *DSM-IV-TR* criteria listed earlier, people with PTSD engage in a wide range of avoidance and numbing behaviors. All of these can be thought of as attempts to control feelings of anxiety or other unpleasant emotions. People with post-traumatic fears will often make efforts to avoid thinking or talking about the traumatic events because remembering feels too painful. They will also stay away from situations that remind them of their traumatic experiences, even if those situations aren't objectively dangerous. A veteran with PTSD might not want to watch a war movie on TV, or a woman who was sexually assaulted might avoid dating. These situations are avoided specifically because they trigger unpleasant memories.

The general withdrawal from the world we often see in people with post-traumatic fears can also be considered a form of avoidance. People with PTSD are likely to do fewer of their usual activities and interact less with other people. Sometimes this is because of external

Can Memories of Trauma Be Repressed?

Some therapists believe that memories of trauma can be repressed, meaning that the person becomes unable to remember the traumatic event (but might still show other signs of PTSD). This idea is highly controversial, however, and there isn't much evidence to support it. Psychologist Richard McNally and colleagues recruited a group of women with PTSD who had been sexually abused during childhood, women who had been sexually abused but did not have PTSD, and women who had not been abused. They showed these women a series of trauma-related words (such as incest) or trauma-unrelated words (for example, mailbox). After each word, participants were instructed to either try to remember the word or try to forget it. Participants were then asked to write down as many of the words as they could remember, regardless of whether they had been instructed to remember or forget the words. The trauma survivors with PTSD showed some problems of memory, but only for the trauma-unrelated words. They remembered the trauma-related words very well, including those they were supposed to forget. People with PTSD don't seem to have trouble remembering trauma. Quite the opposite: they are unable to forget it.

safety concerns; other times, it's because the person simply doesn't want to feel upset, get stressed out, or risk having to talk about his or her experience. As with most forms of avoidance, these behaviors represent an effort to reduce or contain unpleasant emotions, but they backfire by diminishing the person's quality of life.

Exposure Tips for Post-Traumatic Fears

Exposure can be very effective for reducing post-traumatic fears. Because these kinds of fears take two forms (externally directed fears and a fear of memories), your exposure exercises will be most effective if they address both areas.

To address externally directed fears, create a hierarchy that is designed to get you back out into the world and do exposures that feel "risky" (as long as they're not objectively dangerous). If you tend to use any safety behaviors when going out, such as taking tranquilizing medications, cell phones, or weapons of any kind, try leaving them at home. Chances are you don't need them, and they'll just interfere with your ability to make progress. Seek out things that remind you of the traumatic experience. Allow yourself to feel anxious. Notice that your anxiety subsides with time if you stick with the exposure.

For a fear of memories, you'll be using imaginal exposure (as described in chapter 4). The key is to tell the story about what happened. You can do this in writing, into an audio recording device (see chapter 4 for instructions on how to do this on your computer), or both. As with any exposure, you want to make sure that you're not avoiding any parts of it. So, as you tell your story, keep several things in mind. First, *use the present tense.* Instead of saying, "I was walking down the street," say, "I am walking down the street." Using the present tense helps make the mental imagery more vivid. Second, focus on the worst parts. Many trauma stories are long and complicated. The goal here is not to give a lot of background information or to write a novel; rather, you're exposing yourself specifically to those aspects of the traumatic memory that you'd most want to avoid. Third, incorporate lots of details. Focus on the scariest part of the memory, including information about what you see, hear, smell, and taste in this memory. Include information about what you're thinking and feeling in the memory. We want to make sure that you're really getting in touch with the scary memory and not avoiding anything. Finally, repeat this often. If you've written your story on paper, read it over and over again. If you've spoken it into an audio recording device, listen to it over and over.

A Sample Imaginal Exposure Script for Fear of Memories

I'm driving at night. It's raining out, and I can't see very well. Michael Jackson's song "Beat It" is playing on the radio, and I'm singing along. Out of the corner of my left eye, I see something move toward me. I hear a screeching sound, brakes squealing on the pavement. I turn my head to the left, but before I can even see what's going on, there's a loud crunching sound. The left side of my head hits the wall of my car, and I can feel the pain shooting through my head and down my neck. Everything goes black for a while, I'm not sure how long. When I open my eyes, it's still raining and hard to see what's going on. I'm confused. I try to turn my head to the left, but there's a sharp pain in my neck. My head is throbbing, and blood is running into my eyes, I guess I must have cut my head. The airbag on my steering wheel has deployed. It's hard to take a deep breath; when I try to breathe, it feels like someone is stabbing me in the ribs. I look out of the driver's-side window, which is now shattered, and I see another car, a white Toyota, pressed up against mine. The hood of the other car is completely crumpled up as if it were paper. There's a man sitting in the driver's seat, and I can see that he's not moving. His face is covered with blood, and his mouth is wide open. I think that I should help him, but I can't get up. I'm trapped. The air smells like gasoline, and I think my car is about to blow up. All I can hear is the rain pounding on the roof of the car, and "Beat It" is still playing on the radio.

Andrea's exposure hierarchy for her post-traumatic fears is shown in chapter 5. Here are some more examples—but, as always, you'll need to create your own so that the exposure hierarchy gets at your specific fears.

Exposure Hierarchy: Post-Traumatic Fears from a Motor Vehicle Accident

Activity	Fear Level (0–100)
Driving on a busy highway (alone)	95
Driving on a busy highway (accompanied)	90
Being a passenger in a car on a busy highway	85
Driving on a quiet street	80
Being a passenger in a car on a quiet street	75
Downloading the sound of a car crash and listening to it over and over	70
Looking at pictures of car accidents on the Internet	60
Recording the story of my accident and listening to it over and over	55
Writing the story of my accident and reading it over and over	55
Watching a car chase on TV	50

Exposure Hierarchy: Post-Traumatic Fears from a Sexual Assault

Activity	Fear Level (0–100)
Recording the story of my assault and listening to it over and over	90
Writing the story of my assault and reading it over and over	80
Talking to friends about my assault	75
Watching a movie in which someone is sexually assaulted	70
Going on a date with a man I don't know well	65
Going out with male friends	60
Leaving my front door unlocked while I sleep, if my neighborhood is reasonably safe	55

Going for a walk by myself in the evening	45
Attending a support group for sexual assault survivors	40
Reading accounts of sexual assault	40

Exposure Hierarchy: Post-Traumatic Fears from Combat

Activity	*Fear Level (0–100)*
Letting people sit behind me on the bus or the train	85
Recording the story of my combat experience and listening to it over and over	80
Watching a war movie	75
Looking at pictures of combat in a book	65
Smelling gunpowder, foreign foods, and other things that remind me of my combat experience	60
Attending a veterans' support group	55
Writing the story of my combat experience and reading it over and over	50
Sitting with my back to the door	45
Reading accounts of the war	40
Wearing my military uniform	35

PART III

Face Your Fears for Life

Tracking Your Progress

The measure of success is not whether you have a
tough problem to deal with, but whether it's the
same problem you had last year.

—*John Foster Dulles*

About a year ago, I decided that I needed to lose some
weight. I wasn't fat, but I was certainly getting a little fleshy
and didn't really like the way I looked or felt. So I made
some changes to my diet and tried to get a bit more exercise.
People would ask me how my weight-loss program was working,
and initially, I just shrugged my shoulders and replied, "I have no
idea." I really didn't. As far as I could tell, I didn't feel a whole lot
different, and I didn't see a dramatic change when I looked at
myself in the mirror. It was a little discouraging, to tell the truth,
and I found myself wondering whether it was even worth continuing.

But then I weighed myself, and I was surprised by what I saw.
Even though I hadn't noticed anything dramatically different in
how I felt or looked, the scale told me that in fact I had lost a

considerable amount of weight. By actually taking a measure-ment, I had a much more accurate understanding of my progress than I did when I was only guessing. Any doubts about whether my weight-loss program was working vanished right then and there. I was encouraged and excited to continue with the pro-gram—and I made sure to weigh myself more frequently so that I could really see what was happening to me.

As you go through this program of exposure therapy, you might have a similar experience. You're facing fears and getting stronger, but because the change is often gradual, it can some-times be hard to gauge your own progress. If someone asks you, "How's the program going?" your initial reaction might be a shoulder shrug. From day to day, you might not notice that you feel any different. Like me, you might feel discouraged if you don't notice dramatic results right away. You might even find yourself wondering whether it's worth continuing, just as I did.

When you track your progress, however, things go differently. Just as when I weighed myself and had a visual confirmation that I was progressing toward my goals, you'll be able to see without a doubt whether your program is working or not working—and this will be much more accurate than trying to guess. You'll feel more encouraged about the program and will even look forward to see-ing how far you can go.

That's why it's so important to track your progress as you go. You and I both want you to get the absolute maximum benefit from this program, but for that to happen, you'll need to pay much more attention to your own reactions than you did in the past. You, and only you, will determine what's working and what's not, whether to speed up or slow down, and whether changes need to be made. I can give you the tools you need, but it's up to you to use them.

When you track your progress in a systematic fashion, you serve several purposes that are vital to your long-term success: pacing and calibration, problem solving and fine-tuning, and giv-ing yourself a boost in motivation.

Pacing and Calibration

Let's go back to my weight-loss analogy for a moment. One of the things I did was to start exercising, but how hard did I need to push myself in order to lose weight? Did I need to exercise so vigorously that I felt like throwing up or passing out? Did my muscles need to ache so badly the next day that I could hardly walk? On the other side of the spectrum, would a leisurely stroll around the block be enough to help me lose the weight? It's an important question. If I didn't work hard enough, I simply wouldn't get the weight off, and therefore I would just be wasting my time. On the other hand, if I worked too hard, then I would unnecessarily make the process more unpleasant than it needed to be, and this would probably increase the likelihood that I'd get frustrated and quit—which certainly wouldn't serve my aims in the long run.

The American Heart Association came up with a good way to answer this question in the form of the target heart rate. I knew from that organization's research that my target heart rate, given my age at the time, was 90 to 153 beats per minute. So, if I wanted to know whether I was pacing my exercise appropriately, all I needed to do was check my pulse. If my pulse was below 90 beats per minute, I knew I wasn't pushing hard enough and needed to speed up. On the other hand, if my pulse was higher than 153 beats per minute, I knew that I was working harder than I needed to, and I could afford to ease up a bit. In this way, I let my own body be the judge of how hard I should work.

It's the same way with facing fears. We don't have something as precise as the target heart rate in exposure therapy, but we can make reasonable guesses based on your fear level. If your fear level doesn't go high enough, that could be a sign that you're not pushing yourself hard enough. On the other hand, if your fear level goes through the roof, you might want to back off a little and take things more slowly. Pushing yourself too hard won't kill you—fear is not lethal—but it can make the process more unpleasant than it needs to be, which in turn might make you less likely to stick with the program. Everyone's reactions are a bit different, and the numbers might mean different things to various people, so there are no hard-and-fast rules about what your level should be at any given moment. In general, though, I recommend aiming for the middle of the scale with each exposure. As you can see in the following illustration, I usually find that people do best with exposures that put them in the "target zone" of 40 to 80 on the fear level scale. When the fear level is below 40, I usually interpret this to mean that they're not doing things that are scary enough to produce the results they need. On the other hand, when fear levels go much higher than 80, sometimes it's a sign that they're being a bit too ambitious and they can afford to slow the process down by starting with some lower-level exposures.

Of course, every rule has its exceptions, and this is no different. I've known lots of people who decided to just go for it and face their most extreme fears, even though their fear level was 90

The Fear Level Target Zone		
Too High	100	The worst terror I could imagine
	90	
	80	Very scary, I could panic
	70	
Target	60	
	50	Moderately scary but manageable
	40	
	30	
Too Low	20	Slightly nervous, no big deal
	10	
	0	Totally fine, completely calm

The fear level scale.

or even 100. And they did fine. So if you feel like tackling a really high-level fear, don't let me discourage you from trying it! Just know that you probably don't have to push yourself that hard if you don't want to, and that if you're aiming for a fear level in the 40 to 80 range, you're most likely doing just fine.

In chapter 6, I gave you a tracking form to use during an exposure exercise. I definitely recommend using this form, rather than just "winging it," at least at first. Doing exposures without paying careful attention to your fear level is kind of like exercising without checking your pulse: you have no good way of knowing whether you're in the target zone.

The tracking form is also a helpful guide to let you know when it's time to end an exposure. As I mentioned in chapter 6, a good rule of thumb is to stay with an exposure until your fear level decreases by 50 percent or more from its peak—so if your fear level peaks at 80, you should stay with that exposure until your fear level comes down to 40 or lower. Remember, though, that there are always exceptions. If you've been doing an exposure for an hour without seeing a 50 percent reduction in your fear level, it's okay to stop and move on to the next item on your exposure hierarchy. Remember, a lot of research shows that even if you don't see within-session habituation, you can still get good results. So, shoot for a 50 percent reduction, but if it doesn't happen, don't sweat it.

The tracking form can also be a great way to watch yourself getting stronger over time. You might find that an exposure that initially caused your fear level to go up to 80 now only makes it go to 40—that's real progress! We'll get into some more progress-tracking strategies later on.

Problem Solving and Fine-Tuning

When I was working on getting rid of my love handles, I made nice progress for a good long time. My weight was coming down, my waistline was shrinking, and I even had to take my pants in to the tailor for alteration. Then the progress stopped. I had to figure out why. When I took a careful inventory of my behavior, I realized that I had started slacking off on my exercise program. I had also gotten back into the habit of snacking on unhealthy foods again (my wife's chocolate chip cookies are pretty hard to resist). Fortunately, because I detected the "stall" in my progress, I was able to take corrective action quickly. I laid off the cookies and resolved to be more disciplined about going to the gym. I started losing weight again, just as I had before.

The key issue here is the fact that by measuring my progress, by keeping track of what was happening, I was able to detect the problem early. If I hadn't been monitoring my weight on an ongoing basis, I might not have known that anything was wrong—or I might have discovered this fact much later, after my bad habits really had a chance to sink in and become entrenched. It turns out that the seemingly small (and sometimes tedious) task of writing my weight down had saved me a lot of time and effort and helped me get the most out of my weight-loss program.

Even when nothing was going wrong, tracking my weight—actually writing it down—helped me understand just how much work I needed to do. How drastically did I need to cut back on my calories? How hard-core did I need to be with the exercise? Ultimately, the best way to answer that question was to examine how my body was responding. If I wasn't losing weight or wasn't losing it fast enough, that was a sign that I needed to work harder. On the other hand, if my weight was coming down at a reasonable pace, this signaled to me that I was doing fine. Working harder at that point—for example, starving myself or going bonkers with the exercise—would have been unnecessary. In fact, it might have been worse than unnecessary, because it would have made the whole process more unpleasant, decreasing the likelihood that I would actually stick with it.

It's the same way with facing fears. If your fears are not decreasing, that could be a sign that you're not pushing yourself hard enough. On the other hand, if you see that your fears are indeed coming down and that you feel better, you can take that as a sign that you're doing it just right. Pushing yourself harder at that point might not only be unhelpful, it might even work against you by making the process more unpleasant than it needs to be. And if your progress stalls, as mine did, that's a sign that you need to take a critical look at what you're doing so that you can get back on track.

In the appendix is a form for you to track your progress. Notice that this is different from the form I gave you in chapter 6. That one was for tracking your fear level (0–100) within an exposure exercise. This one is to track your overall progress. I've laid it out so that you can track your progress for eight weeks, but remember that everyone is different. If your progress is substantially faster or slower than eight weeks, it's fine. In addition, you can always tweak this form or make your own so that it will be tailored to your needs. I use a Microsoft Excel spreadsheet and graph because I'm pretty comfortable with computers, but good old-fashioned paper and pencil work just fine, too.

You'll see that you are tracking the severity of your fear. This is not the same thing as the fear level, which goes from 0 to 100 and is designed to measure how you feel moment by moment. Here, I want you to take stock of how bad your fear is overall and rate it from 1 to 7, like this:

> During the last week, how severe is/are my _____
> (fear of specific situations or objects, fear of panic-like
> body sensations, social and performance fears, obsessive
> fears, excessive worries, post-traumatic fears)?

7. *Extreme*: Constant, intense distress, extreme avoidance, and/or incapacitating interference in my work, family, or social life.
6. *Severe*: Daily and intense fear, severe avoidance, and/or severe interference in my work, family, or social life.
5. *Marked*: Frequent (almost daily) and intense fear, noticeable avoidance, and/or significant interference in my work, family, or social life.

4. *Moderate*: Moderate distress most days of the week, moderate but manageable avoidance, and/or manageable interference in my work, family, or social life.
3. *Mild*: Occasional, low-level fear, minimal avoidance, and/or slight interference in my work, social, or family life.
2. *Borderline*: No more than minor fear, little to no avoidance, and/or occasional interference in my work, family, or social life.
1. *Normal*: No more fear, avoidance, or interference in my work, family, or social life than the average person experiences.

Start the process now by figuring out which number best describes your fear severity, create a graph, and put a mark over the word "Start" (see the illustration in the appendix). If you determine that your fear severity is 4 (moderate fear), make a mark on the graph that lines up with the number 4 over the word *Start*. Then do the same thing a week from now: decide what your fear severity is, and place a mark over the words *Week 1*. Do it again a week later over *Week 2*, and so on. Just as I weighed myself periodically to see how I was progressing, I want you to mark your graph so that you can see your own progress.

Troubleshooting: Slow Progress, Inconsistent Progress, or No Progress

Tracking allows you to see not only when things are going well but also when they're going not so well. This is a good thing. It's a cue to you that something about the process isn't working and that you have a problem to solve. Here are a couple of questions to ask yourself if you see slow, inconsistent, or no progress:

Am I still avoiding? That is, are you holding back from doing the scarier exposures?
Am I still doing safety behaviors? Even when they're subtle, they can sabotage your progress in a big way. (See chapter 7 for more details.)

Are my cognitive distortions going unchallenged? Are you repeat-edly engaging in probability overestimation? Catastrophizing? Black-or-white thinking? Intolerance of uncertainty? Need for control? If you don't identify these thoughts and really chal-lenge how you think, these negative messages in your head can keep you stuck and may undermine your progress. (See chapter 8 for more details.)

Am I doing the right exposures? Look at your exposure hierar-chy. Does it accurately reflect what you're really afraid of? Does it incorporate the truly scary elements of these situa-tions? (See chapter 5 for more details.)

One patient was making very nice progress for the first four weeks of the program. Her fear severity had gone from 6 (severe) to 3 (mild) fairly steadily. Yet after that, things seemed to stall a bit. Her fear severity wasn't going down and even seemed to go up for a while. Fortunately, because she was tracking her progress, she was able to take stock of her behavior and do a little trouble-shooting. She realized that she had been allowing some safety behaviors to creep back in. If you'll recall from chapter 7, those safety behaviors might make her feel less fearful in the short term (because, after all, they are comforting), but they keep her stuck in the long term. So she was using these safety behaviors to reduce her *fear level* in the moment, at the expense of keeping her overall *fear severity* high. When she got rid of her safety behaviors—that is, when she consciously and deliberately prioritized getting her *fear severity* down, even if that meant experiencing a high *fear level* in the short term, her progress resumed again (remember, short-term anxiety means long-term progress; short-term comfort means long-term problems).

Other people may experience a different kind of problem. Unlike the previous example, another patient had difficulties right from the start. He tried the exposure exercises, but his fear severity wasn't coming down and seemed to hover between 5 (marked) and 6 (severe). This told him that he needed to try something different. He noticed that his exposure exercises had been fairly modest, with peak fear levels around 50. He also noticed that even during the exposures, he was continuing to catastrophize, telling himself that he couldn't stand being this anxious. So he got to work on those trouble spots. He tried some more aggressive exposures, aiming for a peak fear level around 70 to 80. He also used the downward arrow strategy during the exposures, asking himself questions such as, "If I allowed myself to feel anxious, what would really happen? Would it be the end of the world? Or would my fear eventually subside?" With the combined strategy of stronger exposures and thinking more rationally, he started to see results.

> I kept track of my progress on a notepad on my desk at work because that is where I got the most anxiety. Eventually, I noticed that I wasn't reporting any serious anxiety! It motivated me to keep going.
>
> —*Susan*

Motivation Boost

Perhaps most important, tracking your progress is a powerful way to sustain your motivation to keep working on the program. Certainly, when I was trying to lose weight, I had times when I wanted to quit. Going to the gym took a lot of time and effort, and I can only eat so many low-calorie salads before I want to drop everything and find the cookie jar. So I know how important motivation is. Fortunately, when I weighed myself and tracked my progress on my chart, I felt a great sense of accomplishment that reminded me that it was worth it. I even rewarded myself by doing things that I found enjoyable (not by eating the cookies, though).

When you're facing your fears, you, too, might find that the time and effort involved, not to mention the considerable feelings of anxiety you'll experience, can put your motivation to the test.

To keep that motivation level high, you need to remind yourself visually of the progress you're making. As you watch that fear severity line go down, you'll know that your efforts are paying off, and you'll feel more motivated to stick with it. If you're comfortable doing so, use your graph as a way to show off your progress to friends or family members—their heartfelt congratulations will improve your motivation even more! Of course, you can and should reward yourself for all of your efforts. Take the time to pat yourself on the back or treat yourself to something enjoyable (provided that it doesn't involve avoidance or safety behaviors—your equivalent of my cookie jar).

Troubleshooting: Getting Discouraged

Sometimes progress is slow. Sometimes it's inconsistent. Sometimes it's completely absent. I can understand that if you track your progress and see a flat line (meaning the fear severity is not decreasing), this can be discouraging. Don't give up! It doesn't mean that the program won't work for you and certainly doesn't mean you should stop tracking your progress. Quite the opposite: when you track your progress, you can see clearly when things are working and when they're not. You've probably noticed, from the preceding several chapters, that there are lots of variations of exposure. You can go gradually or all at once; you can use in vivo or imaginal exposure; there are safety behaviors to give up; you can choose to challenge specific scary thoughts; and so on. When progress slows or stops, that's your cue to change strategies. Try something new. I know a patient who seemed "stalled" with moderate-level exposures, so she tried some harder ones and found that she did much better. Another patient couldn't figure out why the exposures weren't working, until she realized that she was performing subtle safety behaviors along with the exposures. After she decided to stop those behaviors, her progress picked up. Yet another woman found that the in vivo exposures weren't working very well, but when she added some imaginal exposures in which she vividly imagined the worst possible outcome of her exercises, she was able to start to get control over her fears.

More often than not, when you make key changes in how you're doing exposures, you'll find that this kick-starts your progress and gets you moving. In chapter 17, I have some additional strategies that you can use on an as-needed basis to supplement your exposure. Remember, slow progress simply means that there is a problem to be solved. You have the tools to solve it.

> I'd hate for anyone who considers doing this program to think that everything just marched along perfectly and at a steady pace. There were days when I felt as if I "just couldn't do it." There were other days when I got through some exposures more quickly than I had anticipated. It was often two steps forward, one step back. It zigged and zagged, but at least if I felt there was some movement in the forward direction, I would get up the next morning and choose to keep going. Seeing my progress truly helped on the days when it felt overwhelming.
>
> —*Rachel*

As I mentioned earlier, when my progress stalled, I realized that this was because I had started to "cheat." I wasn't exercising as much, and I had started to get into the cookies. Was there a part of me that would have liked to keep eating cookies? Of course. And just because I discovered what was wrong, that doesn't mean I immediately had the motivation to change it. Yet I took a mental step back, reminded myself of my ultimate goal and why that was important to me, and resolved to get back on track.

And so it might be with you, too. If and when you see inconsistent or slow progress, you will probably be able to make some educated guesses about what's wrong, but you might find that you need to take a mental step back in order to feel motivated to change those things. If so, take another look at chapter 3. If you took my advice and actually wrote down your answers on that worksheet in that chapter, good for you! That's going to come in handy now. If you didn't, it's never too late. How will life be if you accept the status quo? What might be possible if you keep going with the program and really push yourself?

16

The Long Run

There are very few monsters who warrant the fear we
have of them.

—*Andre Gide*

The chapters you've read so far and the exercises you've been
trying have all been designed with one central aim: to help
you free yourself from fear. You've learned about fear and
how it works. You've constructed an exposure hierarchy and have
been working on facing your fears in a gradual, systematic manner.
You've eliminated your unhelpful safety behaviors and addressed
inaccuracies in how you think about scary things. You're tracking
your fear severity over time, and hopefully you are pleased to see
that it's coming down. Your efforts are paying off!

These short-term gains are important, and you should congratulate yourself for them. I want to take a step back now and talk about
the bigger picture. After all, if you're going to invest your time and
energy into this program, I want it to pay off for you not only today
but tomorrow, the day after that, and so on, for the rest of your life.
Now that you've seen how the process works, and you've proved to

yourself that freedom from fear is indeed possible, how do you keep that fear under control over the long term? Once you've mastered a fear, how do you make sure it doesn't come back?

Let me start this discussion with a little preemptive decatastrophizing. Remember from chapter 2 that fear is perfectly normal and healthy. It's designed to save your life in case of a threat. No one is free from fear all of the time, nor should we be. There are some things, such as real and imminent danger, that we're supposed to be afraid of. Fear is your friend. Of course, it's possible to have too much of a good thing—and our friend fear is someone we'd like to see in moderation, rather than all of the time. Yet remember, the experience of fear itself is not necessarily a bad thing; it simply means you're human.

> Have I slipped? Yes, at times! But I quickly return to the proper track because I don't want my fear to beat me again. I don't avoid places or situations with my children, and if I realize that I am doing this, I can snap out of it quickly. I also talk to people about my fear—my openness with others not only validates that lots of people have fears and phobias, but it also keeps the process very real and alive for me, to keep encouraging my growth and to maintain all I have learned during the last few years.
>
> —*Michelle*

Yet sometimes fear can come back in a big way and may lead to more avoidance and problems in functioning. How does this happen? One thing we know is that fear is never "erased" from the brain, no matter how much exposure you do. Rather, exposure teaches you new ways to manage fear and new ways to think about things that scare you. In physical terms, your amygdala (the part of your brain that sounds the fear alarm) never does shut off completely; rather, your frontal cortex (the part of your brain that is involved with rational thinking) simply gets better and better at managing it.

Why does this matter? Because it means that once a fear has been learned, it is never really unlearned. Even people who have been extremely successful in beating their fears might find that the fears pop up from time to time throughout their lives. This is no reason to be discouraged. All significant behavioral change works this way. Perhaps you've experienced this personally, or maybe you've known someone who lost weight, quit smoking, or accomplished some other important change in his or her behavior. That person will tell you that slips happen. The weight, once lost, can start creeping back on, or an individual might start craving a cigarette after abstaining for months or even years. Does this mean that the person's initial success didn't really matter? Or that the program didn't work? Certainly not. It just means that, realistically, changing your behavior over the long run is hard and requires maintenance. In many respects, you're never really "done." The person who lost weight needs to make sure the weight doesn't come back; the person who quit smoking needs to be sure not to fall back into the habit; and you will need to make sure you keep beating your fear. In this chapter, I'll discuss ways to keep that fear under control in the long run.

> I have had my ups and downs. I have had little anxiety attacks here and there—but they don't keep me from going out or anything. I have come close, but I try to talk myself out of it. I think my fears are going to stick around a little bit, for the most part, because I am a hypochondriac, and my health is always going to be there. I live in my body, so it's hard to ignore it! I have gotten a lot better at identifying what I am scared of and at explaining to myself what is actually going on. I have become much better at helping myself—so it is not as frightening when I experience fear as it was before.
>
> —*Susan*

Psychologist Mark Bouton has been studying this phenomenon in animals for many years. His research suggests four basic ways that fear can return after successful treatment. They are (paraphrased):

1. *Fear-related traumatic experience*: Sometimes things simply don't go the way we expect them to, even with the best of planning. And sometimes the very thing you're working on—facing your fear—will go badly. If you're working on a fear of public speaking, someone might laugh inappropriately while you are giving a speech. If you're working on a fear of driving, you might get in a fender-bender. If you're working on a fear of spiders, a spider might bite you. These risks are usually small and are not a good reason not to do the exposure; however, if these things happen, be prepared for a return of fear.

2. *Fear-unrelated traumatic experience*: If something very frightening or painful happens, even if it's not directly related to your fear, you might find that your fear comes back. So, even though you've been working on, say, a fear of public speaking, an unrelated but scary experience such as a car accident can cause your fear of public speaking to get worse. It seems that simply experiencing a high level of fear, regardless of the reason, can "reactivate" your fear system—and because your brain is already predisposed to direct its fear reaction toward something (such as, say, public speaking), it will often choose that thing again as an outlet.

3. *Change of context*: If life throws a curveball at you and presents you with a frightening situation that is different from what you had practiced, your brain might be unprepared and may respond in a fearful manner. So, for example, if you are working on a fear of driving and have mastered driving around your neighborhood, you could find your fear returning the first time you have to drive in an unfamiliar place. Psychologist Susan Mineka and colleagues have shown that something as simple as changing rooms can trigger a return of fear. After conducting a

successful exposure therapy for a fear of spiders, she had some patients go back later to the same therapy room to approach a spider, while other patients went to a different room to approach a spider. The patients who were tested in a different room showed more of a return of fear (although, overall, they had still improved). This same group of researchers even demonstrated that how you feel inside can serve as a change of context. They conducted a similar study, but this time they had patients do exposure exercises with or without caffeine in their systems and then tested them later with or without caffeine. Sure enough, patients who changed internal contexts (exposure with caffeine and tested without caffeine, or exposure without caffeine and tested with caffeine) showed more of a return of fear than did patients whose exposure and testing were the same in terms of caffeine (either with or without).

4. *Time*: Sometimes, simply going a long time without doing exposures can allow fears to creep back in. Let's say you beat that fear of flying, and you're feeling pretty good. Yet it just so happens that you don't have to fly anywhere for the next year. When you finally do get on the plane after a year of not facing that fear, your brain can kind of forget what it has learned, and you could experience a fear reaction again.

So even after you've successfully beaten a fear, there is always a risk that fear-related traumatic experience, fear-unrelated traumatic experience, a change of context, or the passage of time can work against you and may lead to a return of fear. Let's start by discussing how to prevent fear from returning in the first place.

Sometimes I felt as if my fear was lingering in the wings, waiting for a chance to sneak back in. When that happened, I would turn and face it, and tell it to "Back off." I remembered the hell I'd been in and how I never, ever wanted to go back there again, so I would just start doing a mini-exposure with whatever was bothering me, and I'd do it long enough until the urge to perform a compulsive act was gone. It seems to me it was like ending a diet program . . . when faced with the challenges that might make one overeat and start old patterns again, what do you do? Give in and have a binge? Or realize where that might take you and choose to handle it another way? I found that if I "nipped it in the bud" as quickly as possible, the temptations to perform compulsive acts got fewer and fewer, until I realized one day that I hadn't been bothered by my fear in weeks, then months.

—Rachel

Preventing a Return of Fear

Making Exposures Work for You

The first strategies for preventing a return of fear involve the *amount* of exposure you do. As a general rule (and remember, there are exceptions to every rule), more is better.

Do Exposure Exercises a Lot

Especially early in the process, you should make a point to face your fears every day, even several times a day if you can. Once a week probably isn't going to cut it. When I talk to people whose fears have returned, I often find that these fears were only marginally controlled to begin with. Don't merely beat your fear; crush it!

Get Creative

Certain in vivo exposures, such as flying in airplanes, simply aren't possible for most of us to do regularly. Yet with a little creativity, you can still find a way to do mini-exposures, even when you can't afford the plane ticket. Watch movies about flying. Read about airplanes. Do imaginal exposures in which you vividly imagine yourself on a plane in severe turbulence. Similarly, some fears of catastrophic events (for example, a worry that someone will break into your home and harm you) can't really be addressed with direct exposure, but you can certainly face those fears indirectly and creatively. Keep a window open while you sleep. Try leaving the door unlocked if your neighborhood is reasonably safe. Do an imaginal exposure of a scary image of someone breaking in.

Make Your Exposures Long

Whenever possible, try to stay in exposures for a prolonged period of time. Remember the 50 percent rule I discussed earlier? That's the rule that tells you to stick with an exposure until your fear level has decreased by 50 percent or more. Follow it whenever possible. I know that sometimes it will seem unnecessary, and you'll say, "Oh, come on, my fear level has dropped by 25 percent, isn't that good enough? Can't I stop now?" You'll thank yourself later if you can stick with it until you get the full 50 percent reduction.

Stay with the Program

When you beat a fear, it's natural to say to yourself something like, "Woohoo! I'm all better! Now I can stop doing these exposures!" Research shows us that you'll get the best results in the long run if you keep going with the exposures. That is, even though you may feel as if your fear is gone, keep doing exposures anyway for good measure.

Doing Exposures

The next set of strategies involves *how* you do exposures. These points should be familiar to you, because I discussed them earlier in this book, but they're important enough to be worth repeating here.

Change Up the Exposures

Don't just expose yourself to one thing over and over again and expect long-lasting results. It's important to expose yourself to the full range of things that scare you. Let's take a fear of bugs as an example. If you made a point to catch a caterpillar in your backyard and are holding it, congratulations! That's a great thing to try. Yet understand that in doing so, you might not be addressing your fear of other kinds of bugs. It will be important that you keep going with the program and find different species of bugs to practice with.

Change Up the Context

Just as it's essential to change what you expose yourself to, it's equally important to change where, when, and how you conduct exposures. Let's stay with the fear of bugs for a moment. You're working on exposing yourself to multiple kinds of bugs, which is great, but also think about where you are doing your exposures. Have they all been in the backyard? If so, your brain might not be prepared for a chance encounter with a bug in the house. You need to take the exposures inside. Bring the bugs in and try the exposures in your kitchen, for example (be sure to release the bugs unharmed back into the yard when you're done). Have your exposures all been conducted during broad daylight? If so, try doing them at night. You're teaching your brain, "It's safe this way, too." Also, pay attention to your internal state. Do you do exposures only when you feel happy? Healthy? Mentally prepared? That's all well and good, but what's going to happen when you're faced with a challenging situation in a different circumstance? To be ready for it, you'll need to conduct exposures under multiple *internal* contexts as well. Do exposures when you feel bad. Do exposures when you have the flu. Do exposures when you're tired. Do exposures when you're stressed. Do exposures when you've been drinking caffeine. This way, you minimize the number of curveballs life can throw at you.

Stay in the Zone

Remember that there's an optimal working zone on the fear level scale. If your fear level is too low, you're probably not accomplishing much. If it's too high, you're probably making the process more unpleasant than it needs to be. Shoot for a fear level that is moderate to high but not extreme. You'll probably find that the more you can stay in the correct fear zone, the better results you'll get over the long term.

Keeping Fears Gone for Good

Finally, let's take a look at what steps you can use, going forward, to prevent the return of fear after you've completed this program.

Don't Let Safety Behaviors Come Back

Remember from chapter 7 that safety behaviors are like crutches: helpful if you really and truly need them but completely unhelpful otherwise. If you've been performing safety behaviors for a long time, you might find that they're a hard habit to break. Yet it is absolutely necessary that you watch for them and don't let them back into your life. Imagine someone who needs crutches for a while because of a broken leg. Eventually, she gets her cast taken off, starts walking again, and strengthens her leg muscles. So far, so good. But now let's imagine that one day she says to herself, "Gee, I'm really tired today. Let me get those old crutches out of the closet, just this once." So she does, and perhaps she even feels a bit better. Yet when she starts to use her crutches again unnecessarily, her leg muscles will start to wither away again. So it is with beating fear. You have been strengthening your "courage muscles"—the skills you need to cope with scary situations—and you don't want those skills to wither away. Keep the crutches—your safety behaviors—in the closet, even when you're tempted.

> My fears never left completely. I have to make a conscious effort to try to dismiss my fears, force myself to attend social functions, and interact with people. The more I do it, the easier it gets.
>
> —*Steven*

Keep an Eye on Your Thinking

Cognitive distortions are habits, too. In chapter 8, we reviewed several of these, including probability overestimation, catastrophizing, black-or-white thinking, intolerance of uncertainty, and need for control. This isn't an exhaustive list, and perhaps by now you've identified some other ways in which your thinking might be "off." Just like any other habits, these cognitive distortions can creep back into your life, too. When they do, the result can be a gradual return of fear. So even after you've "finished" this program, it's important to catch these cognitive distortions whenever they come up and work to correct them, rather than simply let them lie.

Make Exposure a Way of Life

At the beginning of this chapter, I mentioned that you're never really done when it comes to beating fears. In the last chapter, I told you a little about my efforts to lose weight. I got the weight off, felt a whole lot better, and congratulated myself on a job well done. So, was I finished? Nope. Ongoing weight management is a lifelong practice and requires permanent changes to my lifestyle. From now on, I have to watch what I eat and make sure to exercise. I can't go back to my old way of doing things. For me, as with other people who want to keep the weight off in the long run, it's necessary to make weight management a long-term priority. I don't want to be a "yo-yo dieter" who thinks of weight management as something one does for discrete periods in discrete ways. I have to act like a healthy person from here on out. So it is with you. Ongoing freedom from fear, like any other major change, takes long-term efforts, and you may well find that you have to make important, perhaps even major, changes to your lifestyle in order to hang onto your progress. Just as I have to act like a healthy person from here on out, you have to act like a courageous person from here on out—and then you will be one. Your task, therefore, is to take every opportunity to do what used to scare you, whenever you can. Here are only a few examples:

I overcame a . . .	*Now I have to . . .*
Fear of public speaking	Speak up in meetings, give toasts at parties, offer to do presentations at work—in short, take every opportunity to speak in front of others.
Fear of driving	Offer to drive when going out with friends, plan driving vacations, go for recreational drives on weekends—in short, take every opportunity to drive.
Fear of snakes or spiders	Clean the basement; walk on the grass, rather than on the pavement; visit museums with animal exhibits; go camping—in short, take every opportunity to come into contact with snakes or spiders.
Fear of flying	Schedule vacations that require air travel, offer to fly to meetings or conferences for work, plan to visit friends or family members who live far away—in short, take every opportunity to fly.
Fear of contamination	Volunteer at a hospital, plant a garden, use public restrooms, clean up after pets—in short, take every opportunity to become contaminated.
Fear of something bad happening to my loved ones	Sign my kids up for sports and attend their games, encourage my family members to go out on their own, even praise them for taking some reasonable risks—in short, take every opportunity to cope with risk.

| Fear of traumatic memories | Volunteer at a veteran's hospital, a women's shelter, or the Red Cross; read (or even write) books about subjects that are related to my experience; plan recreational activities in the area where the event occurred—in short, take every opportunity to face the memories and master them. |

You may need to come up with your own lifestyle changes, but hopefully you get the basic idea. If you think of exposures as an "exercise," as something you do for a while and then stop, you'll probably do less of them. You'll also probably limit the context of your exposures, increasing the likelihood that your fear will return. Instead, try to think of exposures not only as something you do but as part of who you are. You used to be an "avoider." Now try being an "approacher." You used to shy away from activities that frightened you; now I want you to seek them out and embrace them. This way, exposure is an integral part of your daily activities, not merely something you do at specified times during the day.

Prepare for Challenges by Remembering the Program

Sometimes you know that a challenge is coming up. Perhaps you have a public speech scheduled or you're about to get on an airplane. It's important to psych yourself *up*, rather than psych yourself *out*. Instead of worrying about how hard it's going to be and telling yourself you can't do it, remind yourself: This is what I've been practicing. I can do it. Mentally walk yourself through the exposure exercises you did, and remember your successes.

> ## Quick Guidelines for Preventing the Return of Fear
>
> - *Make your exposures longer than you think you need to.* Even after your fear level has decreased, keep it going a bit longer.
> - *Do lots of exposures.* Do them whenever you can, wherever you can, even after you feel as if you've beaten your fear.
> - *Do exposures often.* Try to do at least one exposure exercise a day. Don't spread them out too much.
> - *Don't distract yourself or use safety behaviors.* These things simply get in the way of learning not to be afraid.
> - *Expose yourself to lots of scary things and situations.* For example, if you're afraid of spiders, do exposures with a variety of different spiders, not only one.
> - *Expose yourself in many different environments and contexts.* Do your exposure exercises in multiple places, under varying circumstances—not only when you feel fine.
> - *Keep your exposures challenging but not extreme.* Remember that exposures are most effective when your fear level is moderate to high.
> - *Remember your program.* If you know that a challenge is coming up, remember the good work you've done and remind yourself that you can do it.
> - *Watch for cognitive distortions.* Probability overestimation, catastrophizing, and other unhelpful ways of thinking can creep back in, so be sure to catch and correct them when they do.
> - *Make exposure a way of life.* Don't think of this only as a "program" or an exercise. Instead, think about how to integrate exposure into your ongoing lifestyle.

Coping with Setbacks

Sometimes, despite your best efforts, slip-ups do happen. There's a good chance that I will find myself dipping into the cookie jar at some point in the future, and there's a good chance that successful fear beaters will occasionally feel increased fear or will fall back into avoidant patterns. This isn't terrible. Remember from chapter 2 that anxiety and fear are very normal, even adaptive, emotions. Remember as well from chapter 3 that more than a quarter of the population has, or has had, a diagnosable anxiety disorder. So I think I can safely predict that you'll feel anxious and afraid at some point. What is important is how you react to that fear when it comes.

Researchers who study recovery from alcohol and drug problems have identified what they call the "abstinence violation effect" in their patients. In treatment, these patients are told to stop drinking or using drugs, and that's sensible. Yet setbacks do happen, and people slip up. Some patients get back on the wagon after these setbacks, and others spiral down into their old habits. Why do some people bounce back from setbacks and others don't? It seems that whenever people believe that they must abstain from substances all of the time, forever, and that there will be terrible consequences if they fail to meet this goal, they are setting themselves up for failure. Slip-ups happen, and when they do, someone with this black-or-white mind-set is likely to think, "Oh, no, I've failed! What's the point of even trying?" Thus, a setback (a temporary glitch in your progress) spirals into a relapse (a long-term return to your old way of doing things).

For people who have beaten their fears, when setbacks occur in the form of increased fear or avoidant behaviors, it is important not to fall into this pattern of black-or-white thinking. Psychologist Lars-Göran Öst has come up with some very handy instructions for coping with a return of fear, which I'll paraphrase here:

- *Remind yourself that a return of fear is normal and predictable.* It's not a disaster. Everyone experiences fear at least some of the time.
- *Remind yourself that fear does not mean you've had a relapse.* Rather, a setback is a temporary failure to manage a situation that you have managed before.

- *Restrict the setback.* If you start to feel fearful of one situation, try not to let the fear spread to other situations.
- *Get back in there.* As soon as you can, reenter the situation or the activity that's frightening you. Continued avoidance only makes things worse. Stay in the situation until you feel better.
- *Use appropriate coping strategies.* When you face your fears, remember to think realistically and stay away from distraction and safety behaviors.
- *Try something easier.* If you just don't feel up to reentering the scary situation, that's fine—try a lower-level exposure, and work your way back up to the scary situation.
- *Make a public commitment.* Family and friends can be a great resource in your battle against fear. If you can, tell your loved ones about your exercises and how important it is for you to face your fears. Ask for their help and support.

Focus on Functioning

I've saved the best (well, at least in my humble opinion) for last. Want to really beat these fears and keep them under control for the long term? Then you'll need to make a conscious effort to extend your progress beyond mere fear reduction. Decreased fear and avoidance are great, but ultimately these changes need to translate into improved functioning.

Go back and look at the worksheet at the end of chapter 3. There, you listed what the future holds for you if you face your fears. It's time to turn that imagined future into a reality. Think about what you've been unable to do because of fear. Think about what opportunities you've passed up or the subtle (or not-so-subtle) handicaps you've put up with because of fear. Now make a plan to reclaim those aspects of your life, now and forever. What will your new life look like? Will you get a new job? Have an improved social life? Go back to school? Engage in more activities with your family? It's not for me to say what your life should include; that's your decision. Yet I do want you to identify at least one specific aspect of your life in which you intend to function better, not merely feel better. If there's any magic bullet to long-term fear beating, this is it. It's hard, but don't skip it!

At the end of the chapter is a sample form I'd like you to re-create in your notebook and fill out. Write down your specific functional goals, and list the concrete steps you intend to take toward those goals.

Here's a completed example:

My Fear-Free Life Plan

Specific Functional Goal(s) I Will Pursue:
1. Go back to work
2. Start dating again
3. Travel

Concrete Steps I Will Take toward My Goal(s):
Goal 1
- Update my resume
- Network with my old colleagues
- Look through classified ads

Goal 2
- Join a social club
- Agree to go out with friends to places where I might meet people
- Research online dating sites

Goal 3
- Pick a location to visit
- Talk to a travel agent to make plans
- Purchase a ticket and make hotel arrangements

Now it's your turn. What functional goals will you pursue in your fear-free life? What specific steps will you take toward those goals?

```
My Fear-Free Life Plan
Specific Functional Goal(s) I Will Pursue:
1.
2.
3.

Concrete Steps I Will Take toward My Goal(s):
Goal 1
    •
    •
    •

Goal 2
    •
    •
    •

Goal 3
    •
    •
    •
```

A sample of the fear-free life plan.

Supplementing the Face Your Fears Program

Courage is not the absence of fear, but rather the judgment that something else is more important than fear.

—*Ambrose Redmoon*

My sincere hope is that this program will point you toward a fear-free future and will give you the tools that you need to beat your fear, once and for all. I would like nothing more than for this program to be the last thing you have to do to stay healthy. I am confident that if you follow the instructions in this book and really work hard at it, you'll obtain results that can transform your life.

That having been said, I realize that everyone is a bit different, and there's no "one size fits all" solution. No program can benefit everyone, and I have seen some people who simply don't get better, despite their best efforts. More frequently, I have seen people who just can't dedicate the time, energy, and motivation that are necessary to make exposure therapy work. I know that if you're like many people with anxiety-related problems, even when you do see success, you might still have some lingering fears that just don't seem to go away. If you find that you're still experiencing anxiety and fear even after trying this program, this chapter is for you. I'll describe some specific strategies to supplement your exposure program.

Strategy 1: Try Again

Trying again may seem like a no-brainer recommendation, but it's worth considering. Before you search for alternative strategies, I'd like you to take a good, hard look back at the work you've done so far in your exposure therapy program. Specifically,

- *Did you incorporate exposures that really get at your fear?* Remember, an exposure works only if it truly targets what you're afraid of.
- *Were your exposures in the target zone?* Exposures that are not scary enough don't accomplish much; exposures that are too scary probably make you needlessly uncomfortable and make you less likely to stick with the program.
- *Did you do enough exposures?* For exposures to work, you need to do them as much as you can, at least once a day, if at all possible. It's also important to get as much variety in your exposures and their contexts as you can.
- *Were your exposures long enough?* It's important to stay with an exposure until your fear level decreases by 50 percent or more, if possible.
- *Did you get rid of your safety behaviors?* Performing even subtle safety behaviors can make the exposures less effective.

If your answer to any of these questions was no, then it seems that you haven't given exposure therapy a fair shot. This program can work for you, but it takes effort. Consider rededicating your-self to beating your fears and giving it your all. I know you can do it!

Strategy 2: Clear a Path in Your Life

Sometimes life gets chaotic. People lose jobs. Relationships begin and end. Loved ones get sick. Bills pile up. When things like this are going on, it can be awfully hard to find the time and the men-tal energy you need to focus on beating your fears. So take a moment and think about what else is going on in your life. Is there room in your life right now to make facing fear a priority? If there isn't, no program is likely to be very helpful to you right now. So you have a couple of options. First, you could always delay this program until life settles down a bit. As long as you're not signifi-cantly caving in to fear-related avoidance or using life stress as an excuse not to face your fears, there's no harm in putting this book on a shelf for the time being and returning to it after some other aspects of your life have gotten under control—for example, if you're in the middle of a relationship breakup or you have a seri-ously ill relative, it's perfectly fine to wait a while before restarting your exposure program.

The other strategy is to deliberately and purposefully clear a path in your life for beating fear. Although some stressors, such as a dissolving relationship, will eventually stabilize one way or the other, other stressors might not. You might have a permanently busy job, with no relief in sight. Or you might have young kids who require a lot of attention and energy. When these kinds of stressors are competing for your time and attention, simply wait-ing for the situation to resolve is unlikely to help. Therefore, you might need to take more assertive action toward making room in your life so that you can work on your fears. Are there any tasks that you can delegate to others, at least temporarily? Can you put off anything for a little while so that you can make yourself stron-ger? Can you rearrange your schedule a bit? Can you get others to agree to give you a little personal time while you work on your program? Usually, if beating your fear is a true priority for you, it's possible to clear a path—but it will take work and dedication.

Strategy 3: Use Exposure Boosters

Certain strategies can be added to exposure therapy to make it more effective, at least for some people. These strategies aren't meant to be replacements for exposure; rather, they're intended to augment what you're already doing.

Skill Building

Sometimes, overcoming a fear requires more than simply facing it. For some people, it's equally important to make sure that they have and can use the appropriate skills that are necessary to manage the situation. Let's take the example of someone who is afraid to drive. An exposure program would probably be a good idea for this person, and as you can probably imagine, we'd encourage him to create an exposure hierarchy, ranking different driving scenarios according to his fear level, and to work his way up the hierarchy, staying away from safety behaviors and watching for cognitive distortions. Sounds like a great idea—but what if, in addition to being a fearful driver, he is also an *unskilled* driver? It's not hard to imagine, especially when you know how often fear and avoidance are linked. Someone with intense fears of driving might not have spent much time behind the wheel and therefore may never have learned to drive well. In that case, an exposure plan might not do much good (and could even be dangerous) all by itself. In order to beat the fear, therefore, this person needs not only to face the fear with exposures, but to work on building up his driving skills—for example, by enrolling in driver's education classes.

The same thing can be said of many people with social and performance fears. Speaking in front of others is a skill that can be learned. Some people are truly gifted speakers, with a natural charisma and flow to their presentations. Others, not so much. Now, it's not necessary for a person to be the world's greatest speaker in order to feel okay about giving a speech, but it certainly helps to have at least a minimal skill level. Otherwise, a straightforward program of exposure therapy might actually be setting this person up for a negative experience—speeches might go badly because of his lack of skill, leading him to feel even worse. In cases like this, I often recommend that people join organizations such as Toastmasters, which are specifically designed to help people learn and practice the fundamentals of public speaking in a supportive and friendly environment.

Some people with excessive worries find it difficult to solve problems. They seem to get overwhelmed easily and have a hard time figuring out what to do when problems, even small ones, come up. So instead of solving problems, they often resort to worrying about the problems so that they feel as if they're doing something productive. Of course, when we step back and look at this pattern, we can see that it makes no sense—worrying is not a good substitute for problem solving. Well, problem solving is a skill, too, just as driving and public speaking are. Some people are really good problem solvers, whereas others might be lacking in this skill. Yet just like every other skill, problem solving can be learned and practiced. Psychologists Arthur and Christine Nezu developed a training program for problem solving that may come in very handy for people who need to learn this skill. They break the problem-solving process into these discrete steps:

- *Define the problem.* The philosopher Charles Kettering is quoted as saying, "A problem well-defined is a problem half solved." Often, it's hard to define exactly what the problem is, and there seems to be problem on top of another problem on top of yet another problem, in a big jumbled mess. So the first step is to slow it down and define, as clearly and succinctly as possible, what the problem is. Stick to the facts.

- *Generate possible solutions.* This step involves brainstorming, which means using your creativity to come up with as many possible solutions to the problem as you can. Don't judge or critique them just yet; that comes next. For now, go for quantity over quality, even if the solutions seem ridiculous.
- *Select the best solution.* Start to narrow down the brainstorming list by eliminating solutions that are unrealistic or impossible. Get rid of any that would likely not be helpful or would cause more problems than they would solve.
- *Carry out the solution.* Make a plan to actually implement your chosen solution. If necessary, pick a specific day and time to do it.
- *Evaluate the outcome.* Determine whether the solution was helpful. Did the problem you identified actually get better? If so, congratulate yourself. If not, make sure that you defined the problem accurately, and go back to your list of possible solutions for more options.

Relaxation

I know, I know. I just got through making a big speech in chapter 7 about how relaxation isn't very helpful. For most people, it isn't, and for people with a fear of body sensations, it can even lessen the effectiveness of exposure therapy. But, as I've said before, all rules have their exceptions. I have seen some people who seemed to benefit from relaxation exercises. In particular, people with excessive worries and a persistently high overall level of anxiety and tension might do well with some relaxation. So I add it here as a supplemental alternative, with the warning that it's not a substitute for exposure, and if you have a fear of panic-like body sensations—that is, you tend to catastrophize or overreact to your own physical signs of anxiety—relaxation exercises are probably not for you.

In the early twentieth century, physician Edmund Jacobson developed a program called progressive muscle relaxation (PMR).

The basic idea behind PMR is to tense, then relax, the muscles of the body in a step-by-step fashion. These steps not only make the body feel calmer, but they can also help promote mental and emotional calmness. There are lots of variations of PMR, but here is a relatively straightforward one.

- *Setting.* Find a quiet room where you won't be disturbed. Turn off the ringer on your phone. Sit in a comfortable chair, or lie down.
- *Quiet.* Sit quietly for a few moments. Notice how you are feeling and what thoughts are in your head, but don't try to change them just now.
- *Tense.* Make a fist with your right hand and squeeze it tightly. Hold it like that for about ten seconds. Notice what all of the muscles in your hand feel like. Be aware of what it feels like for these muscles to be tense.
- *Relax.* Relax your hand. Let all of the tension go. Notice what it feels like for the muscles to relax, and see how much better that feels. Let the hand become loose and floppy.
- *Repeat.* Now do the same tense-and-relax cycle for each of the following muscle groups, one by one:
  - Tense and relax your left hand.
  - Tense and relax your right hand.
  - Tense and relax your bicep muscles (both sides).
  - Tense and relax your chest muscles.
  - Tense and relax your neck and shoulders.
  - Tense and relax your nose, forehead, and jaw.
  - Tense and relax your stomach muscles.
  - Tense and relax your buttock muscles.
  - Tense and relax your thigh muscles (both legs).
  - Tense and relax your calf muscles (both legs).
  - Tense and relax your feet.
- *Breathe.* Spend about five minutes paying attention to your breathing. Try to breathe slowly and evenly, rather than

deeply. For most people, about four seconds to inhale and about six seconds to exhale is a good pace.

- *Practice.* Like so many other things, PMR is a skill that has to be learned and practiced. It might feel awkward or weird at first, but if you make a point of practicing this skill every day (or more frequently, if possible), you'll find that it becomes easier and more natural.

Applied Tension

This strategy is helpful for the approximately 50 percent of people with a fear of blood and injections who tend to faint when they are exposed to frightening things. The technical term for this kind of fainting is *vasovagal syncope,* and it comes from a sudden drop in blood pressure, which results in blood pooling in the legs (due to gravity). When blood pools in the legs, it's diverted away from your brain, which leads to fainting. Vasovagal syncope is not usually dangerous, but, as you might imagine, exposure doesn't work very well if you're unconscious! The solution to vasovagal syncope is called "applied tension," systematically tensing the muscles of your body to prevent blood from pooling in your legs.

One note of caution: applied tension is useful only for people who really faint during exposure. Nearly all of the time, these will be people with blood- and injection-related fears. Lots of people might *feel as if* they're about to faint (those of you with a fear of body sensations, listen up), but they rarely actually faint. For those people, their fear of fainting represents a probability overestimation, rather than a true likelihood of fainting, and applied tension would not really help matters. It could merely serve as a safety behavior. So if you really and truly faint—that is, you reliably lose consciousness during exposure—use applied tension. If you don't reliably faint (or have fainted only once or twice), but merely *fear* that you will faint, treat applied tension as you treat all other safety behaviors—stay away from it.

In their book *Overcoming Medical Phobias: How to Conquer Fear of Blood, Needles, Doctors and Dentists*, psychologists Martin Antony and Mark Watling describe a method of practicing applied tension, which I'll paraphrase here.

- Find a comfortable position in a quiet spot, where you won't be distracted. You can be sitting in a chair or lying down, whichever feels best to you.
- Tense the muscles in your legs, arms, and torso. Hold the tension until you feel a warm feeling or a "rush" in your head, usually ten to fifteen seconds.
- Relax the muscles and rest for thirty seconds.
- Repeat this process four more times.

Another way to prevent fainting during exposure is to sit or lie in a reclining position. If you have fears of blood, injections, or blood draws, and you are prone to fainting, it's perfectly fine to ask your doctor or lab technician to allow you to lie down during the procedure.

Strategy 4: Consider Disorder-Specific Self-Help Programs

As I mentioned in chapter 1, this book is intended to be transdiagnostic, meaning it is meant to apply to a wide range of people with a variety of different fears. There are pros and cons to taking this approach; one con is that there might be subtle aspects of specific anxiety disorders that get missed. For example, there are many subtypes of obsessive-compulsive disorder and specific phobias that I haven't discussed in this book. Similarly, many subtleties of posttraumatic stress disorder, generalized anxiety disorder, and social phobia might require extra attention. I've designed this book to hit the main points that should be common to all of these disorders. If you find that this program isn't quite doing the trick, however, you might want to consider a workbook that is more tailored to your specific problem (see the Resources section at the back of this book).

Strategy 5: Seek Professional Therapy

Although self-directed treatment can help many people, some problems are just too entrenched or too complex to solve by yourself. Furthermore, many people with anxiety-related problems also suffer from other mental health concerns, such as depression or substance use, which might require a more comprehensive approach to treatment. Sometimes you simply need to call in a pro. So, how do you go about finding the right professional to help you? The Yellow Pages or the Internet will give you a dizzying array of clinicians, with a variety of specialties and backgrounds, but not much information to help you pick one. Here are some general suggestions to guide you.

Select a Professional with Expertise in Cognitive-Behavioral Therapy (CBT)

This will narrow down the pack substantially. The program in this book is based on CBT, and it makes sense to select a professional with compatible expertise. Besides, as you already know from chapter 3, CBT is the most evidence-based treatment for anxiety-related problems.

Consider Individual vs. Group Therapy

There is ample research showing that fear-based problems can be treated very effectively using individual (one-on-one) therapy, group therapy, or both. Many people with fear problems like going to groups because it helps them feel less alone to speak with other people who are suffering from the same issues. Others find group therapy helpful because it requires them to interact with other people—which is beneficial if they have social or performance fears. Group therapy is often less expensive than individual therapy, as well. If you decide to join a therapy group, however, make sure that it's a CBT-based group and that the other people in the group are really struggling with the same kind of problems that you are. Teaming up with others to work on the problem is a great idea; sitting around talking to people with whom you have little in common is not so great.

Decide What Kind of Professional You Want

Many different types of clinicians can provide CBT competently. Here are some basic descriptions that apply to many (but certainly not all) of these professionals.

- *Psychologists.* In most US states, psychologists have doctoral degrees (usually a Ph.D. or a Psy.D.) from graduate programs approved by the American Psychological Association. Clinical psychologists also have a one-year clinical internship, and one to two years of supervised postdoctoral experience are generally required to receive a license. Psychologists must also pass a national and a state examination to become licensed.

- *Clinical social workers.* A clinical social worker must have a college degree, plus at least two years of graduate training in a program accredited by the Council on Social Work Education. Certified social workers have a master's or a doctoral degree in social work (usually an MSW or a Ph.D.) from graduate programs approved by the Council on Social Work Education, have had two years of postdegree experience in the practice of social work, and must have passed an examination given by the Academy of Certified Social Workers (ACSW).

- *Psychiatrists.* Psychiatrists are medical doctors, usually with an M.D. or a D.O. degree. Most (but not all) have had a five-year residency program in psychiatry after medical school. Psychiatrists who have board certification have had two years of postresidency experience practicing psychiatry and must have passed an examination given by the American Board of Psychiatry and Neurology.

Psychiatrists can prescribe medication; relatively few are trained to provide CBT.

- *Professional counselors.* Professional counselors usually have master's degrees (most often an M.A. or an M.S.) from an accredited university. Certified counselors typically have graduate training in counseling and must have passed an examination given by the National Board of Certified Counselors.

Look for Professionals in Your Area

As you can probably guess, simply going online and searching for "therapist" won't necessarily bring you to the right person. Instead, try one or more of these strategies:

- The Association for Cognitive and Behavioral Therapies (www.abct.org) has an online search tool that allows you to narrow your search by state and by areas of expertise.
- The American Board of Professional Psychology (www.abpp .org), the National Register of Health Service Providers in Psychology (www.nationalregister.org), and the National Association of Social Workers (www.naswdc.org) have online search tools for psychologists and social workers that allow you to narrow your search by location.
- Call the university psychology, social work, or medical school psychiatry departments in your area and ask for a referral.
- Call your local community mental health center and ask whether there is a CBT therapist on staff.
- Ask for recommendations from your family physician, friends, and relatives.

Ask the Right Questions

During your initial telephone or in-person conversation with the clinician, it's important to get enough information to decide whether this is the right person to treat you. Any competent and honest clinician should answer these questions readily; if not, consider looking elsewhere. Ask questions such as

- What are your training and qualifications?
- How much experience do you have treating problems like mine?
- What is your level of expertise in cognitive-behavioral therapy?
- What goals will we pursue in treatment?
- What approach or strategies are you likely to recommend?
- What are the costs of treatment? Do you accept my health insurance?
- What is the likely time frame of treatment? How frequently will we meet, and how long will our meetings be?

Strategy 6: Consider Medications

Finally, some people will benefit from adding medications to their program of exposure therapy. Although it might make intuitive sense that adding one good treatment (medications) to another good treatment (exposure) would give you much better results than would either treatment alone, the scientific findings have been inconsistent on this topic. Some studies have indeed shown that patients who receive medications with exposure therapy make more progress than do patients who receive exposure therapy alone. Other studies, however, suggest that adding a medication doesn't improve the results of exposure therapy for the average person. This is one reason that I don't automatically recommend that everyone take a medication. Another reason for caution is the side effects. All medications have them, and they can range from mild to serious. Most people don't experience serious side effects, and taking medications is not a big deal. Personally, though, I prefer not to expose someone to potential side effects unless it's necessary that we have to (that is, the benefits clearly outweigh the costs).

If you find that your exposure program by itself isn't helping as much as it should, it might make sense to consult with a physician (this can be your primary-care physician or a psychiatrist) about starting a medication. In the following list are some of the more commonly used medications for anxiety-related problems. Bear in mind that this is only a partial list. There are many more medications that are used for anxiety and a lot more information (both good and bad) about each medication that I did not include here. If you want to try a medication, I recommend that you

Medication Class	Examples	FDA Indications for Anxiety Disorders	Most Common Side Effects	Comments
Selective serotonin reuptake inhibitors (SSRIs)	Fluoxetine (Prozac) Paroxetine (Paxil) Sertraline (Zoloft)	Panic disorder Obsessive-compulsive disorder Social phobia Posttraumatic stress disorder Generalized anxiety disorder	Nausea Dizziness Headaches Sexual dysfunction Insomnia Agitation Anxiety	SSRIs may be associated with increased suicidal thinking and behavior, especially in children and adolescents.
Serotonin-norepinephrine reuptake inhibitors (SNRIs)	Desvenlafaxine (Pristiq) Duloxetine (Cymbalta) Venlafaxine (Effexor)	Panic disorder Social phobia Generalized anxiety disorder	Decreased appetite Weight loss Insomnia Agitation Anxiety	Sexual side effects may be somewhat less in SNRIs than in SSRIs. People with high blood pressure should be monitored carefully. SNRIs may be associated with increased suicidal thinking and behavior, especially in children and adolescents.
Tricyclic antidepressants (TCAs)	Amitriptyline (Elavil) Clomipramine (Anafranil) Imipramine (Tofranil)	Indicated only for obsessive-compulsive disorder (clomipramine); however, a good deal of research suggests that TCAs can be effective for a range of anxiety problems.	Dry mouth and nose Blurry vision Constipation Cognitive impairment Dizzy spells Weight gain	TCAs are not commonly used as a first-line treatment for anxiety because of less favorable side effects, compared to SSRIs or SNRIs. Overdose can be fatal.

Benzodiaze-pines	Alprazolam (Xanax) Clonazepam (Klonopin) Lorazepam (Ativan) Diazepam (Valium)	Anxiety (broadly) Panic disorder	Drowsiness Dizziness Impaired con-centration Impaired coordination	Benzodiazepines carry some risk of addiction. In addition, "as-needed" use of benzodiazepines may reduce the effectiveness of exposure therapy. Can have severe interactions with alcohol.
Monoamine oxidase inhibitors (MAOIs)	Phenelzine (Nardil) Selegiline (Emsam) Tranylcypro-mine (Par-nate) Isocarboxa-zid (Mar-plan)	None	Insomnia Dizziness Lightheaded-ness and low blood pres-sure	MAOIs may be useful for some patients with severe social phobia. They are not commonly used as a first-line treat-ment for anxiety because of the need for signifi-cant dietary restriction (certain foods can trigger severe elevations in blood pressure) and the risk of drug interactions.
Gamma-aminobu-tyric acid (GABA) analogues	Gabapentin (Neuron-tin) Pregabalin (Lyrica)	None	Dizziness Drowsiness Weight gain Impaired coordination	Preliminary research sug-gests that GABA ana-logues might be useful for social phobia and generalized anxiety disorder.
Beta-adren-ergic blockers (beta blockers)	Propranolol (Inderal)	None	Diarrhea or constipation Dizziness or lightheaded-ness Drowsiness or fatigue	Beta blockers may be helpful for time-limited performance anxiety (e.g., public speaking).
Atypical anxiolytics	Buspirone (BuSpar)	Generalized anxiety disorder	Dizziness Nausea Headache Nervousness Lightheaded-ness	Buspirone may be less sedating than some other medications.
Cognitive enhancers	D-cycloser-ine (Sero-mycin)	None	Drowsiness Cognitive impairment Nausea	Preliminary research sug-gests that although d-cycloserine does not reduce anxiety, it might make exposure therapy more effective when used concurrently.

educate yourself about the medication you are considering, by talking with your doctor, as well as looking at the package insert and/or Internet sites such as www.webmd.com or www.drugs .com.

If you find that this book alone doesn't give you the results you need, don't worry. People are different, and no one treatment is effective for everyone. Often, finding the right treatment or treatment combination involves a process of trial and error. It may be that the solution is as simple as recommitting yourself to work hard on the program, or you might need to augment your program with some of the exposure-boosting strategies described in this chapter. If going it alone just isn't working, there is always the option of obtaining CBT or medication from a trained professional. The bottom line, however, is that I do believe there is a right treatment for everyone.

Now the ball is in your court. It's up to you to face these fears and beat them. You have the tools that you need—gradual exposure, restricting safety behaviors, and addressing scary thinking patterns—and you know how and where to get additional help if you need it. It's my sincere hope that you'll feel a whole lot better after you use this program and that you'll let me know how you're doing (at the time of this writing, I can be found on Facebook, Twitter, and www.drtolin.com). I wish you the best of success in your life beyond fear.

Appendix

The list below shows a breakdown of the costs of anxiety disorders in the United States, in billions of dollars (although the study was conducted in 1999, I have converted the amounts to 2010 dollars).* Most of the costs are due to nonpsychiatric medical treatment. That is, individuals with anxiety disorders have a tendency to overutilize primary-care physicians as well as specialists, such as cardiologists, gastroenterologists, and emergency room physicians.

Direct nonpsychiatric treatment costs	$36.5 billion
Mortality costs	$1.9 billion
Total workplace costs	$6.5 billion
Direct pharmaceutical costs	$1.2 billion
Direct psychiatric treatment costs	$21.1 billion
Total	**$67.2 billion**

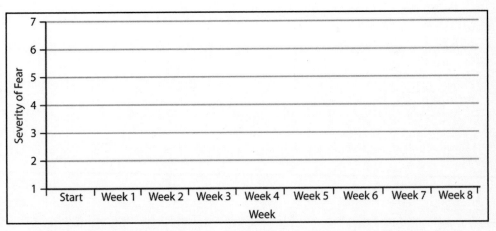

A sample form to track your progress. See the section "Pacing and Calibration" in chapter 15 for the discussion.

---

*Greenberg, P.E., et al. (1999). The economic burden of anxiety disorders in the 1990s. *Journal of Clinical Psychiatry*, 60, 427–435.

Notes

Chapter 2: What Is Fear?

31 *"Captain! The ship can't take much more of this!"* Eddie Murphy, *Delirious* (Home Box Office, 1983).

36 *the odds of being involved* Aircraft Owner's and Pilot's Association, 2005, www.aopa.com.

36 *if my thought process* National Highway Traffic Safety Administration, 2004, www.nhtsa.gov.

36 *because the leading causes of death* Centers for Disease Control and Prevention, 2009, www.cdc.gov.

Chapter 3: Why Face Fears?

59 [Figure]*The lifetime prevalence of anxiety disorders* R. C. Kessler, et al. Lifetime prevalence and age-of-onset distributions of DSM-IV disorders in the National Comorbidity Survey Replication. *Archives of General Psychiatry*, *62*, 593–602, 2005.

63 [Figure]*Percentage of patients in Barlow's study* D. H. Barlow, et al. Cognitive-behavioral therapy, imipramine, or their combination for panic disorder. *Journal of the American Medical Association*, *283*, 2529–2536, 2000.

Chapter 7: Eliminating Safety Behaviors

125 [Box]*Social psychologist Daniel Wegner has done* D. M. Wegner, et al. Paradoxical effects of thought suppression. *Journal of Personality and Social Psychology*, 53, 5–13, 1987.

125 [Box]*My colleagues and I have studied* D. F. Tolin, et al. Thought suppression in obsessive-compulsive disorder. *Behaviour Research and Therapy*, 40, 1255–1274, 2002.

125 [Box]*Psychiatrist Robert Goisman surveyed 231 people* R. M. Goisman, et al. Utilization of behavioral methods in a multicenter anxiety disorders study. *Journal of Clinical Psychiatry*, 54, 213–218, 1993.

129 [Box]*Psychologist Henny Westra surveyed forty-three people* H. A. Westra, et al. Naturalistic manner of benzodiazepine use and cognitive behavioral therapy outcome in panic disorder with agoraphobia. *Journal of Anxiety Disorders*, 16, 233–246, 2002.

Chapter 9: Beating Fears of Specific Situations or Objects

164 [Box]*Psychologist Ronald Kleinknecht surveyed members* R. A. Kleinknecht. The origins and remission of fear in a group of tarantula enthusiasts. *Behaviour Research and Therapy, 20,* 437–443, 1982.

Chapter 10: Beating Fears of Body Sensations

174 [Box]*Psychiatrist Kees Verburg and colleagues* K. Verburg, et al. Discrimination between panic disorder and generalized anxiety disorder by 35% carbon dioxide challenge. *American Journal of Psychiatry, 152,* 1081–1083, 1995.

Chapter 11: Beating Social and Performance Fears

187 [Box]*Psychologists Kathy Veljaca and Ronald Rapee* K. A. Veljaca and R. M. Rapee. Detection of negative and positive audience behaviours by socially anxious subjects. *Behaviour Research and Therapy, 36,* 311–321, 1998.

Chapter 12: Beating Obsessive Fears

198 [Box]*Psychologists S. Jack Rachman and Padmal de Silva* S. Rachman and P. de Silva. Abnormal and normal obsessions. *Behaviour Research and Therapy, 16,* 233–248, 1978.

Chapter 13: Beating Excessive Worries

211 [Box]*Psychologists Lizabeth Roemer and Susan Orsillo* L. Roemer, S. M. Orsillo, and K. Salters-Pedneault. Efficacy of an acceptance-based behavior therapy for generalized anxiety disorder: evaluation in a randomized controlled trial. *Journal of Consulting and Clinical Psychology, 76,* 1083–1089, 2008.

Chapter 14: Beating Post-Traumatic Fears

221 [Box]*Psychologist Richard McNally and colleagues* R. J. McNally, et al. Directed forgetting of trauma cues in adult survivors of childhood sexual abuse with and without posttraumatic stress disorder. *Journal of Abnormal Psychology, 107,* 596–601, 1998.

Chapter 16: The Long Run

254 [Box]*Quick Guidelines for Preventing* Adapted in part from M. J. Boschen, et al. Relapse of successfully treated anxiety and fear: theoretical issues and recommendations for clinical practice. *Australian and New Zealand Journal of Psychiatry, 43,* 89–100, 2009.

Chapter 17: Supplementing the Face Your Fears Program

263 *A problem well-defined* A. M. Nezu, C. M. Nezu, and M. G. Perri. *Problem-Solving Therapy for Depression: Theory, Research, and Clinical Guidelines* (New York: John Wiley & Sons, 1989).

Resources

Suggested Reading

Chapter 2: What Is Fear?

Beck, A. T., et al. (1985). *Anxiety Disorders and Phobias: A Cognitive Perspective*. New York: Basic Books.

Bouton, M. E. (2005). Behavior systems and the contextual control of anxiety, fear, and panic. In *Emotion and Consciousness*, ed. L. F. Barrett et al., pp. 205–227. New York: Guilford Press.

Bouton, M. E., et al. (2001). A modern learning theory perspective on the etiology of panic disorder. *Psychological Review, 108*(1), 4–32.

Davis, M. (1997). Neurobiology of fear responses: The role of the amygdala. *Journal of Neuropsychiatry and Clinical Neuroscience, 9*(3), 382–402.

Delgado, M. R., et al. (2006). Extending animal models of fear conditioning to humans. *Biological Psychology, 73*(1), 39–48.

Mowrer, O. H. (1960). *Learning Theory and Behavior.* New York: John Wiley and Sons.

Schafe, G. E., and J. E. LeDoux (2004). The neural basis of fear. In *The Cognitive Neurosciences*, 3rd ed., ed. M. S. Gazzaniga, pp. 987–1003. Cambridge, MA: MIT Press.

Williams, J. M. G., et al. (1997). *Cognitive Psychology and Emotional Disorders*, 2nd ed. New York: John Wiley and Sons.

Chapter 3: Why Face Fears?

Barlow, D. H., et al. (2000). Cognitive-behavioral therapy, imipramine, or their combination for panic disorder: A randomized controlled trial. *Journal of the American Medical Association, 283*, 2529–2536.

Borkovec, T. D., and E. Costello (1993). Efficacy of applied relaxation and cognitive-behavioral therapy in the treatment of generalized anxiety disorder. *Journal of Consulting and Clinical Psychology, 61*, 611–619.

Cuijpers, P., and J. Schuurmans (2007). Self-help interventions for anxiety disorders: An overview. *Current Psychiatry Reports, 9*, 284–290.

den Boer, P. C., et al. (2004). Why is self-help neglected in the treatment of emotional disorders? A meta-analysis. *Psychological Medicine, 34,* 959–971.

Foa, E. B., et al. (2005). Randomized, placebo-controlled trial of exposure and ritual prevention, clomipramine, and their combination in the treatment of obsessive-compulsive disorder. *American Journal of Psychiatry, 162,* 151–161.

Gould, R. A., and G. A. Clum (1993). A meta-analysis of self-help treatment approaches. *Clinical Psychology Review, 13,* 169–186.

Heimberg, R. G., et al. (1998). Cognitive behavioral group therapy versus phenelzine therapy for social phobia: 12-week outcome. *Archives of General Psychiatry, 55,* 1133–1141.

Keane, T. M., et al. (1989). Implosive (flooding) therapy reduces symptoms of PTSD in Vietnam combat veterans. *Behavior Therapy, 20,* 254–260.

Kendall, P. C. (1994). Treating anxiety disorders in children: Results of a randomized clinical trial. *Journal of Consulting and Clinical Psychology, 62,* 100–110.

Menchola, M., et al. (2007). Efficacy of self-administered treatments for depression and anxiety. *Professional Psychology: Research and Practice, 38,* 421–429.

Newman, M. G., et al. (2003). Self-help and minimal-contact therapies for anxiety disorders: Is human contact necessary for therapeutic efficacy? *Journal of Clinical Psychology, 59,* 251–274.

Öst, L. G. (1989). One-session treatment for specific phobias. *Behaviour Research and Therapy, 27,* 1–7.

Chapter 6: Conducting Exposures

Craske, M. G., et al. (2008). Optimizing inhibitory learning during exposure therapy. *Behaviour Research and Therapy, 46,* 5–27.

Kozak, M. J., et al. (1998). Process and outcome of exposure treatment with obsessive-compulsives: Psychophysiological indicators of emotional processing. *Behavior Therapy, 19,* 157–169.

Chapter 16: The Long Run

Boschen, M. J., et al. (2009). Relapse of successfully treated anxiety and fear: Theoretical issues and recommendations for clinical practice. *Australian and New Zealand Journal of Psychiatry, 43,* 89–100.

Bouton, M. E. (2002). Context, ambiguity, and unlearning: Sources of relapse after behavioral extinction. *Biological Psychiatry, 52,* 976–986.

Öst, L. G. (1989). A maintenance program for behavioral treatment of anxiety disorders. *Behaviour Research and Therapy, 27,* 123–130.

Rachman, S. (1979). The return of fear. *Behaviour Research and Therapy, 17,* 164–166.

Specific Phobias

Jonathan Abramowitz (2009). *Getting Over OCD: A 10-Step Workbook for Taking Back Your Life.* New York: Guilford Press.

Martin Antony and Randi McCabe (2005). *Overcoming Animal and Insect Phobias: How to Conquer Fear of Dogs, Snakes, Rodents, Bees, Spiders, and More.* Oakland, CA: New Harbinger Publications.

Martin Antony and Karen Rowa (2007). *Overcoming Fear of Heights: How to Conquer Acrophobia and Live a Life Without Limits.* Oakland, CA: New Harbinger Publications.

Martin Antony and Mark Watling (2006). *Overcoming Medical Phobias: How to Conquer Fear of Blood, Needles, Doctors and Dentists.* Oakland, CA: New Harbinger Publications.

Tamar Chansky (2004). *Freeing Your Child from Anxiety: Powerful, Practical Solutions to Overcome Your Child's Fears, Worries, and Phobias.* New York: Three Rivers Press.

Edna Foa and Reid Wilson (2001). *Stop Obsessing!: How to Overcome Your Obsessions and Compulsions.* New York: Bantam Books.

Victoria Follette, Jacqueline Pistorello, and Stephen Hayes (2007). *Finding Life Beyond Trauma: Using Acceptance and Commitment Therapy to Heal from Post-Traumatic Stress and Trauma-Related Problems.* Oakland, CA: New Harbinger Publications.

Debra Hope, Richard Heimberg, and Cynthia Turk (2010). *Managing Social Anxiety: Workbook, A Cognitive-Behavioral Therapy Approach*, 2nd ed. New York: Oxford University Press.

Robert Leahy (2006). *The Worry Cure: Seven Steps to Stop Worry from Stopping You.* New York: Three Rivers Press.

Susan Orsillo, Lizabeth Roemer, and Zindel Segal (2010). *Mindful Way through Anxiety: Break Free from Chronic Worry and Reclaim Your Life.* New York: Guilford Press.

Ronald Rapee (2000). *Helping Your Anxious Child: A Step-by-Step Guide for Parents.* Oakland, CA: New Harbinger Publications.

Barbara Rothbaum, Edna Foa, and Elizabeth Hembree (2007). *Reclaiming Your Life from a Traumatic Experience: A Prolonged Exposure Treatment Program Workbook.* New York: Oxford University Press.

Gail Steketee and Randy Frost (2006). *Compulsive Hoarding and Acquiring: Workbook* New York: Oxford University Press.

David Tolin, Randy Frost, and Gail Steketee (2007). *Buried in Treasures: Help for Compulsive Acquiring, Saving, and Hoarding.* New York: Oxford University Press.

Online Resources

- The Anxiety Disorders Association of America: www.adaa.org
- The Association for Cognitive and Behavioral Therapies: www.abct.org
- The International OCD Foundation: www.ocfoundation.org
- The International Society for Traumatic Stress Studies: www.istss.org
- The National Institute of Mental Health: www.nimh.nih.gov/health/topics/anxiety-disorders
- Sharecare: www.sharecare.com
- WebMD: www.webmd.com/anxiety-panic

Finding Professional Help

- The American Board of Professional Psychology: www.abpp.org
- The Anxiety Disorders Association of America: www.adaa.org
- The Association for Behavioral and Cognitive Therapies: www.abct.org
- The International OCD Foundation: www.ocfoundation.org
- The National Association of Social Workers: www.naswdc.org
- The National Register of Health Service Providers in Psychology: www.nationalregister.org
- WebMD: doctor.webmd.com/physician_finder

Index